HEAL THE PEOPLE
Expanding Human Consciousness
for a Global Awakening

Praise for Heal the People

"Kristin is truly a gift to the world. Her youthful exuberance and mystical wisdom come together in her book *Heal the People* to redefine healing and awakening in this new age. What is written in these pages in not just for the people of the world now, but lays the foundation for future generations who will see themselves not as survivors on a harsh planet, but as carriers of divine wisdom and love."

—**Rhys Thomas**, founder of the Rhys Thomas Institute of Energy Medicine and bestselling author of *Discover Your Purpose: How to Use the 5 Life Purpose Profiles to Unlock Your Hidden Potential and Live the Life You Were Meant to Live*

"This book is breathtaking. It tells the story of healing, self-discovery, and coming into a life of purpose. Raw, honest, uplifting… let this book invite you deeper into everything life has to offer you. Kristin's vision for a world full of healed humans will inspire you."

—**Jacob Nordby**, author of *Blessed Are the Weird* and *The Creative Cure.*

"We are only healthy to the degree that we are conscious and we are only conscious to the degree that we are healthy. Through autogenesis the body automatically heals itself. This is our birthright. Cut yourself, and watch the body heal. This applies to the mental, emotional, physical and spiritual bodies. *Heal the People* equates to what all the ancient sages have said: balance is the key, and know thyself. This book will deliver you further down the path of KNOWLEDGE."

—**Troy Casey**, the Certified Health Nut. Life coach, healer and author of *#RIPPEDAT50*

"Kristin Johnston is one of the most amazing people I have ever met. When I got the chance to interview her on my podcast I was blown away by the amount of knowledge she had on a variety of subjects. Her book *Heal the People* is a remarkable and candid book documenting her own personal journey. She is an amazing writer with a wide breadth of knowledge. I found myself enthralled chapter by chapter at her unique and powerful story. You will learn so much in reading this. *Heal the People* is not just another by-the-numbers book on spirituality, it's a powerful personal story that will inspire everyone who reads it."

—**Brian Scott,** author of *The Reality Revolution*, CEO of the Advanced Success Institute and host of *The Reality Revolution* podcast

"*Heal the People* is not just a call to action, it is a mantra to uplift all of those struggling with despair, hope and desire. Kristin Johnston's noble adventure to find the value of her beautiful life is a love song to all those needing to understand the mysteries of existence. In going from the depths of despair to the height of spiritual awakening, Kristin puts the human back in humanity. The intensity of her dedication, the power of her words and the value of her spirit is what makes this sweet book a salve to the soul of those in need of healing, purpose and love. Kristin dedicates her words to the enlivening a passion for the adventure of life itself. Her infectious love for the incarnational experience is a gift to all who hold this delightful book in their hands and let it into their hearts."

—**Alan Steinfeld,** author of *Making Contact*, and host of *New Realities*

"*Heal the People* is a wonderful, healing journey to the core. Truthful and gritty, yet hopeful and enjoyable to read. It flows beautifully and is filled with captivating stories and lessons that waste no time.

It firmly and gently activates the reader instantly toward authentic healing and inspires that which is good, real, and of love. Sharing her raw personal story along with her knowledge and profound realizations with the clear intent of nourishing her readers, Kristin distills the essence of healing, spirit, love and God. She does so in such a way that every reader will feel comforted, hopeful, inspired and stronger. A perfect book for our times!"

—**Jonathan Glass**, M.Ac. Ayurvedic
Practitioner, author of *Total Life Cleanse:*
A 28 Day Program to Detoxify and
Nourish Body Mind and Soul

"Kristin is a brilliant woman with a timeless soul. Her wisdom expands many lifetimes and her ability to tune in and heal those around her is uncanny. I've seen firsthand what she can do and will forever be grateful to have come across her. *Heal the People* is her fascinating story that we all have the gift of getting to discover."

—**Justin Stenstrom**, author of
Elite Mind: A Real-World Guide to
Overcoming Anxiety, Conquering Depression,
and Unleashing Your Inner Confidence

"There is great power in this book simply because of the consciousness it was written from. As you read it, it lets something in cellularly, so change is happening within you during your read. Many of us do not consciously meet the depths of our own grief, despair, or fear, so we don't communicate from these spaces. Because of Kristin's courage to walk this journey and let such profound wisdom come through, there is the tincture of deep, authentic compassion within her words that allows healing to happen.

"This book will serve as a great opening for those who have suffered and not known how to bridge the gap between despair and peace. Especially with meeting the depths of opioid addiction, the hopelessness and helplessness of which I've seen hundreds of times in my career as an Emergency Medicine doctor, this is a powerful bridge to a space of truth and peace. Having personally met my own fear, depression, and despair to emerge into consciousness, I know how unthinkable it can seem that there may somehow be a purpose in our journey. Kristin's willingness to bring this to light, instead of succumbing to the ideas of the mind and keeping it suppressed, is a testament to the power she has cultivated for the reader to receive."

—**Kim D'Eramo**, D.O., Founder of the American Institute of Mind Body Medicine and bestselling author of *The MindBody Toolkit*

HEAL THE PEOPLE

Expanding Human Consciousness
for a Global Awakening

KRISTIN JOHNSTON

**Heal the People: Expanding Human
Consciousness for a Global Awakening**
Copyright © 2022 Kristin Johnston

Produced and printed by Stillwater River Publications.
All rights reserved. Written and produced in the United States of America.
This book may not be reproduced or sold in any form without the expressed,
written permission of the author(s) and publisher.

Visit our website at **www.StillwaterPress.com** for more information.

First Stillwater River Publications Edition

ISBN: 978-1-955123-89-1 (hardcover)
ISBN: 978-1-955123-80-8 (paperback)

Library of Congress Control Number: 2022901390

Images from *The 5 Personality Patterns* by Steven Kessler © 2015.
Used with permission. For more information visit
www.The5PersonalityPatterns.com

1 2 3 4 5 6 7 8 9 10
Written by Kristin Johnston
Cover design by Mike Johnston & Matthew St. Jean
Interior book design by Matthew St. Jean
Published by Stillwater River Publications, Pawtucket, RI, USA.

Publisher's Cataloging-In-Publication Data
(Prepared by The Donohue Group, Inc.)
Names: Johnston, Kristin, author.
Title: Heal the people : expanding human consciousness
for a global awakening / Kristin Johnston.
Description: First Stillwater River Publications edition. |
Pawtucket, RI, USA : Stillwater River Publications, [2022]
Identifiers: ISBN 9781955123808
Subjects: LCSH: Consciousness. | Johnston, Kristin. | Enlightenment. |
Spiritual healing. | Change (Psychology) | LCGFT: Self-help publications.
Classification: LCC BF311 .J64 2022 | DDC 153--dc23

To Mia, for loving me despite and beyond my humanness.

To my parents, the most genuine people I know, whose hearts are immeasurable in size. Thank you for modeling the virtues of compassion, honesty, loyalty and generosity, and teaching me to embrace the beauty of a simple life.

To my husband, Mike. Thank you for understanding me and how my mind behaves. Your love has allowed me to heal in ways you may never understand. Thank you for making this journey into wholeness by my side — you are the greatest man I've ever known.

To my brother for always being there, believing in me and supporting this mission, even when you didn't understand it. You deserve the world.

To my children, Cye and Rhythm, for being my sacred mirrors, my noble friends, and my constant reminders that the *work* is never truly done. I know what love is because the two of you exist.

To all of the authors, modern-day mystics, and researchers who have come before me, a list far too great to name, who have paved the way in sweat, tears, and determination, those who have devoted their entire lives to making information like this accessible.

But most importantly, *this book is for the people*, whose names are known or unknown, that walk in the light of their own truth. To the diverse group of generations destined to join together at this time, to harness the power within, and to shift the current paradigm ruled by competition, fear, and division into one of collaboration, cooperation, unity, and love.

When all the broken-hearted people living in the world agree,
there will be an answer. Let it be.
—The Beatles

CONTENTS

FOREWORD

A re you ready to heal?

Be prepared to be inspired, opened and cleansed by this remarkable book.

I met Kristin Johnston about ten years ago, when she floated into the Energy Medicine School where I was teaching. She was waiflike: beautiful and ethereal. Like a cross between a fairy and a badass angel.

I loved her on sight.

My daughter, who was a child back then, loved her too and called her Mermaid Girl because of her blue and green mermaid hair and other-worldly smile. She was, is, and always will be a soul sister to me.

Back then, she had a wispy sort of energy, like she had one foot here on earth and the other foot off planet somewhere. It was easy to think she could choose to leave if she wanted to. I didn't know at the time that she was in the grips of her powerful opiate addiction; I just knew that she was like one of those wild animals who wander into your back yard and desire company at the same level that they fear being seen.

I wasn't really aware of Kristin's struggles until she beat her addiction and told me the whole miraculous story, which I will leave for her to tell you. Since that time, her spirit, now unchained and expanded, grew and blossomed into the amazing mystic and healer that she is now.

She told me back then about her vision of her future and assured me that someday soon, she was going to heal the people.

This book that you hold in your hands, is a guide, a gateway and a recipe book so that you can follow in Kristin's footsteps. In it, she maps out the path to liberation and includes all the wisdom you need to bring yourself into a higher state of consciousness.

It will teach you how to open your mind and your heart. And how to claim your power back by truly understanding and accepting with reverence who you really are. And then it will show you how to live a life of integrity and harmony with yourself and the world as you open to loving all the parts of you and living from your truth.

Shift happens.

You are waking up—the proof is in your hands.

Kristin is a powerful, inspiring and compassionate guide on your journey and this book is your map.

Dig in, drink it up and may you be blessed on your journey.

—Lisa Campion,
Author of *The Art of Psychic Reiki*
and *Energy Medicine for Empaths*

PREFACE

In gratitude to those who've come before.

*"If I seem to have seen further, it is only by
standing on the shoulders of giants."*
—Isaac Newton

I will always remember January 31st, 2012 as the first day of the rest of my life. A little dog named Pablo nestled comfortably at my feet as I sat huddled on Angel's living room couch. Angel was basically a stranger to me, a woman I'd met only hours before, but somehow, I was comfortable trusting her with my life. Clouds of cigarette smoke filled the room around us as I watched her weigh out the finely powdered root bark of a profoundly hallucinogenic plant. I shivered, feeling a cold sensation of chills rush up my spine, followed by an abrupt wave of heat, and I began to sweat. I wasn't sure if I was sweating because I was nervous or because I was about to be sick, when she handed me the capsule to take. Although some parts of me were still reluctant, I knew that this was a now-or-never moment in my life. And even though I was nervous, I knew there was no turning back, so I swallowed the little brown pill and went upstairs to lie down before the medicine started to kick in.

I walked slowly through Angel's dimly lit hallway, the mid-afternoon sun shining faintly through a window set way up high in a large corridor, its rays gently illuminating a winding wooden stairwell. Angel's house had a distinctly antique feel to it—it wasn't warm like a home that had been lived in or well loved—but it wasn't completely devoid of character either. In some strange way, it felt alive with an energy that was entirely unique. With a cross-roads kind of vibe, it felt a bit like an old train station that at one time housed many boarding passengers; only, the passengers never stayed very long, just long enough to get to their next destination. I wasn't exactly sure how, but I could feel the presence of the many souls once liberated in the exact location where I now stood.

What I didn't know at the time, was the spirit contained within the capsule I just swallowed was about to free me from nearly a decade of agonizing self-imprisonment. It would become the most life-altering experience of my 23 years on the planet. I was journeying with the African plant medicine iboga, one of the most powerful psychedelics known to man.

A faint buzzing sound hummed just behind my ears, like that of a dull lawn mower running somewhere off in the distance. I couldn't tell where the sound was coming from, but it was completely drowning out any distracting mind chatter I might have otherwise been experiencing. My head which felt heavy and tired rested comfortably on a small stack of soft pillows while my consciousness ventured somewhere *far* beyond what we consider to be average, everyday reality. At one point I found myself in the vast expanse of infinite space, visiting with distant relatives of otherworldly origins. Moments later, I would find myself returning to my past so I could reexperience painful emotional traumas from my youth, heartaches and pains that as a child I didn't have the tools to process. Some will actually say that journeying with ibogaine can be likened to 15 years of psychotherapy—and I would have to agree, it's really *that* powerful. In just a few short days, this incredible plant has a way of guiding us back to the places throughout life where our souls became fragmented and we lost contact with who we really are. Luckily for me, I'd only been on the planet 23 years, and albeit real, my wounds weren't exceptionally deep—not to mention I'd already begun the work of healing from them. A couple years prior to this experience I'd begun studying the healing arts and was currently enrolled in my second of a three-year energy medicine school called the *Healer Training Program*—HTP for short.

Three entire days passed while I remained in this altered state, my body wrapped snuggly in a cozy down comforter, as vision after vision passed before my mind's eye. So much of what I experienced during that journey was deeply meaningful and profoundly therapeutic. Some might even say, cathartic. At one central point I found myself in the midst of an intense euphoria—the pinnacle experience of human liberation— when my life mission, and the title of this book *Heal the People*, revealed itself to me.

In the dark recesses of my mind I observed something unknown as it began to take shape. I watched intently until the unknowable object finally took on the form of something I could recognize. It turned out to be the brightly colored yellow cover of a paperback book. I studied the blank cover for a moment, until bold black letters began to arrange themselves down the front face of the book. First the letter *H*—then *T*—then *P*. The letters *HTP* hovered over the cover, suspended vertically down the book's surface, they hovered there only for a moment, until things began to move again. I watched the letter *H* as it transformed into the word *Heal*. The letter *T* became the word *the*. And the letter *P* became the word *People*. As soon as the words became legible, a crowd of people appeared. This crowd resembled a rally, some type of peaceful, powerful gathering. Thousands gathered around this book chanting, "*Heal the people! Heal the people!*" Louder and louder the words rang inside my head until finally I sat up, my eyes wide and full of wonder. In this radically altered state of consciousness I was trying to make sense of what I was seeing, but my soul didn't need an explanation. I knew that this was *my* book, and for perhaps the first time in my life I felt a legitimate reason for my existence.

As mentioned, I was currently enrolled in an *HTP*, a *Healer Training Program* where I was learning many techniques and strategies for healing and becoming a *whole-hearted* person. And now this synchronistic appearance of a book titled *HTP* for *Heal the People*, accompanied by a crowd wild with passion and enthusiasm for exactly this information? There was no way possible in my current state of consciousness, I could have conjured that vision. I realized then that this book meant something substantial to my life. It felt like something I was destined to bring into the world —it was my *deliverable*. In that moment, I came to realize that a force much greater than myself was making contact with me, and if I was willing to allow it, it would work with me, and through me, to bring about a positive change in the world.

But, *heal the people*? How could I possibly heal the people when just 24 hours prior I found myself huddled in the stall of an airport bathroom crushing what remained of my drugs—which was probably enough to tranquilize a small elephant—before snorting them. You see, I wasn't experimenting with psychedelics because I thought it would be a good time. I was journeying with iboga as a final and desperate attempt at creating a better life for myself. I was only 23 years old, but I'd been a drug addict for 7 years, and by society's standards, drug addicts are basically the bottom of the barrel. They're an unsightly blemish on the face of humanity, second only to the panhandling homeless person defiling your local street corner—and at the time, that's how I viewed my addiction too, as a shameful embarrassment. I hadn't yet come to realize that a divine hand often uses our deepest pain to help reveal our greatest calling.

I could have never imagined the woman in the airport bathroom, riddled with guilt and shame over her unmanageable behaviors, would one day become somebody's mother, somebody's wife, and a person that she could be proud of. *That* woman would grow to become a healer, a spiritual teacher, and a community leader. She'd eventually become so emblazoned with passion for the art of personal transformation that she'd inspire all who came to know her.

How is a metamorphosis like that even possible, you might ask? This book tells not only the story, but of the alchemical process that makes such a radical transformation achievable. Heal the People isn't just *my* story, the story of how one woman conquered her demons and healed her life—it's a guidebook for all humans, everywhere. Heal the People was written because humankind is destined to undergo a profound shift in consciousness. *Now* is the time, and *we* are the catalysts. The system laid out in this book is designed is to help us understand who we are, and why we're here. It was created to restore harmony and balance within us as individuals, so we can restore harmony and balance to our collective, and hopefully to our planet. Heal the People is not just a systemic approach to healing—it's a call to radical *awakening*.

Personal disclaimer: I do not have an MD. or Ph.D. after my name. I have no fancy degrees, other than from the proverbial school of hard knocks. Through personal research, and the trials and errors of my own life, I've discovered what it means to *awaken* and *heal*. I've come to realize that there are very basic necessities for living a balanced and fulfilling life, and I've decided to compile my insights and to share what I've learned in hopes that it may be of service to those who continue to struggle—who believe that they are defective in some way, who go to bed at night questioning whether *this* really is all there is to life, or simply a fellow human being who's busy doing their part to save the world. The ideas that I share are not my original ideas. I've learned from many great teachers, healers, and more books than I can name as well as from my own lived experience. I don't claim to own any of this material, because I don't believe these spiritual truths can be claimed. They come through us, but from a source much higher than ours. When these ideas are shared amongst men and put into practice, magical things begin to happen—even if we can't exactly explain how.

Although the inspiration for this book was born of an addiction, the principles for comprehensive healing are all-inclusive. They're applicable to anyone and everyone who's human, especially those interested in pondering the depths of spiritual truth. It doesn't matter where you are in your life—whether you're young or old, healthy or unwell, single or married, employed or unemployed, satisfied or searching—this book can guide you into deeper levels of personal fulfillment and personal understanding, awakening you to your soul's purpose in this lifetime. This book was written for those who seek the innermost levels of healing and awakening. *Are you ready?*

INTRODUCTION

"Enlightenment is not a change into something better or more,
but a simple recognition of who we truly already are."
—James Blanchard Cisneros

For as long as human history has been recorded, man has sought to understand himself and his place within the universe. For eons we've looked to the stars, cast runes, read cards and sought the advice of wise counsel from seers and sages for guidance and direction. On some level, we all long to know who we are and why we're here. It seems to be a fundamental longing within humanity to connect to this deeper sense of meaning and purpose in our lives. This search for meaning and desire to create something real and authentic seems to weigh heavily on the mind of many and is only becoming more intensified with the rapidly growing pressures of modern-day life. It seems the further we stray from our essential nature and the authenticity we desperately seek, the more afflicted we become, and the louder the call to awaken and heal. Right now, the call is so loud its deafening, and you're hearing it, otherwise you wouldn't be reading this book.

The passageway that lies before you isn't a step-by-step manual, or a how-to book. It's an offering of assistance, a directional aid, and a guiding light onto a seldom walked trail. You won't find this road to be paved, or landscaped, or even easily discovered—it's private and rather secluded—its edges overgrown, brush and foliage spilling onto it, untamed and wild. While traveling this path, you can expect to encounter numerous variations of yourself, many misleading. You'll be asked to awaken all that's concealed with yourself, to reunite with the essence of your own authenticity, and thereby, with divinity as a whole. I didn't write this book because I think I have something to teach you, I wrote this book so I can help you chip away at the layers of energetic debris that stand between you and what your soul has always known. Consider it a guide to assist you on the path to awakening your highest potential—a tool to help you reclaim all of your fragmented parts, so you can fully embody the brilliance you came here to express.

By picking up this book, you've been called on to clear the way within and without, to cut back the overhanging branches, to tread down the tall grass, and to embark on a sacred, inner journey. In the days of old, this pilgrimage was walked only by devout seekers and those willing to forgo the ordinary aspects of a worldly life. The time has finally come for *all* of us to discover this ancient trail, to wake up to our inherent powers, and to heal absolutely; for the more who discover and walk this path, the more accessible it becomes to others. Collectively, we'll pave the way towards a bright and inspiring future—not just for the fortunate few—but for *all*.

This book is the material manifestation of lifetimes of study, the fusing together of ancient wisdom, age-old magic, modern day principles, cutting-edge neuroscience, and personal experience in order to obtain the secrets to healing. It's designed to initiate an alchemical process within the psyche of you, the reader. If you allow it, it will awaken you to the many complex layers of your own unique human experience, purify you of unwanted states of consciousness, and deliver you from the destructive grip of your own unconsciousness. It will elevate you step-by-step through each of your energy systems, ascending you into your highest form, into union with your pure, unlimited potential.

In the coming chapters, I'll share personal stories of my own awakening journey and the tools that helped me most along the path. We'll cover the secret power hidden in your pain, and the potential for transformation encoded within your human energy blueprint. We'll be exploring, in depth, the human chakra system; what it is, how it works, what it needs, and how to properly care for it.

- We'll cover the various stages of chakra development, and what each stage means for us as evolving beings.
- We'll learn about the formative life experiences that have the most impact on our chakras
- We'll discuss personality types and traits that manifest as a result of our energetic expression.
- Most importantly, we'll cover what we can do to do to heal ourselves by restoring each of our chakras to a state of harmony if they've fallen out of balance.

After reading, you will come to realize that your entire life is simply a reflection of how you've learned to manage your energy. Once equipped with this information, you'll never again be without the awareness and the tools you need to live your life in a balanced, harmonious way. This is the most powerful work a human is capable of, and it's more important now than ever before. With each initiate who does the work to reclaim the essence of their soul, the collective energy grows, adding momentum to a much larger awakening that's taking place now.

In our not so distant past, this type of work was known only to a few rare and uncommon individuals. People like monks, yogis, mystics, and scholars were the exceptional few who got to experience such transcendental states of awareness, where the secrets of the universe poured forth like water from the mouth of a running stream. These remarkable human beings had souls sharp enough to pierce through the veil of illusion, revealing to us all the glimpses of our own divine potential. And this is precisely why these unusual luminaries have left such a lasting impact on the world around them—over time they've changed humanity, gradually raising us up to the precipice where we currently sit—on the brink of radical transformation.

Thanks to powerful souls that have come before ours, and those of great wisdom; men like Gandhi who taught us to *be the change*, so we can see when our world is off tilt and in need of redirection; John Lennon who encouraged us to *imagine* a world that is better than the one we currently live in; and Martin Luther King Jr., who showed us how to *dream* bigger than our current reality, demonstrating that belief and unshakable faith united with forward action is what it takes to make a dream come true. Each of these incredible leaders are wonderful examples for the powerful change that becomes possible when people come together and align their bodies with their minds and hearts and unite over shared mission. Right now, our mission is to *heal*.

Despite the apparent chaos on the surface, we're currently living in a Golden Age of possibility, a blessed time in history pointed to by many of our ancient civilizations, a time when anyone willing can access the power of these prodigious souls. In fact, we're *all* being called in some way to do the work of the masters. We are each being asked to uncover the truths of who we really are, to share our most authentic selves and to transform the world with our love. But if we're going to do that, we're going to need guidance and direction. We're first going to need to learn to navigate the fundamentals of what it means to be a human, *being*.

If you're reading this book it's because you've been called to awaken at this precious time. You're prepared to discover the depths of your being and to reconnect with the essence of who and what *you really are*. Maybe you've been soul searching for a while, or maybe the indwelling spirit within you is just now being roused. Perhaps it's been the desire to heal from a trauma, depression, disease, or addiction that's called you to pick up this book; maybe it's an inquisitive nature, or an intuitive knowing that there simply has to be *more* to life. Maybe it's the calling to discover a deeper sense of meaning and purpose. In any case, I'm glad that you're reading, because herein you'll discover the truth of who you are, why you're here, and exactly what it takes to come alive.

My hope for you is that through reading this book you awaken to what has been stored in your heart and begin to identify all that has prevented you from truly living. My wish is that, in time, you'll remember that the answers to who you truly are and what you seek are now, and always have been, *within you.*

Heal the People

A BRIEF PERSONAL HISTORY

"If a man for whatever reason has the opportunity to lead
an extraordinary life, he has no right to keep it to himself."
—Jacques-Yves Cousteau

Mission is the highest form of motivation, and I've noticed that people motivated by mission tend to have a common thread. Most of them have experienced some sort of personal adversity, some great obstacle, or challenge they had to conquer within themselves in order to discover what their soul was really made of. Pain was most often the catalyst that delivered them into their purpose, and my story isn't much different. My invitation to heal came when, finally, the suffering caused by an opiate addiction became too great to bear. What I didn't realize then was that my soul had been crying for my attention long before an addiction ever developed. Most people would assume that for someone to turn into a drug addict they must have had some horrific experience, or trauma in early childhood—but that just wasn't my story—my life was great growing up. I excelled at sports, had lots of friends, and my family was deeply caring and truly wonderful.

My mother, Laurie, was the archetypal woman: very beautiful, poised, and professional. With dark hair and deep-set brown eyes, a slender figure, and a smile that could illuminate a room; she turned heads wherever she went. I idolized my mom; her beauty, grace, and gentleness were qualities I always aspired to emulate. My mother lovingly doted on my father, my brother, and me. She was always sure to provide us with the best of everything, even if that meant taking care of herself last. She made sure there was never a question as to whether her family was loved by her.

My dad, Bruce, was the quintessential male: handsome, strong, dominant, and hard working. He was a man of few words, but his presence, honor, consistency, and humility remain unparalleled. In a world full of men with undeserved confidence, my dad is a most humble and deserving man. Even without a father to guide him, he turned out to be the most stable, dependable man I've ever known.

My parents were a happily married couple; some even considered them soulmates. My brother, Kyle, and I were close in age and had a great bond, so I knew I always had a friend growing up. By all society's standards, we were the picture-perfect family. I was never abused, neglected, molested, or abandoned like so many people who suffer from addiction. My childhood was full of companionship, fun, love, and togetherness. If I hadn't experienced any real wounding or trauma, why then did I still feel so isolated and detached? Why was I such a depressed adolescent?

The answer—probably for the same reason that the majority of people on our planet experience general feelings of underlying unhappiness and unease. Because instead of living authentically, I'd adapted to my surroundings and unconsciously created a persona that wasn't entirely mine. I was taught in a very subconscious way that the world was not a friendly place, and that the only way to survive was to become good at seeming unemotional, so I adapted. I stopped being me and started being what the world around me told me I should be in order to survive. I learned early on that crying was for pussies, sensitivity was a sign of weakness, and if you couldn't kick somebody's ass, then you just weren't worthy of the fight. So I developed a false self that was hardened and insensitive, and I created a personality around the need for toughness. As a compassionate, empathic, creative soul, this was the energetic equivalent of suicide.

I also absorbed the idea that life wasn't fun—that it wasn't designed to be enjoyable—it was just something you had to endure. These types of beliefs weren't exactly spoken aloud. Inheriting them was merely a by-product of being a member of my family. No matter what kind of family you're born into, you'll be sure to inherit its programming. This form of program is what many call the *tribal mind* which I'll be elaborating on in much greater detail later on. For now, it's enough to say that our familial beliefs are some of the most influential programming we receive as children. This is a type of *initiation* into our family pattern, and it occurs on a very sub-conscious level. It happens so far below our own awareness that we often don't even know it's there. The unconscious allegiance to our family is so strong that most of us will live our lives unconsciously defending it, no matter how dysfunctional it is. Sometimes our inherited programs are positive and beneficial, but other times they can be quite harmful to us—especially later in life when upholding them no longer serves our growth. Awakening to our soul often means rewriting the internal script of our tribal inheritance.

In my case, the inherited dysfunction came by the way of chronic communication issues, the inability to deal with any and all emotional discomfort, and creating a personality that was entirely unlike my authentic self. Not knowing how to manage my emotions led me to needing to escape them. Like many, I learned early on that substances and habits like cigarettes, booze, disordered eating, self-harming, and orgasms helped me avoid unwanted emotional states—and I certainly utilized all options to curtail many of my emotional discomforts. By the time I reached my early teens I'd already developed a number of full-blown addictions. I'd also invested so much of my energy into avoiding my feelings and being what I thought was expected to fit into my family and society, that I completely lost touch with who I *actually* was.

In the summer of 2005 I was only a kid, but I was making adult decisions that were going to significantly influence the direction of my life. I was falling in love with a really cute, charismatic older guy named Deven, and I was totally infatuated with him. As silly as it seems to me now, Deven was a guy I never imaged would date a girl like me. He seemed pulled together, and I was young and inexperienced. I was surprised when he invited me over to his house one night in July, but I played it cool and gladly agreed, trying not to sound too anxious or overly excited. That night, he asked me a question that would alter the course of my life forever.

"You feel like breathing tonight, K?"

"What's that?"

"You know—*oxygen*—OxyContin? I think you'll like it."

I really didn't have a clue what he was talking about, but at the time I probably would have done anything he asked.

Not too long after we arrived at his house, a guy we called Brains pulled a couple of small blue pills from his front pocket. He started to scratch some type of coating off of them, and once it was off he placed them both inside a folded twenty-dollar bill and used a lighter to crush them up on the kitchen counter. Once the pills were ground into a fine powder, he pulled a credit card from his wallet and used it to carefully separate the pile into equal lines. He grabbed a ballpoint pen off the table and quickly disassembled it. It was obvious that he'd practiced this routine many times before. Removing the ink part from the pen, he tossed it aside, keeping only the hollow plastic tube. He lifted the empty pen to his nostril and gave a quick sniff. I watched in disbelief as the powdered pill disappeared instantly into his nose. Coughing slightly, Brains leaned back into his chair with an emphasized sigh, and it was as if the entire room experienced his immediate relief. He passed the empty pen over to Deven, who repeated the exact process of lifting the tube to his nostril, quick sniff, and just like that, the powder was gone. When Deven handed the tube to me, I didn't really think twice about it. I just reacted. As soon as the powdered pill hit my bloodstream, I felt as though I was being wrapped in a snug, warm blanket, instantly removing any fear or discomfort that I'd previously held in my body. I could taste the bitter pill as it dripped down the back of my throat, but after about ten minutes, my immense euphoria was replaced by sudden and intense nausea. When someone slid a shot of Captain Morgan's over to me, the smell of it made my stomach turn somersaults. I just sat there with my face pressed into my hands, disoriented and sweating. I managed to make my way out to the driveway, where I emptied the contents of my stomach into some nearby shrubbery. I'm still not sure how I made my way home that night, but I do know that when I got there I lay awake in my bed, staring at my ceiling, wondering how in the hell anyone could possibly enjoy that drug. I swore to myself then and there that I'd never do it again.

If only I had kept my promise.

That was my first introduction to a drug that held my spirit hostage for almost a decade, a drug that led me by the hand directly into my own personal hell on Earth. Paradoxically, the desperate desire to free myself from its grips also led me on an epic spiritual quest, which eventually revealed to me a direct pathway back to heaven—and this book is my way of sharing what I've learned along the way.

A GLOBAL AWAKENING

"The world will not be destroyed by those who do evil,
but by those who watch them without doing anything."
—Albert Einstein

I think we can all plainly see that our world is not well. In fact, we're very clearly in a state of collective dis-ease. Not only are our political systems wildly out of balance, but our educational, agricultural, religious, ecological, economic and social systems are struggling as well. The world we're living in is not a reflection of a harmonious system. Rather, it's an intentional design that was created to benefit the few at the expense of the many and we've just about reached our breaking point. Something must shift, and fortunately for us, the shift has already begun taking place within the hearts of humanity. People are waking up. Despite the apparent chaos on the surface, the conditions are finally ripe for a global awakening to take place. Though the question remains—is humanity ready for this type of shift?

There's an image I've recently seen floating around social media of a board game being played by a bunch of wealthy old men with white hair wearing business suits, the game play resting on the backs of human slaves. The truth concealed within the graphic image is profound yet simple; the slaves simply need to stand up and the game topples over. It's time for humanity as a collective to stand up against the injustices of our world. Only, this revolution doesn't need to resemble the civil wars of the past that were fought against oppression; on the contrary, what must happen now isn't a fight *against* anything at all. Rather, it's a movement *towards* peace, a movement *for* unity. Today's revolution isn't a war at all, it's an opportunity for the maturation of the human race, an evolution in our consciousness. What's being asked of each of us is that we no longer choose to remain complacent, and that we no longer behave like toddlers waiting for someone else to take care of us or clean up the mess we've made. We must each become willing in our own way to take responsibility for ourselves, discover the truths of who we are and to live our lives as a powerful example of transformation and possibility.

It's been said that these much larger systems we find ourselves apart of are only a reflection of the collective mind of humanity, and that can only mean one thing; our individual systems are wildly out of whack and could use some serious healing. If chaos and crisis precede transformation, then we are gearing up for a global metamorphosis. Universal change begins with individual change, so if we need a global healing that means change must begin with us. We are each responsible for the awakening and transformation of our world.

On an individual and social level, we're experiencing more (and more extreme) cases of addiction, mental illness, cancer, obesity, diabetes, autism, and all sorts of other afflictions that are rapidly growing and threatening the continuity of our species. Present-day, addiction is considered an epidemic that's crippling our nation. Over 81,000 lives were lost in the United States to overdose between 2019 and 2020. Thousands of children are being left without parents, and even more parents are watching their children deteriorate before ever really getting the chance to thrive. At least 50% of adults in our society will suffer from some type of chronic illness. One in two adolescents will suffer from some type of mental health disorder. Over 3.5 million children are on some type of stimulant medication for ADD or ADHD. Does this sound like a healthy society to you?

The nation-wide heartache and desperation have reached a breaking point, and we are left with few choices as to how to react to the current state of the world. We can continue to see the world's problems as happening *out there,* viewing ourselves as too insignificant to make a difference, and hoping that our yearly vote lands a worthy and competent politician in office. We can continue to live as a population divided, gorged on consumerism, absorbing only that which sustains our personal interests until we self-destruct. Or, we can awaken to the deepest fundamental truth—we are all *One.* What we choose to do as individuals impacts the whole of creation, and so, in order for us to solve our problems, we must individually and collectively evolve beyond the level of consciousness that created them.

What I think we all need to understand is that addiction itself is not the problem—neither is cancer, heart disease, global hunger, financial crisis, or personal trauma. These are not enemies in need of eradication. These global illnesses are the collective symptom of a bigger problem that's happening on a much more monumental scale. The real issue is that we have created a world that defies the laws of nature, a world devoid of essential connection, a world of humans disconnected from their souls; where division and separation are our predominant states—a world where fear is exploited and love is suppressed. For many, addictive behaviors are simply the best escape from a world that is so wildly out of balance. When people live in a way that is completely out of sync with natures laws, disease is inevitable. Despite our best technology and best attempts, diseases of all kinds continue to prevail. In fact, it seems we are sicker now than ever before. Why is that?

We're the sickest we've ever been because the vast majority of humans are living out of alignment with the natural order of creation. Our current dis-ease is a manifestation of our individual and collective dissonance, our non-harmonious state of being. It's an indication that something about the way we're living is fundamentally flawed. This dis-ease within our collective isn't necessarily a bad thing, it's a wake-up call—one that potentially becomes life-threatening if we fail to heed its warning.

If you look to nature, you'll see that nothing in nature is out of harmony; everything serves its purpose and works towards the benefit of the whole. Nature has its own brilliance, its own perfect order and intelligence. The problem now is that human beings have come to believe that we're smarter than nature. We no longer see ourselves as a part of the natural world; we see ourselves as the proprietors of it. There was a time in history when every life form was seen as sacred; every plant, animal, mineral, and human played its part in maintaining the balance of this divine world. We took only what we needed, never more. If life was taken to sustain life, be it plant or animal, that life was honored and respected—no part of it went to waste. Every day was full of ceremony, ritual, and celebration. It was well known that a great spirit moved through all things and that spirit was worshipped, in some way, by all. Sadly, the world we've created today would be unrecognizable to our ancestors. Due to greed, arrogance, and the destructive force of human unconsciousness we've fallen out of sync with the rest of nature. Many have forgotten our connection to the sacredness of life, and because of this, we've left very little but destruction and devastation in our wake. We've collectively created a world where mind feels severed from body, thinking has become disconnected from feeling and self is isolated from other; as a result, we feel separate from the fundamentals of what it means to be human. This major severance is why unhappiness, dis-ease, and addiction are so prevalent today. It's also why depression and suicide are at a record high. At this point in history, humanity has but two choices—awaken, or go extinct.

Although the whole world is currently in a state of dis-ease, and will likely remain so if we don't wake up, there is hope for us yet. If those who are called do the work to transform themselves, we can herald in an entirely new age of wisdom on our planet. By restoring wholeness and balance within ourselves, we can begin to restore harmony and balance to our ailing world. We do this with a willingness to awaken and remember who we are, not just from the level of our body or psyche, but by awakening the deepest part of us—*our souls*. We must *awaken* and *remember;* we're not just bodies, we are sentient, energetic beings with access to an infinite supply of creative potential.

This type of healing isn't some alternative therapy or pseudo-science for those that are suffering from disease, or those who identify as wounded or broken—healing is for everyone. This work is about understanding ourselves as human beings, and choosing to return ourselves to what is sacred. It's about reclaiming the fragmented pieces of ourselves lost to the traumas of life and recovering the essence of who we really are along the way. By learning about the impact of our childhood, familial and social programming, we can choose to unlearn what we absorbed that wasn't truth. In choosing to observe and alter our own behavior, we can become a spiritually mature species in the process. And as a healed society, we can start making new and better choices that will positively impact the generations to come. That's what it means to evolve—that's the power of healing.

PAIN AS AN INVITATION

"Not all storms come to disrupt your life;
some come to clear your path."
—Author Unknown

More often than not, people aren't motivated to heal until they're really unhappy, really hurting, or really sick. When the pressures of life become too real, when the capacity for suffering has reached its limit, the cost of remaining the same becomes a price too great to pay—only then, do most become willing to change. I'm curious, *are we there yet?*

When viewed through an appropriate lens, pain and displeasure of any kind can be exactly what we need to awaken the power and potential our pain has to offer us. The inescapable hardships of life—childhood traumas, failed relationships, addictions, diseases, and personal misfortunes can actually be quite exquisite gifts, *if* we're willing to use them as motivation to transform ourselves. If we don't use our personal adversities as fuel for growth, then we run the risk of feeling like we're being *punished* by them rather than *pushed* by them. Experiencing the painful reality of addiction turned out to be the greatest thing that ever happened to me. Feeling so severed from my authentic self and the desperate longing in my heart to be well was the exact catalyst I needed to pursue an awakening path of personal transformation.

Many opportunities for awakening will come in a way that initially forces us to feel uncomfortable. If we're too comfortable, chances are we're not really growing or challenging ourselves. Growth and change are an inevitable part of life— *everything* in life changes—*nothing* stays the same. Once you plant a seed and water it, it will change and grow. Once a new life is born, it will begin to change. Life *begins* and life *changes*—those are its only guarantees. Life wants to evolve because that's its nature, and human beings are really no different from life itself. What distinguishes human life from all other life, however, is our self-reflective conscious-ness that grants us the freedom of choice. This means that we can choose *against* life, we can choose *against* growth. Knowingly or not, we can choose to continue patterns of self-limiting behavior that serve only to keep us safe, and often stuck.

This also means, despite our fear, we can also choose to move through our pain and beyond our limitations. Often, when we've chosen against life's natural movement, invested too much energy in staying the same, playing it safe, giving into fear, or avoiding reality, the universe might sneak in a way to wake us up. Some-times that wake-up call shows up in the form of disease, a misfor-tune, or sudden and unexpected life disturbance. This isn't to say the universe is intentionally causing us pain. Pain is an inescapable part of life; the universe is simply offering the opportunity to grow from our painful experiences.

Once we learn to view life as our greatest teacher, feeling uncomfortable, feeling pain, or feeling unlike ourselves can also be seen as an invitation to heal. The prevailing human experience, however, usually encourages that we avoid discomfort at all costs. And we'll each utilize a myriad of strategies to avert our painful experiences. We'll enlist the help of comfort foods, alcohol, pre-scription medication, sex, drugs, gambling, video games, TV, social media, and anything else we can to avoid actually feeling whatever is causing us pain. But what if pain isn't the problem? What if pain is really just the messenger?

If we look deeply enough into the dysfunction and pain in our lives, we'll often find that most of our reasons for unhappiness actually have their roots in unresolved pain and trauma from the past. Before we had the proper tools for processing our pain and difficult experiences, we learned to repress our feelings, and then we got so good at numbing ourselves from our pain, that many of us forgot how to actually *feel* anything at all. The only way for us to *know* who we are, is to *feel* who we are—so *healing* requires *feeling*.

Many have lived with a lingering displeasure for so many years that they've accepted unhappiness as a way of life. While others finally reach a breaking point at which they can no longer endure a life of discomfort. They've become so depressed, so dissatisfied, or so desperate they're forced to make a choice—to either continue a life of suffering—or go within to find the source of their suffering and to *heal*.

Humans just don't commonly choose a path of healing in comfort. We become willing to heal, most often, when we're desperate and in distress. This is also why many wake up to a healing path only as the result of sudden and painful experience—a near death experience, the loss of a loved one, an illness, a sudden trauma, divorce, loss of a job, crisis, addiction or perhaps, even, a *pandemic*. After such events take place, we can't just go about business as usual anymore. We can't just stay in our own automatic, unconscious life patterns. We're forced to see ourselves and our lives from an entirely different perspective. We can no longer remain the same person we once were; pain changes us and forces us to adapt to new circumstances. But what if we didn't wait for crisis to initiate transformation? What if we chose the powerful path of transformation willingly? And what if the experience of pain is necessary, because without it—we might never evolve?

Painful events can be seen as obstacles in our path, or they can be considered *initiations to our awakening*. Illness, depression, and discomfort can actually be the callings of our spirits to examine the impact of our past, to observe our behaviors, and look at where our lives may be incongruent with our desires. Afflictions can show up in our lives as the exact invitations we need to awaken. Awakened people, the ones who've come fully alive despite life's most grueling experiences, don't often just *happen*, in the same way that diamonds aren't just effortlessly plucked from the earth. It takes billions of years and extreme heat and pressure to create just the right conditions for the alchemical transformation of rough and bumpy coal into its shiny diamond conclusion. Human beings undergo a similar process in order to awaken. They usually become mangled in life's process, shaken down to their cores, until they're so desperate for truth that they willingly strip away all that's flawed within them. Awakened people are as precious and rare as diamonds, and many, if not most, were birthed through some form of intense suffering.

Maybe you were molested as a child. Your ex-husband beat you. You developed a cancer. Your mother was an abusive sociopath. Your father was an alcoholic and a dictator. You've lived a lifetime in the shadow of a highly driven parent and now you're killing yourself by desperately trying to live up to their unrealistic standards of what your life is supposed to look like. You have a deformity. You never got the love you know you deserved. You grew up in poverty. You lost someone who meant the world to you. You were bullied and ostracized in school for being different. You were abandoned. Or, maybe, you're depressed and have no idea what direction you should be going in. All of these painful stories, held tightly our hearts, tethered to a belief that *they're* what's preventing us from fully living, are also holding within their palms the shining key to our glorious freedom.

Without the guilt and shame associated with trauma, one glimpses a dimension of healing not quite visible on the immediate surface of our painful experiences. From a different perspective, you might be able to see that admitting an addiction is far from failure. Recognizing abuse doesn't make you at fault. Acknowledging that you were, and maybe still are, deeply wounded by your parents or your abusive siblings shouldn't make you feel weak. Knowing that you spent your life avoiding the sharp pain of self-hatred; owning that your heartbreak devastated you beyond your personal ability to repair it; or simply admitting that you have no idea what the hell you're doing in life doesn't need to be veiled in painful disgrace.

Instead, it can be revered as the resplendent invitation that it is. Your pain is the pathway back to your heart, a reminder that you are *alive*. It is awakening you to your own inner resilience and strength—you can never resolve it by running from it. Painful events are a summons to do the great work, yet only few will truly heed the call. Running from our pain or trying to numb ourselves to its presence only thwarts our ability to use the experience as fuel for growth. Life's hardships can serve as the sandpaper that polishes our rough edges, like the sharp rocks used by a snake when it's time to shed a skin that's grown too tight. They can be the chisel that chips away packed on mud to reveal a shiny golden Buddha beneath. We can allow our pain to harden us, or we can grant it permission to dismantle our defenses.

Pain is what ushered me into the most transformative part of my life.

THE NEED TO ESCAPE

"The essence of trauma is a disconnection from ourselves.
Trauma is not terrible things that happen to us from
the other side—those are traumatic. But that trauma is
the very separation from the body and emotions."
—Gabor Maté

Dr. Gabor Mate frequently asks the question, "Not why the addiction, but why the pain?" After a lifetime of working with addicts, he's concluded that addicts don't just become addicts for no reason, on some level they're hurt and suffering. Hidden far beneath the layers of habitual, negative behavior is some form of lingering pain. Substance abuse and all other forms of addiction aren't really the problem—they're the solution to pain.

The first time I tried opiates, I wasn't really looking to escape. I was more or less longing to fit in. I think that's why I didn't develop an immediate dependence on them. However, around the time of my 18th birthday, the pain in my life had become so great that I didn't have the tools to deal with it, and escape was the only thing I knew that worked.

At that point in my life, my mom was working as a saleswoman for a mint in our hometown. Her company manufactured coins, or tokens, for places like casinos, arcades, and, coincidently or not, Alcoholics Anonymous and Narcotics Anonymous support groups. After four years of working for them, she started growing suspicious of some of their seemingly dishonest business practices.

Although skeptical, she kept her suspicions to herself until one day in early spring she was called into the President's office where, much to her surprise, she was met by a group of three FBI agents. The FBI was there to investigate as to whether or not the mint she worked for was producing and selling counterfeit currency.

First, how does this level of organized crime find its way into our small hometown? Second, how the hell does my totally innocent and naive mother find herself smack dab in the middle of it?! I just couldn't wrap my head around it.

To make a long story short, without hesitation, my mother agreed to cooperate with the FBI, assisting them in their investigation so they could get to the bottom of the fraudulent activity. As it turned out, her company was indeed producing counterfeit merchandise, and shortly after this information was unearthed, the mint began to dissolve.

My mother has never been the type to question any kind of authority. She's a stand-in-line, follow-the-rules, and don't-ask-questions kind of gal. So, when the FBI asked her to testify against a group of organized crime members, although reluctant, she agreed. She never really questioned whether or not she had a choice. But shortly after she agreed to testify, some bizarre things started happening around our house, and to her specifically.

On May 10th, 2004, I answered a phone call from my mom. It was her 42nd birthday and she'd just received a big, beautiful bouquet of roses at work. She wanted to know who to thank, so she called around to all of her immediate family. The card with the flowers was unsigned, but came in an envelope addressed XXX. "Surprise!" was the only word written on the inside. After numerous phone calls to friends and family, she still couldn't figure out who sent the flowers.

When she started her drive home later that night, she was completely oblivious to the fact that the rear end of her car was rattling and shaking abnormally. That is, until she glanced up to see flashing blue lights in her rearview mirror with accompanying sirens. When she pulled over, the officer approached her car with a look of genuine concern on his face. "Ma'am, are you aware that your rear tire is about to fall off?" he asked, as he pulled out his flashlight to inspect things a bit further. Every single lug nut on my mom's rear right tire had been loosened; three of them had fallen off on the short ride from her office to the on ramp. If it hadn't been for that officer pulling her over, she probably would have lost the tire on the highway, and who knows what might have happened.

Weeks later, the driver's side window of her car was smashed out.

This was just the beginning of numerous threats that continued for weeks. What came next was almost as traumatic, if not worse, than the fear of losing the most important person in my life. I came home one day and noticed that my dad's most prized hunting dog, a fifteen-year-old beagle named Zeb (who was more of a family member than a dog) was acting really strange. He was wobbly and disoriented; he couldn't seem to stand upright without falling over, and we couldn't figure out what was wrong with him. He had been fine earlier in the morning, so we started checking around his cage to see if he had gotten into something. That's when we noticed the antifreeze in his dog bowl. We also found more bowls of antifreeze scattered around the yard and in with our ducks and chickens.

Whoever was threating my mom had now resorted to poisoning our animals.

Zeb never recovered from being poisoned so we had to put him down. It was heart-wrenching and my dad spent the next two weeks in the attic with a shotgun, ready to kill anyone who stepped foot on our property. I was scared; he was really ready to shoot someone. But they never showed up again the entire two weeks he was there. They seemed to know our every move.

They must have known when he went back to work, because that's when the break-ins started happening. The danger of the situation became painfully obvious on the day they broke into our house and poisoned our Chihuahua. Gus was a brown-and-tan apple-head Chihuahua, a gift given to me by an ex-boyfriend, who had quickly become our family dog. He was only two years old and we all loved him very much. I had slept out at Deven's house the night prior and didn't come home until late afternoon. When I got home around 5pm, I realized the bowl in Gus's crate was full of anti-freeze, so we rushed him to the animal hospital where he was stabilized, but it was confirmed that someone had poisoned him.

This was the moment I knew that it really wasn't safe for me to stay at home anymore, so I packed my things and moved in with my aunt. On that very same night, Deven was moving into the apartment directly across the street from her. Could that have been a coincidence? I guess it's possible, but it didn't seem likely. And, I no longer believe in coincidences.

After unpacking a few of my things, I decided to leave my aunt's house. I was anxious, scared, and brokenhearted. I didn't know if Gus would live or die, and if these people were okay with killing animals, how could I be sure they wouldn't kill me or my family? The thought alone was terrifying. Leaving my aunt's house that night, I crossed over Route 1 and stepped into an entirely new destiny. I walked into Deven's new apartment as he was repeating a ritual I'd seen before; he was scraping the blue coating off a small round pill, crushing the pill into a fine powder, and using a credit card to separate the pile of powder into a few equal lines. One by one, we all took turns snorting them, just as we had before—only this time it didn't make me sick at all—this time, *I fell in love*.

When the powdered pill dissolved into my bloodstream, I felt a warm presence embrace me completely, like receiving a soft, loving hug from the divine. I fell back into the down comforter on Deven's bed and it was like falling into a cloud. All of my stress, my fear, my worries, and my heartaches disappeared, but so did my joy, my passions, and my dreams. That night, I fell deeply into a state of blissful oblivion. But I woke the next morning to the familiar pangs of heartache, fear, and anxiety that coalesced with my present reality, only this time I was aware that there was an antidote to my pain. This period of my life became a huge turning point for me. Taking hard drugs to temporarily numb the pain rapidly developed into an all-day, everyday habit.

The attacks eventually stopped, but my dog ended up dying from the poison, I was completely devastated, and I spent the next three years running from my pain. I became a regular drinker, and welcomed just about any type of narcotic offered to me. The drugs and alcohol certainly served to numb the pain on the surface, but were inevitably driving me much further into my own suffering, not to mention they were causing a huge rift in my relationship with Deven. When we finally broke up, I found myself going through an incredibly difficult dark night of the soul. I was heartbroken, seriously drug-addicted, and definitely suicidal. But, born from that place of absolute desperation was a subtle, barely detectable, desire to heal.

When I was desperate and searching, I found myself standing in the self-help section of a Border's bookstore, and that's where I first picked up the book *The Secret* by Rhonda Byrne. *The Secret* is based on the law of attraction which tells us that like attracts like, and that what we think about, we're likely to bring about into our lives. Reading *The Secret* was my first introduction to the idea that I created my own reality and that my thoughts had everything to do with it. While reading that book it dawned on me; I may have been a drug addict, and my life was a bit of a mess, but *I* was in control of my *thoughts*. It was a huge revelation. I started to wonder if maybe the thoughts I'd been thinking had some influence on my current predicament. Could it have been possible that my negative, self-limiting thoughts had created a life of pain, insecurity, failed relationships, and drug addiction?

MYSTERY SCHOOL

"If you want to know who your tribe is, speak your truth.
Then see who sticks around. Those are the people
who get a spot in your blanket fort."
—Nanea Hoffman

By the time I was twenty years old I'd created a personality based on an inner dialogue of questionable-worthiness. Loving myself was a really difficult thing for me to learn. My daily habits and behaviors only reinforced what I'd already thought to be true—I just wasn't a worthy or lovable person. But reading *The Secret* slowly initiated a change in me. After reading, I really started paying attention to what was happening inside my mind. I started taking control of my own thoughts and noticing the impact that had on how I felt throughout the day, and that's when I noticed my life start dramatically changing.

Reading *The Secret* was like falling down a rabbit hole; it introduced me to an entirely new genre of information and opened up a whole new world of inspiration. While I found myself in unfamiliar territory, much like Alice, it felt as though I had somehow been there before. In some peculiar way, this wonderland of information already felt like home. It all felt so familiar that I couldn't help but wonder, was I learning, or I was *remembering*?

My newly found appetite for knowledge inspired me to study the art of Reiki, a Japanese hands-on healing technique that emerged in the 1800s, and I began to read as much as I could on any subject related to healing. Chakras, energy medicine, law of attraction, personal development, and human consciousness—I devoured it all. Almost as if it happened overnight, I was completely impassioned with a love of learning that I'd never before experienced during my traditional education. Sadly though, I knew very few people as deeply fascinated by, or even interested in this new school of thought. The more I tried to share my new-found passion with my family and friends, the more alienated I started to feel. It became painfully obvious that not everyone in my circle was as ready or willing as I was to peel back the layers of pain and dive into the potentials of healing. I wasn't just ready—I was *desperate*.

Once I became aware that my thoughts were powerful creators and started filling my mind with positive books and information that kept me lit up and inspired, my point of attraction definitely shifted. I was now less interested in escaping my pain, and more interested in understanding it. I was still seriously abusing drugs, but I believe the subtle shift in energy from the need to escape to observing my behavior with curiosity was exactly what drew me to an energy medicine mystery school, one that totally catapulted my spiritual growth.

Finding the school was a truly magical moment in my life. I didn't go out of my way searching for it, one day it just kind of just showed up in my peripheral. I was invited to an open house, and as soon as I walked through the doors, I just knew it was a place I needed to be. Everything about the school felt like home. I couldn't really explain it, it just *felt* right. Today, I don't have a single doubt that I was led there by some form of divine intervention. In those early years of awakening, and still to this day, everything seems so full of magic. When I enrolled in energy medicine school, I understood what Harry must have felt like receiving his first owl letter from Hogwarts School of Witchcraft and Wizardry. For perhaps the first time in my life, I felt a deep sense of belonging; not the belonging one feels as a part of a family, but a deeper, more soul-felt sense of belonging *in the world.* The fact that a school like this even existed was assurance that I wasn't alone, and this created a feeling of safety I never even knew I longed for. My classmates, a tribe of like-minded, like-hearted individuals, became the perfect container I needed to grow into the person I was destined to become. After floating around amongst a sea of muggles, I had finally found my kin.

ENERGY MEDICINE

"In every culture and in every medical tradition before ours, healing was accomplished by moving energy."
—Albert Szent Gyorgyi

The school consistently emphasized the importance of discovering and mastering the self; not just the physical self, or the limited ego self, but the *whole* self—including the *soul* self. Prior to awakening, I'd never really considered that there was much more to me than my body or my mind. But all of a sudden, the symbolism was everywhere. It seemed like everywhere I looked, there was a metaphor relating to this goal of awakening the true self. It was mentioned in every spiritual text I read, and even the Disney movies seemed to know this universal secret. I remember watching a scene in Disney's *The Lion King*, where Mufasa's spirit appears in the sky, urging Simba to "remember who you are" and feeling like he was whispering to me. I was finally starting to understand what my journey was calling for—I needed to get to know myself at a deeper level. I needed to start peeling back the layers of conditioning, and reveal who I really was.

Inscribed on the temple of Apollo at Delphi are the words, *Know Thyself*, made popular by the late philosopher Socrates, who taught us that "the unexamined life is not worth living." The truth that underlies this ancient Greek aphorism is ultimately what all mystics, yogis, seekers and saints are directing us towards—the discovery of who we *really* are. And that's exactly what life in the school was teaching. I'd begun dismantling some of the energetic barriers I'd created to protect myself, and started reconnecting to my original nature, my *energetic* nature—the nature of my *soul*—and it felt really, really good.

Self-inquiry, as Socrates taught, is almost always what encourages us to begin asking deep, soul-provoking questions like "who am I?", "why was I born?", and "what is the meaning and purpose of my life?" When I started asking myself these questions, life got serious about delivering the answers. Asking those questions is what lead me to the healing arts of energy medicine.

Studying energy medicine is what woke me up to realize that I was much more than I'd previously thought myself to be. I started to really see myself as more than just a body, more than my personality, and capable of more than my limiting beliefs would allow me to believe. Learning the healing arts also helped me open to and navigate the many complexities that came with simply being human, acquainting me with many aspects of myself and life that I hadn't previously been aware of. Understanding this work changed my life so profoundly that I've spent the last decade studying it and figuring out ways to share what I've learned in hopes that I might be of service to others.

What I've learned is that most anyone who embarks on a journey of self-discovery, be it through yoga, meditation, fasting, cleansing, spiritual discipline or even deep and painful suffering will eventually come to understand; the self they once thought to be true, the self that they protect and defend, isn't actually all of who they are. In fact, most of who we believe ourselves to be is actually impermanent and illusory. When the illusory self sits unobserved in the driver's seat of our lives, suffering is almost always inevitable. But learning to apply the principles and wisdom of energy medicine to daily life is one way to awaken and alleviate some of our suffering. It's one of the ways we can dismantle our *defended* self and awaken to our *true* self—a self which is beyond label and beyond form.

Energy Medicine is basically a combination of rigorous self-inquiry and the intentional application of wisdom, combined with various mind/body optimization techniques in order to achieve homeostasis in the body's natural energetic current. Although energy medicine is certainly gaining popularity, it's still considered a bit of a fringe subject for those who aren't actively persuing a spiritual path. Fortunately for us spiritualists, the emerging science of today is finally catching up with what great spiritual masters and many esoteric traditions have been saying for quite some time; everything in our universe is made up of energy—including *us*! Although the vast majority of us can't perceive it with our physical eyes—*energy*, not *matter*—is the fabric of our existence. And healing ourselves at the energetic level is the most powerful healing we can accomplish.

As soon as life enters our body, so does this energy—which is really the creative impulse of the universe. Some have referred to this energy as *Ki*, *Chi*, or *Prana*. Others have called it source, the field, orgone, zero-point, quantum and even God, amongst many other names as well. Whichever title given, this energy is a living intelligence. It's a force of life that wants to move through us, guide us, take what is intangible, and through our physical vessel, birth it into manifested form. When we're children, this energy blasts through our little systems like firehoses. Unrestricted, it moves in us and we can't help but follow its directive. We'd bounce and flail around, run and shriek, jump and sing. We'd move ourselves not by the rules of a fixed belief system, but rather the innate intelligence that's giving us life.

As children, we spent the majority of our time in this energetic realm. Our experience wasn't necessarily one of matter and material, it was of the invisible world of the formless. We were sensing everything, feeling everything, intuiting everything. As children, we experienced ourselves not as bodies, but as free flowing fields of intelligent energy. Life for an unrestricted child is one epic sensation, sometimes pleasurable, sometimes painful, but a sensational adventure nonetheless. At that point, we weren't creating life; life was creating *itself* through us! We weren't *living* our lives; we were the expression of life itself. And this is the way life is designed to be experienced. But somewhere along the way something happened to the majority of us, and instead of allowing this intelligent energy to guide us into a full body experience, we started trusting in a difference source to guide us instead. The main reason why children live this way and most adults don't is because children haven't yet severed themselves from the vibrancy of their spirit. Children are still connected to their energetic nature. They aren't experiencing life in the way adults do, as something happening *to* them, or as something potentially painful they might need to defend themselves against. In their most natural state, a child perceives life as something fun and exciting, something they're not separate from, but an intimate part of.

So, if this energetic flow is our natural state, what happened to us? What caused this separation between ourselves and our essential *energetic* nature?

In many different ways, and for many different reasons—we learned to restrict the flow of this vital life-force energy. We learned through a process of social conditioning and various pains and traumas to hold ourselves back and separate from our true selves. This is when life stopped being an epic, intuitive, full body sensation, and became more of a mental process instead. These moments of separation between ourselves and our energetic nature landmark pivotal moments for us, and the majority of people still aren't aware that such events ever took place.

There was a brief time during every one of our lives when we were completely and totally free. Our body, our environment and time were these complex mental constructs that we hadn't yet developed the faculty for. We were vessels of pure spirit, replete only with soul; and we were completely immersed in the intimate experience of being *one* with all that is. Before we incarnated into this body, and for a short time afterward, there was no experience of separation between ourselves and the infinite. We were simply a presence, an awareness, a perceiver of consciousness; and at our core, this is still *who we really are.* The idea that we could ever be separate from the infinite is an illusion, one that we like to refer to as *reality.* Most of us carry this connection to source with us through infancy, however, the connection to source energy usually fades with our growing connection to the body, our family, and this material world.

As babies, the light of the universe would shine through our eyes, lifting the spirits of even the most dismal of characters. People are naturally attracted to newborns because they still resemble the heavenly, and on some level, they remind us of our connection to the infinite. They awaken the same soulful quality that remains within us, no matter how far removed from it we may be. Babies haven't yet been domesticated by the adults of this world; their energetic signature hasn't yet been conditioned out of them. They don't know hatred, judgement, fear, or insecurity. They only know love. They only know *presence.* Young children love their bodies and all the fun that being in a body provides. The thought that maybe their bodies aren't good enough, that they're too big or too little, too short or too tall, or *too anything,* doesn't enter their minds until we put it there. Children are unapologetically themselves, and they understand that being exactly who they are is a fantastic thing to be. They haven't yet developed the need for soul-searching because they are still the embodiment of soul. Their essence hasn't yet been buried beneath an illusory identity that they then feel required to uphold. Many have referred to this separate identity as *ego,* which we'll talk about later.

From the instant we're born into this material world, our parents, relatives, and siblings strive to capture our attention. This reliably pulls us from our place in the infinite and into a material, mechanical, and predictable world of form. The more we learn to identify with the material world, the more we restrict the flow of the universe from moving through us, and the denser we become. The moment we gain an awareness of *our* body and all of its parts, *our* name, and *our* gender is the moment we begin to separate from the true energetic signature of our soul and learn to identify more with the personality and material world. The illusion of separation really takes its stronghold when the world of form becomes *reality* and the invisible world of energy becomes *fantasy.*

Once a child firmly establishes himself as a separate entity, he learns to judge his very existence by what he can experience through his physical senses and will continually use the external world to validate himself. Body parts, toys, and personal objects become an extension of self; certain people are made special and given the titles of mommy, daddy, brother, sister, etc. Children will take pride in the ownership of such extensions of themselves and use them to reinforce the notion that who they are as a body and personality is what's *real.* As soon as a child learns to define themselves by their connection to the material world, they begin to slowly lose touch with the unseen energetic realm. Before we're even verbal, we create these illusory identities as a way to reinforce the belief that we're permanent fixtures in our own lives. This somehow feels safer and more predictable to us than the actual truth—who we are in this body is unknowable and impermanent. Our eternal truth is an ever-changing field of *energy,* but as we strive for some semblance of control of our lives, we learn to cling to our material identities.

Our first experiences of painful rejection, abandonment, and disapproval causes us to restrict ourselves and withdraw the flow of this energy from moving through us. In order to avoid pain and to gain pleasure we learn gradually over time and through various life experience to withhold the natural expression of our vital life-force. What results is usually a watered-down version of who we really are—or a supercharged version of who we're not. We become a defended character that's created as a response to our earthy environment. The false-self reflects less of our soul and more of the strategies we adapted for feeling safe; these strategies become the energetic patterns we follow to make sure we can survive in the world we're born into. Our energy current is more like our essence; its similar to our soul's truth. It comes through us, but not from us—we can't change it because we were literally born to express it. It's highly likely that as children, we traded in our authentic selves for a self that reflected the people we grew up around. Instead of emitting our own energetic frequency, we absorbed the frequencies around us. This energetic severance is the underlying cause of most unhappiness and dis-ease in our lives.

This subtle energy that exists within and all around us is meant to flow through our system in the same way it did when we were children, in the same way that water flows through a stream, continuous and unobstructed. An unobstructed river is clean, clear, tranquil, ever-moving and ever-flowing. A river doesn't need to force or restrict its flow, its own innate intelligence will move it where its guided. That's a rivers nature, and it's our nature too. Our life force knows exactly how to move us and how to guide us—it knows exactly how to express itself through us in a way that feels natural and intuitive. But think of a river that's accumulated too much debris; its easily dammed, and eventually, it stagnates. Our human energy system behaves much like a river. It can flow freely through us, and when it does, our lives feel vibrant, vital, ever-moving and ever-flowing; we're literally and figuratively full of creative potential. When our energy is flowing freely it doesn't matter our age, we feel like children, excited just to be alive.

In contrast to that aliveness, our energy body can also collect debris and eventually become obstructed by subtle energies. Throughout the course of our lives, most of us are likely to have collected a host of invisible energetic debris; unresolved trauma, bad habits, toxic thoughts and emotions, stress, fear and phobias all get lodged in the river of our energy. When these traumas and fears go unprocessed, and exposure to mental, emotional, and environmental stress becomes chronic, our energy current loses some of its charge and eventually our whole system can begin to stagnate. This is when our lives start to feel heavy, tiresome, and unfulfilling. It's also when dis-ease can take root in the mind and body. The majority of people will feel this separation as a lack of fulfillment. They will spend their lives in a perpetual state of longing without ever knowing why, endlessly searching for gratification in the external environment and never quite realizing that the solution to their problem can't be found outside of them because the problem lies in the disconnect between themselves and their original nature. The only way to heal this divide is to become willing to remove the blocks in our energy, to unravel our traumas, move through our pain, and reconnect to our true self—our original, *energetic* nature. The recovery and cultivation of our true self as an expression of divine energy is the very essence of energy medicine.

SAYING YES TO LIFE

"The agony of breaking through personal limitations
is the agony of spiritual growth."
—Joseph Campbell

After spending almost two years in energy medicine school addressing my pain and identifying my programming, I was becoming acutely aware of the incongruence between my inner and outer worlds. On the school weekends I felt seen and understood, playful, joyful, and alive. My self-concept of questionable worthiness was starting to fade, and my confidence was growing. With each step I took away from my negative mental programs, the closer I moved towards the true quality of my spirit. In the school I saw myself as knowledgeable, magical, and powerful, but my life outside of school was very different. I was basically a junkie—a painful truth that I tactfully avoided sharing, even with my closest classmates. But I also knew that if I was going to fully embrace my calling as a healer, I needed to make a serious change in my life. I was finally feeling ready to become the person I knew I was capable of being, but that meant doing something I'd been avoiding for almost a decade. It meant facing my addiction and actually saying *yes* to my own life.

One midsummer day while perusing Netflix, I found a documentary called *Facing the Habit*. It was a film that showcased a former stock broker using *ibogaine*, an African plant medicine, to overcome his addiction to heroin. As I lay in my bed watching the film on my computer, a stillness came over me. I began to feel this vaguely familiar sensation, the same sensation I received upon walking into the energy medicine school for the first time—it was an inner *yes*, the gentle stirring of what I now recognize as my soul's presence. I watched this man's detox experience with great interest and curiosity. His detox looked nothing like the traditional protocols I was familiar with. There were no prescriptions, no daily maintenance, no counselors, no meetings, and he didn't experience any obvious pain or withdrawal sickness. The journey he took seemed to be an inward one, with an underlying spirituality to it. There was no doubt in my mind after numerous failed attempts at getting clean, ibogaine was exactly the medicine I needed.

On Thanksgiving Day, 2011, which also happened to be my birthday, my brother handed me a heavy brown paper bag. Inside the bag was an assortment of items, all wrapped individually in a deep purple tissue paper. I unwrapped each piece, one by one, revealing a beautiful collection of crystals—my favorite thing at the time. But instead of being excited, I was left with this sinking feeling in my gut and an emptiness in my chest. I knew that my brother must have spent well over $250 dollars on that collection, and I also knew exactly what I would have bought had I been handed the $250 in cash. The fact that he thought I was worthy of such a wonderful gift actually made me reflect on the seemingly worthless lifestyle I'd been living. As brief as it may have been, that fleeting *aha* moment of clarity was just the catalyst I needed to make a decision. I woke up the next morning knowing exactly what I needed to do, and despite how difficult I knew it would be, I had to be completely honest about what I'd been hiding, and get clear about what kind of help I needed.

That morning, I told my mother I'd been hiding a serious opiate dependency for well over 6 years. She acted stunned. I'm sure deep down she already knew the truth, she'd just been dreading the day it came to surface. As I watched her process what I'd shared, I experienced the deep pains of guilt, shame, and humiliation that often accompany addiction—emotions I'd been avoiding for a very long time. In those moments of discomfort, I came to understand why those who struggle with addiction will try desperately to hide their truth. In that very same moment it became clear, the only way to escape pain is to move through it. After the initial shock wore off, my mom and I were able to sit down and talk about my plans to use plant medicine to heal from the trauma of addiction. She was skeptical, but she supported me, and less than two months later I was on boarding a plane, about to embark upon a journey destined to change my life forever.

Ibogaine isn't drug to me. It's a medicine, a wise teacher, a healer, and a guide—one who just happens to appear in the form of a plant. Shockingly, it seemed that even this plant-teacher knew something about the power of energy medicine! At one point during my journey with iboga, I found myself standing and facing some kind of energy generating tower with very large horseshoe shaped magnets, one in each of my hands. The magnets were the kind you might see in a cartoon. They were big, red, and U shaped, with silver caps on the ends. The energy generator looked like a very large, life sized electrical outlet. It had two slots directly in the center that fit the ends of these magnets perfectly. There I stood with the magnets in my hands, arms outstretched, walking slowly towards the generator. When I plugged my magnets into the sockets, I felt massive jolts of electricity coursing through my entire body. The experience was almost painful, like being electrocuted. When the sensation became too intense, I would unplug and back away from the machine for a couple seconds, only to walk towards it again plugging myself back in. I would receive the same intense charge of energy over and over again, continuing to repeat the process until it felt as though my own energy had finally been restored. Some might say it was only a vision, but I can assure you, this *wasn't* a vision, this was a visceral *experience*. I actually felt the electricity coursing through my body for weeks following my journey with ibogaine. The entire experience realigned me in a way that words fail to express. I can only assume that the effects of my traumas, my poor self-worth, and my toxic lifestyle had caused my life-force energy to become radically imbalanced, and this was the metaphorical equivalent of a jumpstart from the Universe. It wasn't long after my experience with iboga that I found myself naturally gravitating towards things I once enjoyed as a child—writing, making art, exploring nature, playing, and finding joy in the simplicity of connecting with friends. It was as if the natural intelligence that I'd disconnected myself from was finally able to move through me again, and as a result my authentic nature was reemerging. It felt awesome. After ibogaine, I never abused drugs again.

You're probably thinking, "I don't really want to take hallucinogens and get electrocuted just so I can heal my energy." And the good news is, I'm confident that you won't have to! Not everyone needs to journey with ibogaine or get electrocuted by an energy generator to remove the blocks in their system. There's already another system that's quite effective in healing humans energetically, some parts of it dating as far back as five thousand years. This is the system I've been studying for the past decade, and the system I'll be introducing to you next.

INTRODUCING THE SYSTEM

"A good system shortens the road to the goal."
—Orison Sweet Marden

When I silently wondered to myself after my profound experience with ibogaine what it meant to *heal the people*, I didn't quite anticipate that the next 10 years of my life would serve as a boot camp, an initiation by fire kind of training. In addition to that, I could have never predicted that the world would wind up in its current position—that pandemics, politics, news outlets and social media would basically threaten to tear apart everything that humans consider holy and sacred and true. That family members would turn against family members, schools, churches, gyms, restaurants, and small businesses would be forced to close their doors, some of them forever, and that segregation might once again force a percentage of the population into potential exile. The world we're experiencing today was unimaginable to me back then, but somehow, a higher hand must have foreseen these times and chose to prepare me in advance. In hindsight, I can now understand why I've had to experience the rock-bottom-moments of my life; I can see how every obstacle I've ever overcome has been utilized to assist my ability to serve others. And how everything I've ever been through was all so I could deliver this system of healing to you.

According to Dictioniary.com, *a system is an assemblage or combination of things or parts forming a complex or unitary whole.* By that definition we can see how the universe and all of life that exists within it is actually a perfect system, and basically everything that operates within life's system is a system in itself. From the most expansive galaxy systems, all the way down to the smallest colonies of microscopic lifeforms, all of life is really just a system operating within another system. Think of all the systems that we observe and participate in on a daily basis—galaxy systems, solar systems, ecosystems, country systems, state systems, community, school, and family systems, the list goes on and on. From our vantage point, all of these seemingly separate parts might appear as if they're independently operating, but if we can just expand our perspective, the reality becomes clear—all of these things are actually interconnected. We're all participating in one big holographic system, and each and every part is having an influence on all the others. All systems, it doesn't matter which kind, work best when all its parts are working together to benefit the whole, and right now, the human system is struggling to fulfil its role as a healthy contributor to our larger planetary system. But there's one profoundly powerful system that has the power and potential to change all of that. This system has the power to influence all other life systems, from the microcosm all the way to the macrocosm, and that's the human energy system.

The human energy system is a truly genius system that's history dates back over five thousand years, originally appearing in the ancient Indian text of the Vedas. The human energy system, also referred to as the chakra system, encompasses every single aspect of what it means to be both an animal and a soul, to be a human and a spirit, to exist as matter and at the same time, as energy. The chakra system is broken down into seven primary energy centers, each one governing a specific area of the body as well as the level of consciousness associated with it. Each center addresses an aspect of our humanity—our need for survival; our yearning to experience pleasure and a deep-felt sense of power; our desire for love and to express ourselves creatively, as well as our mental processes;

natural intuitive capabilities; our essential spiritual nature; and our desire to connect with a force that's greater than ourselves. We'll be exploring each of these centers in greater detail in the chapters that follow. You may find that I use the words *chakra* and *system* interchangeably. That's because each chakra is essentially its own system; it has its own consciousness, its own function, and its own program. Each chakra, or energetic system describes a basic function of our humanity. I've labeled these individually as the Root System, the Sensate System, the Personal Power system, the Compassionate System, the Creative Communication System, the Psychic Intuitive System, and the Divinity System. When combined each of these systems amount to the entire human energy system. When the individual systems that comprise the human energy system are cleaned up, cleared out, and brought into alignment with the rest of the system, they begin to function as a whole, and this system becomes so powerful that it actually has the capability of activating and entraining other human energy systems into alignment as well.

THE HUMAN ENERGY SYSTEM

"I can tell you that anything that happens in the physical body will happen in the pattern of the energy fields first."
—Barbara Brennan

According to Vedic literature life-force energy is said to move about the body via energy pathways known as *nadis*, which is a Sanskrit word for *tube* or *channel*, and also through intense energy centers known as *chakras*, a Sanskrit word for *wheel* or *disk*. These tubes and channels can't be observed by the naked eye because they don't exactly exist within the human body, they exist within the less perceptible, subtle energy body. I understand that this concept of invisible tubes, vortexes, and chakras can definitely seem a bit lofty to someone who hasn't had any training in seeing or sensing energy, therefore, that's not how I plan to explain them to you. My goal is to break the chakra system down into levels of consciousness so easy to understand that you'll begin to realize you've been speaking chakra your entire life, you just never had a language for it—until now. When the human energy system is broken down in this way, you won't have to be worried about developing a sixth sense or being able to see balls of light spinning around in your body. Instead, you'll be using your own life as a mirror to reflect back to you the health of your energy body, as well as the areas that need work. But because this is a book about the healing power of energy medicine, I think it best to give you a very basic understanding of how energy operates within the energy system, and how that energy is expressed through the human organism.

Many of us are familiar with the oriental symbol of Yin Yang, as it represents a unity experienced when two polarities are brought into balance. It's a simple, yet powerful, image, that illustrates what it means to be wholly-human. As humans, we experience a vast amount of polarity—day and night, sun and moon, male and female, hot and cold, positive and negative. We channel masculine as well as feminine energy. We have a left brain and a right brain. We experience chaos and order, logic and emotion, pleasure and pain. Almost everything about our reality is chock full of contrasting experiences, which is why learning the chakra system is essential to our wholistic-human development. The chakra system teaches us how to integrate the polarities of our humanness, our body with our mind, our emotions with our logic, our inner world with our outer reality, aligning us with the totality of our entire being.

We see the same basic principle of polarity expressed in Hinduism. In Hindu mysticism, the polarities of yin and yang are depicted as two interwoven serpents, Ida and Pingala. These two snakes begin at opposite sides of the base of the spine and once roused, make a spiral ascent upwards towards the crown of the head. Ida, Pingala, and the spinal column they climb are considered the three primary energy pathways, the *nadis*. Ida represents the left, female channel or *yin* energy and Pingala represents the right, male channel or *yang* energy. Each crossing point between the two serpents creates a spiraling vortex, *a chakra*. The chakras are centers within the human energy system responsible for receiving energetic information from our environment, interpreting how that information impacts us, and broadcasting our own energetic signature out into the world. Life-force energy isn't *fixed* in the way that matter appears to be, it's always moving, always fluctuating, always aligning itself and adhering to the potentials and conditions of our lives. That means if our lives are unchanging, it's because our life-force energy is stuck in a holding pattern somewhere in our chakras. When a chakra in our system is blocked or our energy flow diminished, our lives can begin to feel stuck, stagnant, or sluggish and the conscious connection to our vital life-force begins to dwindle. Once this happens, our days become repetitive and our weekly tasks feel tiresome and unfulfilling. If a chakra is blocked, or unable to move enough energy though it, it can begin to feel as if life itself is nothing but a heavy burden that we've been mandated to carry. However, when these energy centers are activated, when they're cleared out and restored to a state of balance and harmony, our bodies are strong, our minds are clear, our lives are vibrant, and we're passionate and enthusiastic about what we're creating. As we learn to cultivate this energy, we effortlessly open channels for divinity to move through us. We become a living embodiment of our own luminous light bodies, rainbow bridges to the heavenly, physical expressions of divinity, and we anchor in an entirely new level of consciousness on our planet.

Energy moves through each of our chakras in a multitude of different ways—our chakras can be *blocked* or *unmoving*; they can be *excessive* or holding too much energy; they can be *deficient*, not holding enough energy; or they can be fluctuating somewhere in between. Chakras can even be both *excessive and deficient* depending upon a situation. In an ideal world, our energy would be *balanced*, flowing freely and evenly throughout of each of our chakras. Chakras serve as our invisible interpreters who speak fluently in a silent, universal tongue; they serve as the interface between our spirit, psyche, and the material world. They've been developing systematically since the time we spent in our mother's womb (perhaps before even) and have been continually influenced by all life events that followed. Birth, infancy, toddlerhood, youth, adolescence, adulthood, and beyond have all left an impression on our energy field and each experience is recorded in our chakras. Each chakra opens and develops sequentially as we grow from infants into adults, each carrying its own specific frequency, characteristic, and information in accordance with our life experience at certain ages and the specific stages of development that accompany that age. Our current lifestyle, habits, behaviors, thoughts, and emotions also have a tremendous impact on our chakras as well. Experiences ranging from trauma to euphoria and the remnants of many unprocessed life experiences are all housed in our chakras. The present health of our body, the clarity of our minds, and the vitality of our spirit are all a direct result of how we've managed our life force energy as it moves throughout our chakras.

From the very moment of our soul's incarnation into human form, our chakras have been absorbing information, interpreting and integrating that information, and then sculpting our lives with it by sending it back out into the universal field. The energy that moves around and through us via our chakra system is both creative and intelligent—it's never not communicating information from within and around us to a much larger field of intelligence. That being said, we're not actually creating our lives with our bodies and minds alone, we're creating our lives through the various aspects of our energy field, namely our chakras. For the majority of us, this process has remained a mostly unconscious one—until now. We've officially entered a time when humanity is waking up to its creative potential in a new and dynamic way and understanding how energy moves in our body and chakras are a vital part of that awakening.

In our most basic understanding of ourselves, perceived through the limitation of our five senses, we're merely physical bodies made of flesh and bone. But from a multidimensional perspective, we're much more complex than that. We're eternal souls experiencing ourselves as temporarily human. Each one of us is a unique composition of light and sound, thought and feeling, energy and emotion—a beautiful expression of both individuality and unity. Imagine your truest self, your *soul self* as a beam of pure white starlight and your human body as the prism through which your soullight shines. The pure white light of your soul is the unified wisdom of perfect, unconditional love, but once your soul incarnates into a human form its range of frequency expands. Instead of radiating one ray of light, it expands to reflect the entire light spectrum, and a much greater potential of experience becomes available—*the human experience.*

The rainbow colors of the visible light spectrum are often used to represent the chakras. Each of the seven colors represents one of the seven primary chakras and a specific level of human consciousness. Chakra energy, like light waves increase in vibration as they ascend vertically upward from the base of the spine all the way up to the crown of the head, each chakra holding a higher degree of frequency than the one that came before. The closer the chakra is to the earth, the denser its vibration and the more relatable it will be to our primal, animalistic instinct. The closer to the crown or the heavens, the higher the frequency, and the more ethereal and spiritual its nature.

Our lower three chakra centers represent our lower self, or the part of us that is closest to our physical, instinctual, animalistic nature.

The first chakra, located at the base of the spine, is known as the root chakra or *muladhara*, which means *root support*. The root chakra is associated with the color red, the element of earth, and represents our physical body, our tribe, and our connection to the material world. It's through the lens of the first chakra that we come to know ourselves as isolated physical entities, experiencing the very real need for food, shelter, safety, tribe, and all things pertaining to physical survival. This is the first chakra we encounter as newly born human beings; it's the solid foundation on which all the other chakras will come to rest.

The second chakra, located just below the navel, is known as the sacral chakra, or *Svadhistana*, which means *sweetness*. The sacral chakra is associated with the color orange, the element of water, and represents our emotional nature, our sensate feelings, and our desire to experience passion and pleasure in life. It's through the lens of the second chakra that we come to know our longings to merge with another, to reproduce, and to experience the sweetness that a physical life can offer us. This chakra adds a dimension to the one that came before, calling us deeply into the world of both sensuality and duality, of color and contrast, of self and other. Here is where the solidity and structure of one becomes the push and pull polarity of two.

The third chakra, located in the center of our bellies, is known as the solar plexus chakra, or *manipura*, which means *lustrous gem*. This chakra is associated with the color yellow, the element of fire, and represents our individuality, our will, and our personal power. It's through the lens of the third chakra that we experience our most autonomous selves, exploring the felt-sense of primal power that arises from acting as an individual with a self-motivating will. It's through this center that we learn the benefits of applying discipline and taking consistent action in order to achieve our goals. The third chakra is where we distinguish ourselves apart from the life we inherited; its where we carve out and sculpt the differences between our personal selves and the tribe we were born into. The third chakra is the home for our ego. It's here that we learn to differentiate between the world we were born into and the world we were born to help create.

These lower three centers are slower, denser, and earthier in their vibration. They represent the part of our humanness that is primal and animalistic by its very nature. This lower-self aspect of humanity is driven by basic instincts, the need for physical survival and all things pertaining to it—nourishment, shelter, reproduction, ego, and power. The lower chakras are a very necessary and powerful facet of our humanness, although they can become destructive when they're out of alignment with the rest of our chakra system. When the lower chakras serve as the primary motivators in our lives, what manifests is typical of Western culture—honoring worldly pleasures like food, sex, money, beauty, and power—often at a much greater expense than the temporary gratification they promise to provide.

The midpoint of the chakra system is arguably the most important chakra to awaken and bring into balance, especially at this time. The heart is the bridge between our higher and lower selves. When activated the heart has the capacity to restore balance to the entire energy system.

The fourth chakra is said to be the seat of the soul within humanity, and because of that, it's often the most sensitive and highly guarded. It's located directly in the center of the chest and is the perfect median between the lower three and upper three chakras. The fourth chakra is known as the heart chakra, or *anahata*, which means *unbroken* or *unstruck*. It's associated with the color green, the element of air and is characterized by higher human ideals of compassion, empathy, generosity, intimacy, and forgiveness. When the heart is closed, often in the case of unresolved trauma, we aren't able to feel love for ourselves or genuine intimacy in our connection to others. A restricted heart may temporarily shield us from pain, yet simultaneously prevent us from experiencing the depth and richness that the human experience offers. In contrast to a closed heart, when the heart center is open, we feel vibrant and alive, full of hope and possibility. We connect deeply with others and really sense our place within life's larger framework. An open heart welcomes all facets of being with an ever-growing capacity for empathy and compassion. The unbreakable *anahata* calls upon our willingness to see, feel, accept, understand, love, and forgive ourselves and others for being imperfectly perfect and infallibly human.

Above the heart exists three upper chakra centers that represent our higher, spiritual selves. These are the chakras emphasized in many new age circles which tend to focus primarily on spiritual development.

The fifth chakra, located in the center of the throat is known as the throat chakra, or *vishuddha*, which means *purification* or *especially pure*. This chakra is associated with the color blue and the element of sound. The throat chakra represents our ability to express the intimate thoughts, feelings, and creative ideas of our inner world and share them with the world around us. Although we communicate ourselves through each of our chakras, the fifth chakra is where the act of conscious expression is directed with both awareness and will. The delicate space between the head and the heart, the fifth chakra creates an audible vibration, giving a tangible expression to what was once only a formless feeling or an idea. The fifth chakra is the power that grants opportunity to consciously and deliberately communicate ourselves, our unique thoughts, feelings and perceptions with the world around us.

The sixth chakra, located at the brow bone, is known as the third eye chakra, or *ajna*, which means *to perceive* or *to command*. This chakra is associated with the color indigo and the element of thought. It represents our mind, our logic, our intuition, and our inner vision. Often associated with the dark indigo color of the nighttime sky, the third eye chakra is probably the most commonly recognized as its the chakra associated with psychic gifts. The third eye chakra is the gateway into the subconscious mind. It speaks to us in not in human tongue but in the langue of dreams, symbols, and archetypes. It's through the third eye and all of its interpretations that we mentally process the world and all of our experiences within it. Many artists, visionaries, and philosophic thinkers have very active third eye chakras.

The seventh chakra, located at the top of the head, is known as the crown chakra, or *sahasrara*, which means *thousand-fold*. This chakra is associated with the color violet or white and the element of ether; it represents our connection to the supreme consciousness of divinity. It is through this chakra that we connect to our own spiritual identity and come to know ourselves not as separate physical beings, but as a unique expression of divinity itself. Here is where we come to the realization we are but a fractal of a much more intricate and infinite pattern. The awakened seventh chakra is what calls us to explore the vast terrain of religious and spiritual endeavor, urging us gently towards a contemplative path, prodding us to ask the unanswerable questions. Who am I? Why am I here? What is the meaning and purpose of my existence?

There's a stark contrast in the human experience between the upper and lower chakras. The upper chakras vibrate at a much higher rate of frequency and are far more ethereal than the primal, lower chakras. The lower chakras represent our physical human identities, whereas the upper chakras represent our spiritual human nature. The upper chakras are less tethered to the planet, assuaging them of the immediate concerns associated with physical survival, granting our consciousness the liberties of exploring the less defined parameters of the higher self. The upper chakras tend to be driven by the desire for truth, intuition, spiritual realization, and

cosmic wisdom; ideals we see canonized in many Eastern traditions. When the upper chakras serve as the primary motivators
in our lives, transcending our humanness through devotional lifestyles, prolonged periods of meditation, fasting, and even extreme
asceticism often become the focus. When the spotlight is focused
solely on spiritual endeavor, often at the denial of our lower chakras,
we can appear detached from reality, living within the confines of
a spiritual mask of superiority, and believing that we are somehow
above the problems of the world.

There's often a great divide amongst Eastern and Western
tradition due to their polarized emphasis on the development of
either the lower chakras in favor of the higher (Western Culture),
or the higher chakras in favor of the lower (Eastern Culture). Ironically, the lower chakras are what gives power to the upper chakras.
It isn't our spirit, but our spirit merged with our humanness that
encourages us to roll up our sleeves and dig into a mess with hope
and willingness that we can actually make things better. Without
engagement from our lower energy centers, our upper chakras are
insufficient in their attempts to better anything at all. In order to
express the true power of our potential, we need the support of our
upper chakras moving in tandem with our lower chakras. Only
when our entire chakra system is firing on all cylinders will we
come to know the real power of what we, as humans, are truly
capable of.

In looking at the current state of our world, we can see that
neither Eastern nor Western tradition has proven superior in their
approach. In fact, both have become equally hazardous. We've
reached a time in history when we can no longer afford to pursue
wealth and power at all costs overlooking the emotional damage it
creates amongst men and the annihilation it's caused to our planet.
Nor can we sit upon our meditation cushion of spiritual excellence,
offering only prayers and mantras in attempt to alleviate the suffering of the masses. The awakening taking place today calls forth

a unified approach, utilizing the best of both Eastern and Western tradition. And this awakened approach is what happens naturally and effortlessly when we awaken and heal each of our chakras. When we understand our lives from this energetic perspective, we'll no longer feel the need to fight or argue with the reality outside of us in order to find peace. We'll become solid in our understanding that peace is the natural byproduct of a world created by balanced individuals. If we want to live in a peaceful world, our job is to create harmony and order within ourselves and then to act in alignment with that peace. By doing that, we organically restore the harmony and order to the world outside of us.

ENERGETIC PROFILING THROUGH CHARACTER STRUCTURE

"When you understand this map of personality,
it's like having x-ray vision and it's like you can see into
other people and you can see what's going on inside them
and how they got distressed and what they need to
come out of their distress. So, it'll help you interact
with other people much more skillfully."
—Steven Kessler

I've found that when knowledge of the chakra system is blended with a profiling system originally introduced to me by my former mystery school teacher Rhys Thomas, at the Rhys Thomas Institute of Energy Medicine the results for personal transformation are absolutely extraordinary. No other system of religion, spirituality, or modality of healing I've ever studied is quite as comprehensive as this one. I firmly believe that when one understands the chronological development of the human energy system and the expression of energy via the chakras, merged with concept of energetic profiling they will be equipped with the only system of healing they'll ever need.

What Rhys Thomas did was elaborate on a brilliant, yet antiquated system of personality profiling originally developed in the

1920's by psychoanalyst Dr. Wilhelm Reich and one of his students, American physician and psychotherapist Alexander Lowen. Their unique profiling system, originally titled *Character Analysis* was based on the notion that there are five distinct personality traits or characteristics that can be identified as an individual's psychological nature. Reich and Lowen believed that these character structures were actually survival adaptations made in response to early childhood experiences as the result of having unmet needs at critical stages of development. What this means is, if during childhood there were deviations from what's considered optimal emotional development and specific needs weren't met at critical life junctures between the ages of birth to six years old, then our original need became replaced with an energy pattern; and if this energy pattern is consistently repeated, it creates a certain type of personality, or *character structure*. It's also noted that these character structures aren't purely psychological, they're also retained in the physical body as a result of chronic muscular tension; so not only can these character structures be observed psychologically, they're actually made obvious in the physical body as well. Alexander Lowen went on to create an entire system of mind/body therapy called *Bioenergetics*, aimed at resolving the physical, emotional, psychological, and spiritual dysfunction caused by the defensive qualities of these character structures.

Since this work was developed in the early 1900's and clinical psychology was just getting established as a recognized field of treatment for mental illness, most of Reich and Lowens' studies were developed around patients that were psychologically unwell, so if you research the original works you'll find that the each of the character structures had pathological names, like the Schizoid, Oral, Psychopath, Masochist, and Rigid. Without a personal interest in modern psychology, or the proper understanding of these character types one might turn away from them simply because of their pejorative names, but almost 100 years later this work has been expanded upon by many other students since the time of its origination. Psychologists and spiritual teachers alike have all continued to enhance the ideas originally presented by Reich and Lowen. Thought leaders like Rhys Thomas, John Pierrakos, Barbara Brennan, Anodea Judith, Steven Kessler and many others have all continued on to expand upon this great body of work, many of them renaming the original character structures so they're more relevant and accessible to modern-day seekers, especially those interested in personal and spiritual growth.

I've studied many different teachers since originally being introduced to this body of work and each one has added another dimension to my understanding of this material, namely Rhys Thomas and Steven Kessler, whose books and teachings have undoubtedly made the greatest impact on my life. There are some contrasting opinions in these newer interpretations of the material, particularly regarding whether or not these character structures are actually inborn soul qualities that existed prior to our childhood development or behavioral tendencies that developed as a result of how early life experiences shaped us into being. I've come to believe there isn't exactly an either/or answer. Both perspectives are relevant and offer equal opportunity to explore the nature of our own unique character development. Both provide a glimpse into how these behaviors can either block our life energy or simultaneously reveal our highest potential. This book aims only to provide a basic, introductory glimpse into the concept of character structure as it relates to the human energy system, however there is far more information available listed in the reference section should you choose to explore it in depth.

Let's briefly examine this concept of character structure and how it relates to energy medicine. As we've discussed, our natural state is one of *presence*. When we're present and living in the moment our energy is flowing freely throughout our system, we're relaxed, and we're living in a state of ease. Our energy body is free of obstruction and we're generally experiencing a sense of peace within ourselves and our lives. But when something disrupts our peace, if we become stressed out or too much energy hits our system, we get overwhelmed and some of that energy needs to be discharged in order for us to return to presence. We have all learned to charge and discharge energy in our own unique way. In an ideal childhood, our parents and caregivers would have had the personal awareness and tools necessary to assist us in discharging our energy and dealing with the emotions of fear, sadness, stress, anger and overwhelm. They'd be able to help us to achieve a healthy level of dependency on them while simultaneously supporting us to develop a felt sense of personal independence but sadly, that's very seldom the case. If as children we weren't able to complete the necessary developmental tasks at age appropriate times, or if we were consistently left with overwhelming feelings and weren't taught healthy ways to discharge our energy, then we still needed a way to defend ourselves against our unmet needs and overwhelming feelings. As a result of our unmet needs, we adapted to our feelings by strategizing energetically to defend ourselves. What this means is, we became really clever at learning how to enhance or restrict our life force energy in certain areas of the body and psyche in order to feel safe and many of us continue to carry the energetic imprints left behind due to stress, trauma, and other negative life experiences. In his book, *The 5 Personality Patterns*, Steven Kessler identifies the five ways in which we unknowingly direct the life-energy flow within the body to defend ourselves and create a feeling of safety. We have five options, all of which we'll try out as children, generally settling on one or two that will become our most used strategies for defense throughout life.

1. We can move our energy **away from others** retreating into the safety of the mind. This pattern results in a *deficient* root chakra and *excessive* upper chakras.

2. We can move our energy **towards others** merging with them on an emotional level. This pattern results in *excessive* emotional centers, the sacral and heart chakras

3. We can move our energy **inward and down**, suppressing our will and anchoring ourselves into the ground as an attempt to endure our surroundings. This pattern results in a *deficient* third chakra.

4. We can move our energy **up and out** creating an explosion of aggressive energy. This pattern results in an *excessive* third and fifth chakra

5. We can **constrict** our energy resulting in a very emotionally arrested, rigid personality. This pattern results in a *blocked* fourth chakra.

These five specific ways of managing our energy through our chakras create patterns in our energy and our body that results in five distinct personality traits. Kessler refers to these defensive patterns in terms of *behavior*, whereas Thomas identifies them by *type*.

- The first energy flow produces what Kessler calls the *Leaving Pattern*, in Thomas' language it creates a *Thinker Defense*; both describe a feeling of disassociation from the body and a felt-sense of safety in the mental realm.

- The second energy flow produces what Kessler calls the *Merging Pattern* and what Thomas has labeled the *Poor Me Defense*; both describe an insatiably needy, almost infantile personality.

- The third energy flow produces what Kessler has identified as an *Enduring Pattern* and what Thomas calls *People Pleaser Defense*; both describe a personality whose life energy is often dictated by the needs and demands of others.

- The fourth energy flow produces what Kessler has identified as an *Aggressive Pattern* and what Thomas has labeled the *Enforcer Defense*; both describe a dominating personality who strives for power and control over others, often by attempting to appear larger or superior in some way.

- The fifth energy flow produces what Kessler calls the *Rigid Pattern* and what Thomas has labeled *Rule Keeper Defense*; both describe a personality that has blocked the flow of emotional energy in favor of logic, order, rules and worldly achievement.

The difference between Kesslers' explanation and Thomas' interpretation of this work is found in the *undefended* qualities of these character structures. Kessler's psychology-based approach to the material highlights the *gifts* we develop as a result of these strategies; for example: a person who displays the *Leaving Pattern* might lack a sense of connection to their body, however this lack of physical grounding allows them become really skillful at navigating the intellectual and spiritual realms.

Coming from a more spiritual perspective, Thomas might argue that this skillset isn't developed as a result of going into the defensive pattern, rather it's an innate soul quality that the individual was born to express. Thomas, who titled his work the *Life Purpose Profiles,* believes that there are five distinct expressions of the soul as they exist in human beings; there are *thinkers, feelers, caretakers, leaders, and achievers.* From Thomas' perspective, our character structure isn't *created* as a result of early childhood experience or defensive patterning, rather, who we are as a soul is being *revealed* by them. Thomas has gone on to identify the *Core Soul Qualities* displayed by each personality type as they come out of defense and move into alignment with the core-self. He has named the core soul quality of each character the *Creative Idealist, Emotional*

Intelligence Specialist, Team Player, Charismatic Leader, and Knowledgeable Achiever.

The true nature of a person's soul will reveal itself effortlessly whenever they're living their lives in a flowing, present, and undefended way—just like it did when we were children. However, these five unconscious defenses can become like hardwired energy formations in our energy body, and they have a very real impact on our physical body, our psyche, our emotions, and our lives. As we age, we get so accustomed to living in these unconscious patterns that they often become our automatic responses to life, especially when life becomes scary, stressful, overwhelming, or if we feel threatened in some way. Many of us have become so accustomed to living with these patterns that we actually believe they are who we are. Since childhood, many of us have lived our entire lives completely ruled by these patterns, others have been able to remain mostly present throughout life, but the majority of us are oscillating somewhere in between. Our goal now is to expand our consciousness and heal our past so we can bring all of our energy and awareness into the present moment. This goal makes it important to learn which developmental tasks are critical to the formation of a healthy human and at which stages of development. We need to understand which chakras have been impacted by trauma and unmet needs, so we can observe where our energy might have gotten stuck in the past. Once we understand that some of our unmet needs in childhood might still be having an influence on our unconscious patterns and behaviors as adults we can actually start the work of healing ourselves. If we can learn to understand how, when, and why we go unconscious as adults we actually gain power over that unconsciousness and then we can make necessary alterations in our own behavior. Once we understand how life energy moves throughout our human energy system, how stress and trauma shape our chakras, and how mismanaged energy effects our perception and our lives, we can move our bodies and direct our minds in a way that intentionally liberates stuck energy. Once our life force energy becomes free from our unconscious patterning we can direct it with awareness to create the lives and relationships we actually desire.

When I was first introduced to this information, it felt like someone handed me a roadmap to life, like a blueprint for becoming a healthy, fully integrated, and spiritually mature human. It was literally like someone turned on a light-switch and for the first time ever, I caught a glimpse of my inner workings. This inner illumination helped me understand why I behaved the way I did and gave me the awareness I needed to correct some of my behaviors that were unhealthy. It helped me better understand and relate to the people I was in relationship with and it also helped me develop a deep sense of compassion for the human condition. Once I learned to apply the wisdom to my daily interactions, my entire life improved and has continued to improve ever since. My hope is that this work will offer you the same opportunity.

In the chapters that follow we'll begin to explore our own energetic anatomy. We'll take a deep dive into each of the individual sub-systems that operate within the human energy system. We'll move systematically through each sub-system and cover in detail how each one developed and progressed throughout our lives. We'll also cover:

- Chakra formation
- The age at which each chakra is developing
- The level of consciousness each chakra governs
- What tasks are necessary at each stage for the development of a healthy human
- What chakra wounds threaten healthy development
- How each system expresses itself energetically in both health and disease and how that energetic expression directly influences the way we live our lives today

- Which character structures are associated with each system
- What we can do to heal at the energetic level of each system

I firmly believe that when this system of self-analysis and energetic-understanding is understood and applied, it creates the perfect template for human beings to begin identifying and reclaiming all of their fragmented parts. To heal is to become whole and realigning ourselves at the energetic level is how we heal. Healed people heal people, and right now, the world needs all the healers it can get.

So, let's dive in.

THE FIRST CHAKRA—
THE ROOT SYSTEM

"When roots are deep, there is no reason to fear the wind."
—Chinese Proverb

Forming the Root

Let's begin where life itself begins, the firm foundation upon which all other life processes will come to rest: the root. The rooting of our human consciousness begins with the inception of our spirit into our physical form, our soul's integration into the human experience. *Embodiment*, or claiming the physical body as our home, is the first fundamental task associated with our human development and its absolutely vital if we want to claim our power as the creators of our own lives. In order for us to be present and powerful in our lives, we must first be deeply rooted in our humanness.

Physical embodiment is a process that begins as embryos in our mother's womb and continues to strengthen and develop after birth and over the following 6-12 months of our lives—long before our conscious mind is able to comprehend what's going on. During our time spent in utero, a link between our soul-selves and our physical-selves is beginning to establish. This is a very sensitive time in our development, as we're absorbing energy and information from our environment—*the womb*—and this information is helping determine whether it's safe for our spirit to become embodied. Not only that, but our physical body is also rapidly developing.

If our mother was adequately nourished, then our growing fetus was strengthened and fortified by that nourishment. If she wasn't, then neither were we. Under the stress of a challenging or fearful experience had by our mother, we too, became submerged in a watery soup of stress hormones. If our mother was joyful or calm, then we shared in her contentment as well. With every contracting emotion or peaceful calm felt by our mothers, we were subject to an identical physical experience. These early formative months had a tremendous impact on our relationship to our bodies and to life, and although we may not remember them, their energetic signature is still encoded within the very fabric of our being.

When the time was right, we and our mother embarked upon our first earthly journey together, the arduous task of physical incarnation—our shared birth experience. Prior to being born, our every need was met upon demand, before we ever knew we had a need. In some way, I think we all long to return to this fetal ideal, where our every need is provided for instantaneously and without our asking. But this short-lived embryonic utopia would come to a halt for us as soon as our gestation period came to completion and our mother's body began to contract. Soon we'd find ourselves squeezing our way through the tight quarters of a birth canal. Upon delivery we were ushered into an entirely new world, a world of bright lights and intense noises, of new smells and strange textures—much different than the safety and comfort of our mother's womb. Our arrival earth-side welcomes us into the contrasting experience of human life, where we are exposed to its cold and comfort, along with its pleasure and pain. For the first time ever, we experience the sensation of our separation, and the very real need for physical survival becomes our reality. The birthing experience and those that immediately follow will convey to us whether the world is safe and supportive or frightening and stressful. The moments that follow birth and our decent into the manifest world will become a signal to our spirit whether it's safe to embody or if remaining in spirit is a more secure option. A traumatic birth experience is enough to create wounding at this very delicate stage of development. Although it will still be many months before our mind becomes consciously aware of our separateness, our root chakra will be receiving and assimilating a great deal of information about the safety of our environment. Our very survival at this stage of development is purely dependent upon others, and whether we are immediately cared for by those who welcomed us into this world—this is the information that programs our root chakra.

During the root stage of life our behavior is purely instinctual and connected to our physical survival and development. We naturally seek the safety and comfort of our mother's warmth, we search for a nipple and involuntarily begin to suck. Once the milk starts to flow we experience the immediate physical satisfaction of being nourished. We cry at the first signs of pain or discomfort, unaware that we are asking the outside world to meet our inward needs. We're learning the basics of surviving as a human, but ultimately, we are utterly defenseless.

The inception into our physical form can be both a delightful integration or a terrifying experience, depending upon the conditions of our arrival. If as infants our immediate survival needs were met; if we were fed when hungry, changed when wet, soothed when upset, protected from the elements and consistently shown love then we learn to accept the world and the people in it as friendly and safe. If, however, we were unwanted, uncared for, or if our parents struggled to meet their own survival needs and our experience was one of scarcity or lack, or if there was any other perceived threat to our survival then we learn to mistrust the world. Whether our infancy was met with love and connection, or mental illness, physical abuse, addiction, chaos, and struggle, these formative experiences are what shape our early perceptions of the world. There will be plenty of other childhood, adolescent, and adult experiences that play a critical role in our perception and the shaping of our unique character, however, all of these future events are built atop our root, a foundation originally set by our early childhood experience, and our immediate familial programming.

Tribal Consciousness

The root has two distinct aspects to it, both equally pertinent to our physical survival; the physical body being one, and the tribe being the other. Before we dive into the fundamentals of creating balance in the physical body, I want to first cover the only reason our body was able to survive its infancy—*the tribe.* The tribe is an absolutely critical element to our survival as humans. Regardless of how independent we pride ourselves in being, humans are pack animals, and pack animals survive by belonging to a tribe. But unlike other animals you might observe in the wild, like a pack of wolves, pride of lions, or herd of bison, the presence of a tribe doesn't just influence our physical safety, the human-tribe affects our consciousness as well. In fact, the tribe holds the greatest impact on our development and has the most direct influence on the adults that we turn out to be. This root-level, tribal-consciousness isn't necessarily intentional, it speaks to the more primitive survival mechanisms put in place solely to ensure our physical safety. Just like animals in the wild, humans experience a time when our physical safety depends on belonging to a group. At birth, each and every one of us came into this world utterly defenseless, unprotected, and impotent, lacking any ability to provide for ourselves. As infants, we couldn't hold our heads up on our own, let alone provide ourselves with food, sustenance, or shelter. We had not a single chance of survival had it not been for a tribe of people sheltering us, feeding us, taking caring of us, and keeping us safe. To some degree, we owe our lives to the tribe, and because of this we pledge an unconscious allegiance to them. Our tribal legacy is downloaded into us like a software program. Mostly unconsciously, but *sometimes* consciously, the beliefs, attitudes, behaviors, customs, and traditions of the tribe will decidedly become our own. Whether we want to or not, we *inherit* the tribe, and until we come into consciousness and learn to decide and act for ourselves, our choices and programs will reflect those of the tribe we were born into. We swear an unspoken oath to uphold our tribal customs, not because they're legitimate, but due to our human wiring for survival. The tribal-mind tells us that the more we behave in a conforming fashion, the more likely we are to survive with the least amount of conflict. Tribal consciousness is the pack-mentality of the human race. Primitive man survived because the tribe knew how to act as one organism. The tribe functioned as a unit—one step out of line by any member, and death would have been a very real possibility. Interestingly enough, human-evolution is presenting us, once again, with a life-threatening opportunity to re-awaken to our tribal power.

Historically, tribes were much larger than they are today, consisting of parents, grandparents, aunts, uncles, extended families, and more. Members of the tribe gathered to hunt, share meals, perform rituals, care for children, and to celebrate the joy of being alive. When there was a threat, tribes gathered to protect and defend one another. Each man, woman, and child had a role within the tribe, and by performing a task or a job, each had their own way of contributing. Having a place within the tribe created a sense of pride and belonging; it was the foundation from which tribesmen derived the very purpose and meaning of their existence.

Modern-day tribes look very different in comparison to those of the past. With the cost of living dramatically increasing, and the stress of modern-day life making a noticeable impact, we see much smaller family units, sometimes containing only a mother, father, and children, sometimes less. The tribal-divide continues to grow as our western drive for independence and personal success at all costs severely impairs our natural instinct for a tribal foundation.

Another truth that's notably heart wrenching, especially given today's prevalence of addiction, disease, and mental illness, is that families are being broken apart and children are being abandoned in numbers greater than ever before. These deeply wounded, displaced children may find shelter in foster care or group homes but still long for a sense of connection and rootedness offered by a tribe. Without the experience of being wanted, loved, and nurtured, children often grow into adults that question their right to exist.

Tribal identification doesn't always adhere to the strict parameters of a family unit either, its consciousness extends far beyond the reaches of our immediate family and continues to shift and readjust throughout our lives. Sometimes those who grew up without a felt-sense of connection to their familial tribe will discover their tribal identity later in life and develop a sense of belonging to a culture or sub-culture, race, or religion. Others will discover themselves in a school, a clique, a particular genre of music, or an industry that resonates with their innermost thoughts and feelings. Many will experience tribal identification in relation to their country, a favored sports team, or political affiliation. Most anything that denotes a sense of belonging within us arises out of our desire for tribal identification and speaks directly to our tribal mind.

Establishing a sense of belonging to something greater than ourselves is essential for human well-being. Without it, the very ground we stand on feels shaky and the likeliness of rooting ourselves into our human experience or discovering our soul's place in the world is significantly diminished. Although the times have changed, the tribal consciousness of man has not. Our tribal mind behaves today in the same way it did way back then. That means in order for us to experience a deep-sense of rootedness in our lives, we each need to develop a sense of belonging, to both ourselves and to the world. If we don't feel as though we truly belong to life, we'll lack a sense of purpose and won't strive for anything more than mere survival. The world is currently overflowing with an abundance of shallow-rooted wanderers and those questioning whether or not they really belong here, but what we need now more than ever are fully-rooted, totally embodied humans, claiming their space, and living their lives on purpose. What we really need is a healed, unified tribe of humans, perhaps more-so now than we ever did ever back then. This is why coming into consciousness around our tribal programs are imperative at this stage of our human-evolution.

We inherit far more than just our genetics from our tribe; our tribe teaches us the fundamentals of human life. It's through the tribe that we learn how to care for our bodies and which foods are an appropriate source of fuel. Tribe members demonstrate how to be in relationship with others and how to (or not to) communicate effectively. The tribe shows us how to relate to money and what's an acceptable amount to make. Their influence helps us determine a whole host of other decisions, like which careers are within our reach; which love interests are approved of; if sexual expression is sinful or a healthy source of pleasure; what romantic relationships should look like; how each gender should behave; how to express our feelings; and how to deal with stress, anger, and other difficult emotions. We absorb all of this information on a level that is mostly pre-verbal. We take in our family patterns both visually and energetically, and then we become loyal to the reenactment of our tribal inheritance.

Again, this is a mostly unconscious process. If we witnessed our parents drinking to avoid their pain, we became likely to do the same. In contrast, if we watched our elders loving, honoring and taking care of themselves, then that too, is likely to become our fate. The longer we stay within our tribe, the more we become indoctrinated by it and the more likely we are to create lives that resemble those of our closest relatives. Generally speaking, we either behave exactly like the other members of our tribe, or alternatively, we may work tirelessly to become unlike the tribe from which we origi-nated. A common term has been coined for those who go against their tribal inheritance; they're called *the black sheep* of the family.

If you're reading a book like this, that term might sound famil-iar to you.

Tribal consciousness is an aspect of humanity that runs deep within our psyche and has a profound effect on our species. It is more than just the inherited influence from the tribe we were born into, and how we relate to our immediate family. The tribal mind bleeds into all of our interactions, particularly those that take place within a group. Remember, the tribal mind tells us that the collec-tive must think, feel, and behave in a similar, conforming fashion, so that we'll have a better chance at survival. But we saw a breaking away from the tribal mind as a great shift began taking place in the 1960's and 70's, when the onset of personal therapy brought about greater opportunities for us to examine our own tribal beliefs. What were at one time deeply-rooted secrets, such as sexual abuse, drug abuse, and confidential family issues, now became topics open for discussion with close friends, a therapist, or some type of sup-portive group of individuals. This open discussion, outside of our tribe, was in and of itself a veering away from the unconsciousness associated with the tribal mind. Now that we're fully into the 21st century, our tribal consciousness, although still deeply guided by the roots of our origins, is continuing to evolve. Talking to quali-fied therapists, healers, and regularly attending support groups is now recognized as normal and healthy for personal growth and development, emotional support, and self-discovery. Individuals are beginning to find their own voice, apart from the tribe, and while this is great step in our evolutionary process, it's still per-ceived as a threat to the unconscious tribal-mind.

Tribal consciousness in an unconscious world can make it incredibly difficult to act in accordance with our own voice, and discover our own personal code of ethics, independent from the groups we find ourselves a part of, be they family, friend circles, support groups, business affiliations, or religious organizations. If one member of an unconscious tribe breaks off and begins to think or behave differently, its generally perceived by the unconscious collective as a threat. This autonomous action isn't always welcome, as it decreases the sense of strength in numbers, and therefore limits the foundational stability of the tribe. Metaphorically speaking, its analogous to removing one leg from a four-legged chair; the chair will still stand, but its stability will be significantly decreased. It's for this reason that when people begin to outgrow or challenge their tribal programs, support group ideologies, or dogmatic religious principles the group will often use fear, guilt, shame, or other tactics to unconsciously persuade its members to return to a position of compliance within the tribe. This is such a common and clear example of *tribal unconscious,* otherwise known as the crab mentality. If you gather a bunch of crabs together in a bucket and one crab reaches the buckets edge in an attempt to escape, the rest of the crabs will rise up and pull him back down. The unconsciousness within humanity does the same thing; our families do it, our friends do it, our spouses do it, and I'm sure there's been a time when we ourselves have done it too. We unconsciously sabotage our own growth and the growth of those closest to us, in favor of what's familiar. The tribal unconsciousness within us wants everyone to stay the same and do the same thing, because to the tribal mind, that signifies survival and anything outside of that is perceived as a threat.

When I was a couple of years into my healing journey, my dad was diagnosed with prostate cancer. At this point, I'd been studying holistic health for a little while, and after doing a bit of my own research, I made a few suggestions to my dad on how else he might be able to approach his situation. His test results revealed that what he had was a slow-growing encapsulated cancer. It wasn't posing any immediate threat to his health and there was a good chance that it had already taken years to develop. I didn't believe there was an urgent need for him to have a major hormone-regulating gland removed from his body, especially one that could have a detrimental effect to his quality of life, before he had at least explored a more holistic approach. I proposed the idea that it might be smart for him to try changing his diet before making any radical decisions. I took the time to start educating him about the power of the nutrition and how important it was to remove the food source that was feeding the disease in his body. He started eating less meat, eliminating processed foods and artificial sugars, increasing his fruit and vegetable intake, and making his own raw-food smoothies daily. This created an unexpected ripple effect, as I had initiated a change process that evidently had become uncomfortable for my mother. My mom had always controlled the kitchen and she cooked the way her mother had taught her to cook. Whatever she made was what we ate and there was never an issue with it—until then. All of a sudden, there were *two* women in my dad's life with contrasting opinions. I was lobbying for faith and the power within my dad's body to heal itself when given the right conditions, and my mom's vote was clearly with the doctors and their modern medicine. Due to my growing knowledge of nutrition, I was challenging the tribal structure of my family. My dad was slowly shifting gears and allowing new information to come into his consciousness. On another level, a big negotiation of power was happening within the tribe. My mother became fearful of the changes my ideas were presenting because they weren't going to affect my father alone. These ideas were going to directly affect her and how she lived her life. They were going to change how she shopped, how she prepared meals, and her own relationship to food. Things around her were changing and her ego, an aspect of the tribal mind, was threatened by the loss of control. This created a huge rift between us, and it lasted for quite some time. You might find that as you elevate your consciousness and start making healthier and smarter choices for your body, it will become a trigger for the tribal unconscious within your family. I'm not sure anything gets more tribal than food.

Eventually, you'll learn to see these defining moments as opportunities to elevate the tribe and influence newer, more beneficial tribal traditions; but be forewarned, tribal changes aren't always met with opens arms. You'll discover in the coming pages that the way humans have learned to relate to food over the last hundred years is one of the many tribal programs in need of some radical shifting.

Darwin was said to have stated, "It is not the strongest of species that survives, nor the most intelligent that survives. It is the one that is the most adaptable to change." Resist as we might, there's no denying it any longer; change has been thrust upon us all. Humanity's very survival is being threatened. Because of this, we are now being asked to upgrade *all* of our systems, and our tribal beliefs are at the *root* of our issues. The deepest truth is that we are all one, but that doesn't mean we are all the same. We're not supposed to be, and we never were. Many of us are going to need to break free from and evolve beyond some of our unconscious tribal systems. Many of these tribal beliefs are still operating within us today and have prevented us from growing. For many of us, this may mean outgrowing our own families, which can be painful, and aligning with a tribe of people that have similar values to our own. In order for us to evolve into unity consciousness, we're being asked to use the power of our minds to dissolve these divisions and borders that have been imposed on us by our families, culture, and society. We must now expand our perception to see that *humanity* is our tribe. Only then will we figure out how to collectively work together rather than against each other.

The Body as a Vehicle for Consciousness

"If we listen to the body when it whispers,
we don't have to hear it scream."
—Author Unknown

As we reclaim our space as powerful members of the human tribe and nurture our right to exist within that tribe, a felt sense of belonging will emerge, and our energetic roots will naturally want to deepen, widen, and strengthen. This increase in energetic resiliency will often be experienced as a growing connection to the earth and to the earthiest part of us—our skin, and bones, and blood—the very flesh of our being.

Energetically speaking, the root chakra represents the slowest and densest form of vibration—*matter*—or in our case, the physical body. The experience of having a physical vessel is the foundational element of our human-being-ness. Without a body, we simply wouldn't be able to experience life on our planet in the way that we do. Our body grants us the ability to see, feel, sense, taste, smell and intuit. Our brains enable us to speak, process thought, recall information, and make critical decisions. Our body is tasked with beating our heart, digesting our food, regulating our hormones, and performing a multitude of other complex functions all so we can experience life, and we're meant to really honor that. Still, many of us take our bodies for granted. But it should come as no surprise that those who value and enjoy their lives tend to take better care of their bodies than those who don't, and those who disregard the care of their bodies will eventually come to pay a greater price.

Our own human body, and the body of our beautiful mother earth have been designed brilliantly, not just to coexist, but to *thrive* in a symbiotic union with each other and with all of life. Nature has provided us with everything we need to flourish as humans—food, hydration, shelter, clothing, and warmth. But our own falling out of nature's good graces has left many of us sick, tired, and struggling. When the body is functioning the way nature designed it to, we won't have to feel that way anymore. We'll have all the energy, vitality, and strength we need to live a vibrant life, just the way nature intended. When the body is in alignment, we'll go to bed restful at night and wake up energized in the morning. We won't struggle to fall asleep or stay asleep and then find ourselves running out for a mid-day coffee because we're crashing halfway through the day. Once we establish a sense of groundedness in our bodies, we'll feel strong, solid, and secure, like the body is rooted to the earth, and the soul is rooted to the body. But this can only happen when we accept the body as a sacred vehicle for our consciousness and learn to care for it as such. We all know what happens to a motor vehicle when the oil isn't changed and the engine isn't serviced. Eventually, it's bound to break down. The vehicle of our consciousness is no different. If our souls aren't fully embodied, and we're not actively taking care of ourselves, we're going to begin breaking down.

Whatever the cause—trauma, stress, or a lack of belonging— far too many of us have become disconnected from our bodies. Perhaps a great many of us never accomplished the task of embodiment to begin with. This great severance between mind and body has created a world disconnected from their essential nature. Souls disconnected from their bodies equals bodies disconnected from our earth, and the result is the planet we live on today. The potential to change that however, is resting in our hands. If we are going to influence the awakening taking place, we must become deeply rooted in our bodies—there's really no exception to this rule. If our bodies are struggling energetically, there is only one solution— *health*. Health is the only real cure for dis-ease, and returning ourselves to nature is the only thing capable of restoring health to physical bodies.

Unless we live off the grid somewhere deep in nature, far removed from modern-day life, we live in a highly processed, artificial, and toxic world. Most of our food has become poisonous, our air polluted, and our water contaminated. Not only that, but our soaps, detergents, cleaning supplies, and body products are all full of chemicals as well. We are consistently exposed to harmful toxins, yet, we expect ourselves to be healthy, and without ever truly caring for our health. The accumulation of all of this toxicity is being reflected in the massive amounts of dis-ease in our society and the vitality, or lack-there-of, in our individual bodies. Given the conditions of the world we currently live in, it's not exactly enough to simply eat our fruits and vegetables and expect ourselves to be healthy. Not all food is created equal anymore, so it's important for us to learn about the foods in our modern-day culture. We must also begin to purify our bodies of what is toxic to them. Once we do, our minds will begin to clear, and we'll start to feel our connection to the earth again. Once we've reestablished a sense of rootedness in our bodies and a connection to our planet, we're far less likely to behave in a way that we know is harmful. The most fundamental aspect of living a rooted life is to understand the relationship we have to our bodies and learning how to properly care for them. Our body is an extension of our souls and everything our soul gets to experience in life rests on the foundational element of our body. If we want to live a life rooted in soul, then we need to create a world of souls rooted in their bodies. But returning our bodies to a state of nature currently means a lot more than just regaining our health, it's become a necessary part of our human evolution.

The evolutionary process is now making a higher degree of consciousness available to us, and humans are being asked to serve as the medium through which this higher degree of consciousness will come to pass. Remember, the body is designed as a vehicle for consciousness, but this higher degree of consciousness won't be able to transmit through us if our bodies are full of junk. The new consciousness is already here, it's already available, but our bodies need to be in alignment and capable of grounding the new charge. Think of the body as a lightning rod and consciousness as the lightning that passes through it. Lightning, or the enormous electrical charge in the sky strikes as an attempt to ground itself and a lightning rod serves as the perfect conduit. Without a lightning rod, the electrical charge might cause a lot of damage as it attempts to ground and bolts of lightning will scatter and strike erratically. But when a lightning rod is made available, the lightning is able to travel through the rod and find an easy path to ground with the least amount of damage. Imagine that there is a highly charged, electricity in the sky—this is the charge of a new consciousness, and human bodies can serve as lightning rods for that new consciousness to ground itself into our world. In order to do this, we need to make sure that our lightning rods are functioning as a clear pathway to the ground, or else the electricity of the new consciousness won't be able to ground itself through us. But we can't ground consciousness, if we aren't first grounded ourselves. The best way to ground ourselves is by claiming our physical space and learning to care for our physical bodies.

Despite how we've chosen to treat them, our bodies aren't machines. They're made of nature, and thus, the body is subject to nature's law. Life and death, the cycles of building up and breaking down of matter are two of mother nature's undeniable laws. These essential life cycles are part of a natural process from which humankind is not exempt from. When the body accumulates too much stress (chemical, emotional, or physical) and toxicity, our root system will start to weaken and eventually will begin to break down. This breaking-down is like broadcasting a signal to mother nature that our life force is running low, and because mother nature is brilliant, she sends her clean-up crew to help decompose us so our creative life force energy can be recycled into something

more useful to the whole. This is when we start to see disease processes take hold of the body. We might start to experience pain
and inflammation, experience fungal and parasitic infections, have
digestive issues, or manifest other physical symptoms that indi-
cate a breaking down of matter. I don't say this to alarm or offend
anyone, but rather as a reminder; our bodies *are* nature, and we
must abide by her laws if we want to thrive in her world.

I was certain that overcoming addiction would be the greatest obstacle I would have to face in my lifetime, but I was wrong.
I couldn't escape my own karmic retribution—the consequences
of my previous actions were unavoidable—and the toll they took
on my physical body was going to make itself known. Pain would
again become my familiar companion. After years of polluting my
body, I began to experience some chronic health issues. They came
one after another after another. I experienced abnormal cellular
activity and various digestive issues, a lump formed in my chest,
and I experienced a severe kidney infection and painful kidney
stones while I was pregnant with my daughter. With each diag-
nosis, I resisted mainstream treatment which always seemed to
include, "Here's a referral to see a surgeon so you can have that
taken out." I consistently left the doctor's office not wondering *how*
to get rid of the issue, but rather, *why* are these issues showing up
to begin with?

Thus began my journey into learning about holistic health. I
started to understand that the body wasn't just a bunch of isolated
parts, each experiencing its own symptoms, rather the body was
a *complete* system. I realized that all of the issues I was experiencing were somehow connected, even if I didn't quite understand
how. I started take some supplements and made tweaks in my diet
here and there, but it wasn't until I started experiencing chronic
skin problems that I really started paying attention to what my
body was trying to tell me. Humans can be so stubborn sometimes! We're so addicted to our own habits and so reluctant to

change that we'll nonchalantly overlook every spark of flame until the house is literally burning down around us. Only then will we run out screaming and asking God why this is happening to us. My body had been trying to tell me for years that it was headed for a breakdown, but it literally had to show up on my face before I was willing to listen.

I wouldn't recommend what I did next to everyone because it was radical and probably a lot harder on my body than it needed to be, but I transitioned pretty quickly from a standard American diet to a strictly raw vegan lifestyle, and I ate that way for about three months. The effect that this shift had on my body, and on my consciousness was entirely unexpected.

After a little over a month, the lump in my chest started to dissolve and within two months it was completely gone. My mind became clear, my energy was through the roof, and I was literally buzzing with life force. The sensation I experienced from eating only raw, living foods actually became so intense at times that I found myself standing outside barefoot in the middle of winter just trying to discharge some of the energy. What I didn't expect to happen as a result of changing my diet was the spontaneous experience of pure bliss and total enlightenment that came with it. A raw food diet served as another great awakening for me, and with it came the full recognition of my soul's mission for this lifetime. For about nine days during this time I lived in a seemingly non-dualistic state of consciousness. I completely understood the dimension of polarity that humans experience living on planet earth, how the forces of good and evil are very real, and that they're both vying for our attention at all times. Simultaneously, I felt an immense connection to a Source that existed somewhere far above and beyond my limited sense of duality. This source was elevated beyond anything of this world. It felt like pure, unadulterated, and unconditional *love*. It could only have been what we humans call God. In those moments, I seemed to remember with perfect clarity exactly who I was and why I had chosen to come here. I knew I was here to help *heal the people*; that it was written in my soul contract, and I knew that I was going to dedicate my life to this service.

This actually turned out to be very challenging time for me because this awakening was a totally spontaneous occurrence and practically no one in my life could relate. It was as if one day I was a stay-at-home mom, taking care of kids, tending to a home, and reading spiritual literature on my downtime and then seemingly overnight, I was on a dedicated mission to write books, and change the world. I'd always felt in my heart that this was my destiny, especially after journeying with ibogaine; I guess I just didn't expect it to unravel in the way that it was. The transition into my newly awakened vigor for service work wasn't exactly a welcomed one, especially by my tribe. I mean, it wasn't unnatural for me to be exceedingly spiritual, but this was different —this was intense—*even for me*. I knew something profound was happening to my energy, but I was really struggling to balance it myself. So I went to visit my former teacher Lisa Campion, who happens to be an incredibly gifted healer and psychic, in hopes that she could straighten me out.

I'll never forget Lisa's feedback. "Oh hunny, she said, you've been pulsed by God." "Of course I have," I thought to myself. As crazy as that sounds, it felt like the only true explanation for the electric storm that was happening inside my body. Meanwhile, as Lisa was balancing my chakras for me, she mentioned seeing something in my future. She said it was a healing center, not only that, but it already existed and it was "all *rainbowy*." She said that one day, my family would own it.

Interestingly enough, a few months later, I had a dream that I was standing inside an empty building in my town. I knew exactly where it was—right on a corner, diagonally across from the street I grew up on. I wasn't alone in the dream, someone was with me but I couldn't make out who. I was explaining to them how perfect the place was and how the size and location were just right. It didn't quite feel like a dream, it felt more like a prophetic experience. And when I woke up, I remembered the building we were standing in. It was the old art store, one that my great-grandmother and I would frequently stop at for colored pencils, paints, and other crafting supplies. It suddenly dawned on me, the building we were in had once been painted rainbow. From root to crown, red to violet, the outer walls of that building proudly displayed the full-color-spectrum of what I now recognized as the human-energy-experience.

After that dream, I had an intuitive knowing that one day I would open a wellness center in that old art store, that somehow it was my destiny. And I clearly remember predicting it to my brother, who doubted the possibility because the store was currently being rented by a limo company. But I didn't doubt the vision.

A few months later while I was driving by the old art store I noticed that the limos were leaving. One by one they were driving out of the parking lot, and another group of men were moving large items from inside the building and packing them into trucks. I pulled in and asked the guys where they were headed. They told me they were leaving the location because a man named Bill, the owner of a local restaurant, had recently bought the building. What are the odds that I happened to be driving by at the exact time they were moving out? It was an eerie feeling, but something strange was definitely happening around me. I couldn't quite piece it all together yet, but I was certainly picking up on the clues.

This was the moment I started to realize that the body is truly a receiver—an instrument of consciousness—and when its signal is clear, we're able to pick up information from realms that exist far beyond the five senses. But in order to do this, the body must be first tuned in to the correct channels. Our bodies must exist in a state of harmonious alignment with our souls and with the natural world. That means there are things about the body and our environment that we must understand. First, we're living in an industrialized society, so most of the food we eat is not real food. Our soil is deficient of nutrients; therefore, our food is lacking necessary vitamins and minerals. Our water supply is contaminated. Our air is polluted. We're constantly being bombarded by unnatural light sources, WiFi, and other dangerous waves of electromagnetic frequencies. Much of this goes unseen, but none of it goes unfelt by the body. The body absorbs the toxicity of our modern-day lives, and if we're not doing the necessary things to detoxify, our bodies become overburdened and struggle to work efficiently.

So, let's talk detox.

Detoxification

> *"To keep the body in good health is a duty,*
> *otherwise we shall not be able to keep*
> *our mind strong and clear."*
> —Buddha

The body has five major detoxification pathways: the kidney, the liver, the colon, the lungs, and the skin. Each of these detoxification pathways help to keep the body clear of illness, infection, and disease. Metaphysically, and metaphorically speaking, they also help keep our human-lightning-rod clear of energic debris.

The *kidney* helps us by filtering our blood and eliminating waste via the urine.

The *liver*, which is probably our most important detoxification pathway, does the tremendous job of helping the body metabolize nutrients and eliminate harmful chemicals, heavy metals, alcohol, drugs, and other toxic substances. It also helps us to regulate a whole host of hormones including our sex hormones, thyroid hormones, cortisone, and other adrenal hormones. The liver is always hard at work behind the scenes, all on behalf of your body.

Our *lungs* do their part by helping us filter out all of the toxins we breathe in through the air around us. For many of us, our lungs have to work overtime, especially if we smoke, work in industrialized factories, or live and work in heavily polluted areas like tightly cramped cities. Believe it or not, the air inside our homes is usually more toxic than the air outside of them. All of the candles, air fresheners, and cleaning supplies that we use to make our homes look and smell nice can actually be quite hazardous to our health. One suggestion might be to fill your homes with essential oil diffusers and house plants to clear the air instead—your body will thank you.

The *colon*, also known as the gut or the GI tract, has a massive impact on our overall health as it houses more than 70% of our immune system. The colon does the job of reabsorbing water and any other absorbable nutrients from food before eliminating the rest via the stool. Hippocrates, the founder of modern medicine, told us that, "All disease begins in the gut." Your gut is teeming with life, as it contains ten times more health-determining bacteria than the rest of your body. We have more bacteria in our bodies than we do human cells. In fact, we're really only 10% human and 90% bacteria! In order to really be healthy, we should be paying more attention to the microbial balance in our gut. In a healthy body, 85% of the gut microbes are *friendly*, while the other 15% is comprised of *unfriendly* or *bad* bacteria. Bad bacteria aren't entirely bad, in fact, they're equally as important to our health as the good guys. Just as a little bit of stress helps teach the body to adapt to stressors, having a little bit of bad bacteria in our guts helps to strengthen and build the intelligence of our immune systems. Too much stress however, will throw your whole system out of balance, as will too many bad bacteria. Unfriendly bacteria consist of pathogens—viruses, fungi, and parasites—which are often referred to as opportunistic. Opportunistic organisms only show up when the right conditions are present for them to thrive. Unfortunately, our modern lifestyle creates the perfect growing medium. The modern

American who's living a stressed-out, 9-5 lifestyle of working, raising kids, rushing from one thing to the next, and eating a standard American diet will most likely have gut microbiomes that are majorly out of balance. Another contributing factor to an imbalanced microbiome is the overuse of antibiotics. Because of the popular use of antibiotics, we're seeing a rapid rise in antibiotic resistant superbugs. This is because antibiotics kill *all* of the bacteria in our guts, not just the bad guys. The friendly bacteria get wiped out just as quickly as the unfriendly bacteria do. The problem with this is that the good bacteria take far longer to recolonize than the bad bacteria. Antibiotics aren't entirely bad, of course. In life threatening situations they're completely necessary and their invention has stopped many epidemics and saved many lives. But they are being way over-prescribed and have left a lot our immune systems severely compromised.

Should it really come as a surprise that 90% of people on the planet have some type of fungal or parasitic infection, one in two get cancer, 133 million Americans are plagued with chronic "incurable" illnesses, and that less than 5% of our human population is completely free from health problems? These are pretty sad statistics for something that's entirely within our power to control. If you've taken a lot of antibiotics over the course of your lifetime, feel as though you have a weakened immune system, or have digestive or other chronic issues, it may be a good indication that your gut microbiome is out of balance. It might be smart to start supplementation with a high-quality probiotic, drink probiotic-rich beverages like kefir and kombucha, or add fermented foods like sauerkraut or kimchi to your diet. You may find all of this beneficial, although no amount of supplementation can provide you with what a healthy, nourishing diet rich in whole foods and a healthy lifestyle can.

The last organ of detox is actually the largest organ of the body, the *skin*. We sweat out toxins through the skin, which is why Native

American cultures have long used sweat lodges ceremonially as purification for the body. The skin doesn't just excrete toxins, it also absorbs 60% of what we come in contact with. That includes pollutants from the air, water, and soil, as well as makeup, hair care products, soaps, household cleaners, laundry detergents, and even the fabrics we wear. When all other detoxification systems are overburdened, the body will begin to eliminate toxins through the skin.

Another system worth mentioning is the lymphatic system. The lymphatic system is essentially our body's sewer system. It's a network of tissues and organs that help rid the body of toxins, wastes, and other unwanted materials. The primary function of the lymphatic system is to transport lymph, a fluid that contains infection-fighting white blood cells, throughout the body. Unlike the cardiovascular system which pumps blood throughout the body via the heart, the lymphatic system has no pump. In order for it to do its job, we have to *move our bodies*. Our sedentary lifestyles of commuting to work, only to sit in a cubicle and eat fast foods on the run isn't allowing our lymphatic system to do its job. When the lymphatic system gets backed up, we're essentially bathing in our own waste product. This is exactly why our own unconscious living and modern lifestyles are slowly killing us.

I'm not a doctor, so I'm not going to be making any specific dietary recommendations. But if you're planning on putting your health into your own hands, which I highly recommend you do, there are some things about our food supply that you need to understand.

Not all food is created equal. Most of what's on the shelves in our grocery store isn't actually food. It's more or less a *food-like* product and when you eat it, your body doesn't know what to do with it. It actually takes more energy for your body to digest, absorb, and eliminate than the food delivers. Over time, these food-like products pollute your system and make you sick. Your sickness will inevitably lead you to a doctor. They will most likely point you in the direction of the pharmaceutical industry, which will provide you with medication, but never educate you on what's *actually* making you ill. Getting yourself healthy is a personal investment. You can choose to invest in your health now, or you can invest in your doctor later. This will ultimately be your own choice. Big industries are benefiting greatly from our ignorance and sickness. Meanwhile, organic farmers are struggling to keep their businesses alive. That's exactly why poor-quality food is affordable and organic food is more expensive. Billions of dollars are invested in marketing, so we would rather have a shiny new iPhone than an organically grown cucumber or a steak from a grass-fed cow. The average American is more concerned with the value of the clothes they wear or the car they drive than the food they consume, and these are just *a few* of the characteristics of our insane world. But if more people like you and I wake up and make better choices for our health, that alone has the power to begin shifting the energy of the industrialized-machine-world we live in.

When I was desperately trying to heal from chronic health issues, I tried many diets, took a lot of supplements, and worked with several different healing protocols. I hired coaches, bought courses, read a ton of books, and spent more money than I care to admit. I eliminated entire food groups for long periods of time and figuring out what to eat became really stressful at times, which only exacerbated my problems. Throughout my experimentation, I actually came to discover that food is but a small fraction of what makes a person well, and what's even more important than what we *do* eat is what we *don't* eat.

Below is a list of foods we should really try to avoid. Obviously, we're all human, and as you'll read in the next chapter, allowing ourselves the experience of pleasurable things, including food, is our birthright; but it's important that we strive for balance, especially when it comes to food. That said, it's next to impossible to avoid certain foods at all times, especially when going out to eat or attending parties, but we should definitely try our absolute best to consume the foods listed below in moderation, if at all.

- *GMOS*—GMO stands for *genetically modified organism.* Genetic modification is the manipulation of plant and animal development, which is done by altering the expression of their genetics. Humans have long been intentionally manipulating the genetics of animals by interbreeding certain bloodlines in order to create award-winning cows, pigs, horses, chickens, etc. Traditionally, this practice was always done within the confines of nature. There's a reason why dolphins don't mate with sharks and cats don't breed with groundhogs. But over the course of the last few decades, humanity has become dangerously arrogant and pretentious in its belief that we can outsmart mother nature. We've begun splicing genes from bacteria, insects, plants, and animals and injecting them into other various plants and species. Most of the GMO crops that are fed to humans were created so they would be resistant to certain insects and pesticides. This means that they can survive exposure to harsh toxins and chemicals designed to kill insects without hurting the plant. This is dangerous for so many reasons. Not only because *we* are consuming all of the toxic chemicals sprayed onto the resistant crops, but also because the scientists that are engineering these crops don't know what kind of effect the biotech is having on the expression of human genetics. It's one big science experiment and we're the guinea pigs! The entire idea seems foolish even to a layperson like me, and yet scientists are doing it, and they're doing it to our food supply. In other words, **avoid GMOs.** The most common GMO plants are alfalfa, canola, corn, cotton, papaya, potato, soy, sugar beets, zucchini, and yellow squash. It's estimated that over 90% of US canola and corn crops are genetically modified. Why does this matter? For one, corn, canola, and soy are found in almost every shelf-stable food in the grocery store. You can be certain that these crops were sprayed with glyphosate, which contains a toxic herbicide. Remember when we talked about the good guys in your gut that are supposed to make up 85% of your microbiome? Glyphosate kills those guys. Not only that, but the World Health Organization and National Academy of Sciences have identified glyphosate residue as a *probable carcinogen*. In 2017 the State of California declared that glyphosate *causes cancer and birth defects*. The biotech industry, supported by the US Government, doesn't want you to know that your food contains GMO's. There's no mandatory labeling and the scientists producing these foods are not required to prove their safety before placing them on your grocery shelves. The next time you go grocery shopping, read the ingredient list of what you're purchasing, especially if it's a processed food like chips, cookies, cakes, salad dressings, popsicles, or any pre-made meal. If you can't pronounce the ingredient, you probably want to avoid eating it.

- *Processed Vegetable Oils*—Processed vegetable oils are structurally more similar to plastic than they are to food and almost all of them are genetically modified. Shelf stable foods are laden with these toxic oils, and so are all commercially made deep fried foods. Scientists have linked the heating of vegetable oils to cancer, heart disease, and even dementia.

- *Conventionally Grown Produce*—Conventionally grown produce is loaded with toxic herbicides, fungicides, and pesticides. These crops are sprayed heavily with chemicals to prevent the infestation of unwanted pests. Unfortunately, the toxic chemicals sprayed on the plants are absorbed by the earth and disrupt the natural microbial balance of the soil. This depletes some of the nutrient sources naturally found in plant foods by over 50%. When we consume conventionally grown produce, the chemical residues left behind disrupts the microbial balance of our guts and places a heavy burden on our major detoxification pathways. Organic food is expensive, so do the best that you can to avoid all non-organically grown plant foods, but if you must buy conventionally grown produce, soak it in a solution of apple cider vinegar and water and rinse thoroughly before consuming.

• *Factory Farmed Meat*—I have personally come to believe that consuming some meat is good for growing a strong and healthy body, but when it comes to animal foods, quality is of the utmost importance. I would rather not eat any than to eat meat of poor quality. Conventionally farmed meats are raised and fed in a way that's not only unethical and inhumane, but is not in accordance with nature's design. Cow, sheep, buffalo, and other commonly eaten mammals are called *ruminants*, meaning they're designed to eat plant matter. Most conventionally farmed animals are fed grains (wheat and corn), which quickly makes them fat. The grains fed to conventionally farmed animals are most often GMO crops. These animals are not meant to eat grain; they would never be found eating it in the wild. The factory-farm conditions these animals are raised in usually leave them very little room to move and force them to live in their own waste. When these animals are fed an unnatural diet, are pumped full of artificial growth hormones, and are living in such tight quarters, they often become sick and so are given high doses of antibiotics to prevent the rapid spread of infection and disease. This is a nightmare scenario for so many reasons. Not only does the quality of their meat decline but when we consume it, we're also absorbing minute doses of antibiotics which disrupt our microbial balance. This leaves our immune systems weak and unable to fend off parasites and bacteria stored in the flesh of these animals. Their living conditions also make their lives a misery, which brings up ethical concerns as well. Factory farming is an abomination for all beings involved. With each purchase we make, we can either support its continuation or support humane farmers.

- *Commercialized Dairy*—Humans have been pasteurizing dairy products for less than a hundred years, due to the fear of tuberculosis, botulism, and other infectious diseases. Before that, milk was consumed raw. Raw milk contains naturally occurring, lactic acid producing bacteria that protects it from pathogens. When milk is pasteurized, it's heated to a very high temperature to kill bacteria. The problem with this is that the heat also kills important enzymes that aid in digestion. Many people with sensitivity to dairy can actually tolerate raw milk because of the enzymatic activity. An additional problem with commercialized dairy products is that they include growth hormones. Dairy farmers inject their cows with a growth hormone to increase milk production for a longer period of time than is natural, which increases the risk of infection by 80%. This, of course, creates the need for even more antibiotics. Dairy products are not necessary for optimum health and commercialized dairy can be quite harmful to humans. If you're weary of consuming raw dairy products, my suggestion is to avoid dairy all together.

- *Bread, Grains, Gluten*—Human bodies aren't designed to ingest as many processed carbohydrates as we've been eating. They were never meant to be such a large part of our diet. Wheat, white flour, and other bread products are wreaking havoc on our digestive systems and are major offenders on our list of processed carbs. Conventionally grown wheat is most likely to be genetically modified, so it's best avoided altogether. Whole grains, seeds, legumes, and some nuts also contain something called *phytates*, or *phytic acid*. Phytic acid has also been referred to as an *anti*-nutrient. Phytic acid can impair the absorption of iron, zinc, manganese, and calcium, and can also create mineral deficiencies in the body. Our ancestors knew about phytates, and this is why they soaked their grains, nuts, and seeds before consuming them. If you're going to consume whole grains, nuts, or seeds make sure to soak them prior to eating. This reduces the phytic acid and makes them more absorbable to the body. Try your best to avoid all foods made with bleached white flour and conventionally grown wheat, including bread. You can always purchase sprouted grain breads if bread is a regular staple in your diet—that's what I do.

- *Refined Sugar*—Sugar does not belong to a food group. Processed sugar is a drug to our brains and a poison to our bodies. Although it's incredibly difficult not to, I'd suggest not eating the stuff very often, if at all. If you need a sugar alternative, have a little bit of raw honey, monk fruit, or stevia. Adequate amounts of below-ground vegetables, like beets and carrots, can also curb the cravings of a sweet tooth.

These are very basic dietary guidelines. The best thing you can do for your body, and for the world around you is to eat *real* food. It's that simple. The hardest part about changing our diet is breaking the addiction we have to food-like products and the chemicals intentionally added to make these foods addictive. If you eat eggs, make sure they're from organic free-range chickens. If you eat meat, make sure it's high quality. Learn where your food comes from and do your best to support local farmers. If it comes from nature and was grown organically without pesticides in high-quality soil, it's probably good to consume.

You also want to consume raw food as often as possible. Raw food, or food eaten in its natural state, contains enzymatic activity. Enzymes can't survive beyond 118° Fahrenheit, so once we cook our food, the natural enzymes have been killed off. Basically, we've robbed our food of its life-force energy. Remember when we talked about chi, ki, and prana, the intelligence contained within all living things? That intelligence is also in our food! When we consume food in its natural state, the prana within us is able to interact with the life-force energy of the food. The body will know exactly what to do with the food we eat, how to absorb its living waters, where to send its nutrients, and how to eliminate the rest. Once we cook our food, it's no longer *alive* with that intelligent life force. This doesn't mean it's completely devoid of nutrients, it just means that our bodies become responsible for doing all the work to break it down. I'm not suggesting that you eat *all* of your food raw, although that diet does work really well for some, especially those in warmer climates. Just make it a point to eat plenty of foods in their natural, raw state as much as your body allows.

Our bodies only come equipped with a certain amount of enzyme storage; think of this as your enzyme savings account. If you continually make withdrawals by eating cooked food, and don't make regular deposits by eating raw foods, you'll go into a deficit. When we eat a diet of overcooked, highly processed foods, our bodies need to work overtime to produce more enzymes, which can have a negative impact on our immune systems. This lowers our ability to protect ourselves from disease. It will eventually slow down our digestive systems, leaving food that's undigested in our guts for longer than desirable. Mother nature then sends her clean-up crew in to break down the excess and our guts become a breeding ground for unwanted visitors. When we incorporate living food into our diets, the enzymes in our food assist in the digestion process and help our bodies by continuing to break food down once it's been eaten. This allows for better nutrient absorption, and that's why a fresh green salad is traditionally served before a meal.

Even if you're struggling with a condition that's challenging to your health, your body is always working on your behalf. The idea is to help your body when and where you can and as often as you possibly can. There are a few ways you can assist your body when it comes to enzymes and digestion. The first one is actually very simple; be present while you eat and chew your food. When we chew our food well, enzymes in our saliva are excreted to help us break it down. When you're present with your meal, your mind is letting your body know that it's time to eat. Have you ever seen a commercial with a big, juicy cheeseburger or a pizza and your mouth starts to water? That's your body's way of getting prepared to digest that meal! When you're watching television while eating, your mind is giving your body all sorts of mixed messages and good digestion is not likely to be one of them. So, take some long, slow, deep breaths before you eat and signal to your *parasympathetic nervous system* that it's time to rest and digest. One of the worst things you can do for your body is to eat when you're stressed out. When you're stressed out, your sympathetic nervous system is activated. This means your energy is being sent to your extremities, preparing your body to run or fight, *not* to the vital organs necessary for digestion. So, when it's time to eat, eat. Don't watch videos or TV shows, don't argue with your family; be present, eat, chew, and enjoy your meal. You can also supplement with a high-quality digestive enzyme for extra help.

It may take some time for your body to heal itself, especially if you've been living an unhealthy lifestyle for a while. But if you get rid of the offending foods and start introducing more of the right foods, your body will begin to balance itself out. Please don't forget—the decision to make lifestyle adjustments and heal your relationship to food doesn't just heal your body—it also heals the planet. We heal the planet by healing its people.

Owning the rights to a physical vehicle comes with just a few more requirements. Along with real food, we need:

- *Quality hydration.* We want to be drinking at least half our body weight in ounces of high-quality, purified water every day. In an ideal world, we would all be getting clean drinking water from a natural spring, but most of our natural waters are polluted, and our municipal water supply is likely far worse, containing over 30,000 possible pollutants. Water plays many vital roles in our quest to stay healthy and it's our responsibility to provide our bodies with adequate amounts of clean water. I suggest a home filtration system, not just for the water you drink, but also for the water you bathe in. Remember, the skin absorbs 60% of what it comes in contact with in less than 26 seconds. If you're bathing in it, you're basically drinking it.

- *Rest.* One of the most highly overlooked nourishments to the body actually has nothing to do with food or water, but with our need to *rest.* The body rejuvenates and repairs itself during moments of deep, dreamless, and restful sleep. There's simply no questioning it; getting adequate amounts of sleep is a major contributor to our well-being. Sleep came more naturally to our ancestors who weren't afforded the luxuries of the modern world. They didn't have the convenience of electricity, tablets, TVs, a light source at the flip of a switch, or an iPhone, so their wake and sleep cycles were aligned with the natural rhythms of day and night. This is called our *circadian rhythm* and the more in tune with it we are, the better off our bodies will be. There are various contributing factors that lead to a disrupted sleep cycle, stress being one of them. It's smart to prepare your body for sleep by turning your television off at least two hours prior to going to bed. Instead of scrolling your phone, read a book. If you are going to stare at your phone, at least make sure your turning on the blue-light blocker to protect your eyes. Let your brain relax and reduce the amount of stimulation coming in from your external environment. Just because we can't see Wifi and electromagnetic frequencies, doesn't mean they aren't having an effect on our bodies. We are just energy, after all, so I also recommend either turning your devices off, putting them on airplane mode, or leaving them out of your sleeping space all together.

- *Air* is another critical element to physical health and vitality. The body can go three weeks without food, three days without water, but can't go three minutes without air. After only three minutes, the brain and body will begin to shut down. The ancient Yogic Masters were well educated not only in the power of aligning the body through physical postures (*asanas*), but also in understanding the power of breath. They mastered their breathing through a practice called *pranayama*, a series of breathing techniques used to control the flow of prana (life-force energy) throughout the body. Deep, rhythmic breathing is so good for the body. It does far more than just oxygenate our cells; it also creates alkalinity in our blood, which helps boost our immune system and protects us against potentially harmful pathogens. The great majority of the world is living in a state of chronic stress, and this activates the sympathetic nervous system which causes our breathing to become shallow. It also broadcasts a signal to the body that we're in physical danger. When our fight or flight response is activated, the body's energy moves away from our vital organs and into our extremities in preparation to run or fight. This weakens our immune system and inhibits our ability to think clearly. Many of today's stressors aren't exactly due to real-life threats, rather, they're caused as a result of our own fearful thinking. The practice of conscious, controlled breath-work helps to activate our parasympathetic nervous system which affects our rest and digest response by sending a signal to our brains that we are, in fact, okay and aren't facing any immediate threats. This allows us to be present to what is right in front of us.

- *Movement* is another requirement for living in a healthy physical vessel. Modern-day humans don't move their bodies nearly as much as our ancestors did, who needed to either hunt, forage, or farm in order for their basic survival needs to be met. Instead, many of us sit all day long in front of computer screens, inside cubicles, or in classrooms with harsh fluorescent lighting. When we're done working, we rush to the gym and beat our muscles into submission so we can *look* like healthy people. We might forgo the attempt altogether, order a pizza, and live like couch potatoes. There's something fundamentally wrong with the way our society lives and it's time we start paying attention to what's really making us sick! The bottom line is that we need to move our bodies every day. Exercise stimulates our lymphatic system, which helps clean up some of the mess inside us created by modern-day living. Movement doesn't have to be difficult; it can be as simple as taking a nice walk every night after dinner or making time each morning to do some light yoga or stretching before you start your day. Adopting a daily yoga practice is my primary recommendation for incorporating daily movement and bringing balance back to the entire mind/body/spirit system. It doesn't have to be strenuous. As long as you're making the effort to move, your body will thank you.

Cleansing

"The microbe is nothing, the terrain is everything."
—Louis Pasteur

Long ago, before the world became nearly as toxic as it is today, cleansing and detoxification were common practices for health and longevity. Even in a time *before* we had massive amounts of air pollution, industrial waste, electromagnetic radiation, and an onslaught of toxic chemicals being added to all our food and water, humans understood the importance of cleansing and giving the body adequate time to restore itself. The ancient masters knew that the cleaner the body, the clearer the mind; the more purified our system, the better we feel and the closer to Source we become. Somehow, it seems we've lost our connection to this wisdom. If you think about it realistically, cleansing isn't just a *suggestion*; it's an essential if we don't want to live in filth. We need to empty the trash or it's going to rot and our house is going to stink. We clean our kitchens, bathrooms, houses, and cars regularly—we wash the outside of our bodies and brush our teeth—but we don't pay very much attention to what's happening *inside* of us. Until it hurts, of course; then we go to the doctor and rely on the medicine they provide to make us better. But does medicine really make us *better* or does it just temporarily prevent us from hurting? What if a vast majority of the diseases in our bodies are caused by the fact that we simply stopped taking out the trash? For a majority of us, our inner ecosystems have become stagnant wastelands, and we just can't *see* the filth. It's really not our fault that we don't understand this; no one taught us about our inner landscape. Humans generally only think about what we've been taught to think about, so now might be a good time to question—why didn't we learn about internal *health* in health class?

We don't learn about health because trillions of dollars are generated annually as a result of us staying sick. If you become your own physician and heal your own body, you no longer rely on the establishment for your healthcare (unless of course there's a major accident or injury, in which case, trauma care is unparalleled.) I want to be clear here, I'm not against modern medicine. In fact, it saved my ass when my kidney became severely infected during pregnancy, and I believe our general life expectancy is much greater because of it. *But is our quality of life better?* Just because you aren't experiencing sickness doesn't mean you're healthy. Many of us have normalized mediocre health because we've forgotten what genuine health really feels like. If you're dealing with any type of chronic illness in your body, there are plenty of options worth exploring outside of mainstream medicine.

Cleansing, detoxification, and diets that are nourishing to the body aren't taught in healthcare because they're the greatest threats to our modern-day sickness for profit healthcare *industry*. Medicine isn't really about health anymore, it's about business. If you're currently struggling with your health, it's important that you understand that all healing and regeneration first begins with detoxification. Health can't be cultivated in a toxic system. Only when the system is cleansed can adequate nourishment take place.

I wish I could give you a one-size-fits-all detox protocol, and there are loads of people on the Internet trying to sell you theirs, but every person has a unique body with unique needs. What I can offer you is this: my personal experience and what cleansing protocols I've used (and continue to use) to detoxify my own body.

- *Fasting*—some people are really extreme when it comes to cleansing, and I've also taken that approach. What I've learned is that too much of a good thing can actually be a bad thing and a simple approach is always a solid approach. Our bodies really do love to eat and eating is super satisfying to our senses, but if you're feeling tired, sluggish, overweight, or cloudy-headed, it might be a good idea, every once in a while, to give your body a rest from eating. Digestion requires a great deal of energy. When all our energy is invested in digesting large meals, we may not have the energy we need for healing and regeneration, especially if our bodies are overloaded with toxicity. If you're totally new to cleansing and detoxifying, try a water fast one day a week, or have a couple of days of freshly pressed juices to give your body a welcome break from digestion. I recommend juice fasting over water fasting as an introduction, as juice contains a variety of vitamins, minerals, and enzymes that your body can use to regenerate itself. You can always work your way up from there if you feel inspired to go further.

- *Raw Living Food Diet*—eating a diet of raw, living foods changed my entire life. I wholeheartedly believe that we should all be consuming as much raw, unprocessed food as we possibly can, and directly from nature. This is the way that humans were always intended to eat. Our planet is primarily made of green plant material and water, not Cheese-Its. This should tell us something about what we need to be consuming. Include lots of green foods rich in chlorophyll, like raw salads and leafy vegetables in your diet, as this is incredibly beneficial to the body. If you have compromised digestion and can't tolerate much raw food, try adding some very simple green juices like cucumber, kale, cilantro, and green apple. You can also try adding spinach to a smoothie with a variety of fresh berries and sprouts. Just remember—the simpler the better.

- *Parasite Cleansing*—if you eat meat, you should parasite cleanse, period. This is especially true if you eat pork. I know, it's pretty weird to even think about, but we consider it completely natural to deworm our pets but not ourselves. Because *they're* animals, right? I hate to break it to you, but humans are animals too and we're just as susceptible to parasitic infections as our dogs and cats are—especially if we treat our pets like family and allow them all over our furniture and in our beds. I've made parasite cleansing a regular part of my detoxification routine. A couple times a year, for a minimum of ten days at a time, I'll eat a primarily raw diet and take an anti-parasitic herbal blend of clove, wormwood, and black walnut hull. You can also add fresh garlic, ginger, and turmeric root to your meals. It's not about the microbes in your body as much as it is the environment of your inner ecosystem. If your body's full of toxicity and stagnant waste, you'll attract pathogens. They don't go away on their own, nor will they go away with a course of antibiotics or antifungals. They'll only go away permanently when you make your inner environment inhospitable to them.

- *Dry Skin Brushing*—brushing your skin with a naturally-made dry brush is an ancient technique for stimulating the lymphatic system. You can purchase a dry brush online or at any local health food store. I like to do this just before I shower. You always want to brush your skin gently but firmly in short, swift motions upward and towards your heart. Start at the feet and move up the ankles, calves, legs, hips, and then onto the abdomen; brush the front and back of your torso and keep moving upwards toward the chest.

Once you're finished brushing your lower body, move to the hands and brush upward from your hands towards your armpits, one arm at a time. Brush over your chest and collarbone. If you have a brush with a long handle, you can brush your back, ending with your face and neck.

• *Hot/Cold Showers*—alternating hot and cold showers also stimulates the lymphatic system, as lymph vessels contract when exposed to cold and relax in response to heat. The lymphatic system doesn't have a pump like the heart. If we aren't moving our bodies, our lymph system isn't flowing and won't be able to do its job of cleaning up the waste in our bodies. When the lymph starts contracting and relaxing in response to the alternating hot and cold water, it starts to pump lymph fluid throughout the body, flushing toxins and pathogens out of areas that may have become stagnated. Conscious breathing through cold exposure also helps to train the body how to better handle moments of stress. When the body is exposed to cold, our body goes into shock; our diaphragm restricts and our breathing becomes shallow. Essentially, we enter fight or flight mode. If we can train ourselves to breathe slowly and deeply while being exposed to the cold, we can retrain our bodies to manage the effects of stress. Stress can be brought on by thoughts and emotions about things like late mortgage payments and child support; it can also be from physical stress like working out and doing manual labor; or it can be caused by viruses, bacteria, fungi, and other pathogens in the body. I understand that cold exposure isn't for everyone, and I used to absolutely hate it; but with practice I've come to enjoy it, and I'm sure my body thanks me for it.

• *Yoga*—yoga is another practice that I've learned to love wholeheartedly. Yoga is similar to cold exposure in the sense that you're deliberately putting yourself into stressful positions and breathing your way through them. Not only does yoga help the body to handle stressful situations, it also opens and aligns all of the energy centers and redirects the flow of energy throughout the body. In fact, this is why so many people report deep, therapeutic benefits, and often embark on their own healing journey as a result of practicing yoga. It gets all the old stuck and stagnant energy in our bodies moving and flowing again, so we can heal ourselves and become clear conduits for allowing divine energy to flow through us.

These are just a few of my favorite detoxification practices. There are plenty more out there, like saunas, colonics, red-light therapy, etc. All you have to do is run a Google search and you'll have plenty of information at your fingertips for how to detoxify your life. It just takes a little discipline. It's also a smart idea to check in with your primary care physician or hire a specialist before starting any intense protocol as they can be intense on the body and it's always good to have professional support.

More important than any of these health suggestions, however, is a *reason* to make them a top priority. We need an answer to our *Why?* We need to feel a sense of connection to what we're doing and know wholeheartedly the reason we're doing it. If we don't have a big enough connection to our choices, they'll be way too easy to just blow off. We'll just pick up a pack of donuts and binge-watch *Shameless* instead (not that *I've* done this before . . .). But honestly, we must have a reason to want to be better than we were the day before. We need motivation, and the highest form is *mission* motivation. A *mission* is something that arises from deep within you—from the diamond center of your being, from the very core of your soul. We each have one. When you discover yours, the health of your physical vessel becomes an easy priority. It's okay if you haven't discovered your own personal mission yet, just get behind someone who has and figure out how you can use your unique gifts to help! My mission is to *Heal the People* so we can heal the planet! Welcome aboard!

For a more comprehensive understanding of exactly how to move your body and what to eat, why, and how much, I highly recommend reading the book *How to Eat, Move, and Be Healthy* by Paul Chek.

Character Structure

Creative Idealist
(Thinker)

| Distant fearful eyes, head tilted, body core tight, disjointed limbs, left to right or top to bottom imbalance | "Mad scientist", tall vertical energy, no eye contact, introspective, fidgety, wandering |

According to Thomas: The Creative Idealist/Thinker
For more information visit www.4dhealing.com.

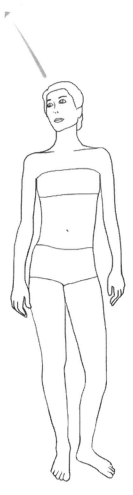

According to Kessler: The Leaving Pattern
Images from The 5 Personality Patterns by Steven Kessler © 2015. Used with permission.
For more information visit www.The5PersonalityPatterns.com

The character structure most closely associated with the Root System is the *Creative Idealist*. The *Creative Idealist* describes the highest potential of this character, which is revealed when they're able to release their energetic defense and allow their soul quality to be expressed. We cover both the soul-quality and the defensive-quality of this character in the section on the Root System, due to the fact that this structure has the most difficult time rooting themselves into the human experience. This is why Kessler has identified its energy-pattern as the *Leaving* pattern. When threatened, a *Creative Idealist* will simply leave. They'll either leave physically, by leaving the room, or if this isn't a viable option, they'll leave energetically by leaving their body. It doesn't take much to overwhelm them, simply being alive or the thought of having to do something outside of their comfort zone, can be enough to overwhelm a *Creative Idealist*. Thomas calls the defensive-quality of this character structure the *Thinker,* because their tendency is to live entirely in their minds, completely disassociated from the world underneath their feet. This makes them highly *deficient* in their Root System.

The *Thinker* personality is how a *Creative Idealist* energetically defends themselves from feeling overwhelmed and is characterized by the spinning thoughts of an overly analytical mind. It's often this lofty, ungrounded quality that makes creative people appear to be unrealistic dreamers, and unrelatable to the rest of the world. If the *Thinker* is one of your favored energetic defenses, you'll tend to live your life with ceaseless mind chatter, ruled by excessive thinking, fear, and insecurity. You'll have a tendency towards over analyzing everything, down to the most minute of life experiences, while never really coming to any concrete conclusions. You may be overwhelmed by the simplest of tasks and have a very difficult time being present in your life. You might struggle in areas that appear effortless to most, like meeting your own survival needs, holding down a steady job, and taking care of yourself. Honestly, you might just forget about the basic needs of your body because that's not really where you spend the majority your time.

For those of us who identify as *Thinkers,* the deficiency of energy in the root causes us to be tall and thin, or otherwise-frail, our bodies lacking in a sense of stability, solidity, and groundedness. We might be clumsy, or accident prone; a simple a gust of wind might be enough to blow us over. A lot of *Thinkers* struggle deeply with their humanness and will turn to drugs because they're an easy escape from the body. *Thinkers* will tend to use substances as an outlet to keep themselves up and out of their bodies, retreating to the safety of their minds where they're free to explore the limitless expansion of their spirit. However, their habitual drug use will often lead them to the same sensation of physical imprisonment they were originally trying to escape, only amplified (this is what happened to me.)

To live life within the *Thinker's* defense is to never truly claim the body or physical existence as their own. According to Kessler, this pattern originated in the very early stages of life when the spirit was unable to complete the developmental task of *embodiment*. From a psychology-based perspective, this pattern is thought to have been created due to a birth trauma, physical abuse, or neglect at a very early age. Anything that might cause an infant to question their physical safety or ability to survive might manifest as a *Leaving Pattern* or *Thinker Defense*. Remember, a felt sense of safety is necessary for embodiment; *Thinkers* never feel safe and thus, never fully *root* into their bodies. Due to their lack of connection to the physical body, any experience that causes a *Creative Idealist* to feel unsafe, afraid, or overwhelmed will catapult them into the vacant, ungrounded, spinning energic pattern of their defense. When *Creative Idealists* are caught in the defensive patterning of the *Thinker* they will have a very challenging time grounding themselves into the material world. In their mind, they may be super-hero's, full of fantastic ideas and idyllic daydreams, but their lives and bank accounts will tell a much different story.

Until they come into the core-soul-quality of their character, *Thinkers* will generally have a difficult time amassing any sort of material wealth or prosperity. Their energetic structure doesn't really allow for it and their inability to stay consistently grounded to the material plane only makes matters worse for them. Material abundance is a very earthly quality, and *Thinker's* don't readily identify as *belonging* to the earth. If you ever talk to a *Thinker*, they'll often tell you they feel like they're from another planet or they just don't feel as though they're from here. Many will tell you their real home is off-planet somewhere, like Andromeda, the Pleiades, or someplace else in the stars.

The goal of a *Thinker* is to come out of their head and into their body, down from the stars and onto the earth. In order to do this, they will need to feel safe and supported enough to do so. Once they're able to cultivate a general feeling of physical safety, it will become easier for them to manifest their ideas into the physical plane. Because they spent a great deal of time untethered to the world of form, they naturally become very spiritual, or intellectual, sometimes both. With access to visionary states of consciousness, their ideas usually reflect their expanded states of awareness. *Thinkers* who are able to re-connect to their bodies, and establish a steady ground on which to build will become individuals capable of stretching humanity's vision, pushing us steadily forward in our evolutionary process. A *Thinker*'s primary goal is to find a *worldly outlet* where they can express their *out-of-this-world* ideas and talents. But that first requires them to accept that although they often feel like a stranger, they may, in fact, belong in this world.

When I first learned about the character structure of the *Creative Idealist*, with all its unique struggles, fears, gifts, and talents, it felt like someone had spoken directly into my own soul. I often felt as though planet earth just wasn't my home and longed to experience a deeper-sense of belonging if not here, then anywhere—even if that meant leaving my own body.

I struggled my way through school, taking refuge in art and many other creative endeavors, until eventually I dropped out of high school in favor of homeschooling. *Creative Idealists* tend to be loners, bonding with only a select few people who really get them. I'd spend most of my days in the comfort of my own imagination and as soon as I was introduced to mind altering drugs, I'd use them too, to escape from myself. After learning about this character structure, it was incredibly comforting to know that I wasn't the only one who felt the way I did and struggled in many of the same ways that I had. But, according to the psychological-model of character structures, I didn't exactly meet the criteria that constituted the makings of that particular personality. My birth wasn't traumatic, I wasn't neglected or abused and as far as I know, I was a very loved and wanted child. But why then did I identify so strongly with this structure? The answer: because it wasn't created in response to this life, it is the nature of my soul. Which is why I have chosen to share not just the defensive qualities of each character, as many psychologists might choose, but to also include the core-*soul*-qualities as defined by Thomas.

Even still, after learning all about the nature of my character, I didn't actually come down into my body until sometime after graduating energy medicine school. In fact, it was during my spontaneous, raw-food induced spiritual awakening that I dreamt about my growing need for embodiment. Right around the same time that I was remembering my mission as a soul, I had a dream that my "spiritual legs" were still coiled high inside my body and I could feel my soul-self all twisted up inside my torso. Standing parallel to the feet tucked up inside my torso stood a very small, Asian man, just barely reaching 5 feet tall. His skin was old and tanned, but without any wrinkles, and he had a long, thin, white beard that came down into a point a few inches below his chin. He was encouraging me to put my feet down, telling me that it was okay and that I was safe—but I didn't exactly trust him. When I refused his offer to ground myself, he placed his hands on my feet, which were still tucked up somewhere inside my belly, and began to gently tug on them. I could feel the energy of him pulling my spiritual feet down into my own physical feet, urging me to step fully into this world. As soon as I surrendered to the pull, I woke up from the dream.

When a *Thinker* finally relaxes out of their defensive position, they become willing to step fully into their core soul quality and role as a *Creative Idealist*. While their personality is still similar to that of the *Thinker*, the characteristics of the *Creative Idealist* differ in the sense that they become highly purposeful and grounded in their ideas and in their action.

Creative Idealists are born to create. They are able to make manifest in the world what one might only dream about in their mind. They are the artists, visionaries, mystics, scientific, musical, and mathematical geniuses. They help us to see the world through a different lens, stretching our minds and expanding our vision. Their energy runs slightly different to that of their defended counterpart. In defense, the *Thinker's* mind is split off from their body creating a detached, dissociated persona and a tilted head that often appears disconnected from the rest of them. But when connected to their core, the *Creative Idealist* is able to run all of their energy through a very linear channel capable of connecting to their mind and creating in their reality. *Creative Idealists* effortlessly connect to heaven, and then have to work at bringing it down to earth. This energetic current usually results in a tall and thin, or otherwise slender but stable body with little density.

Although they've accepted their position as being in the world, they still prefer to spend most of their time in the mental realm rather than the physical, unless they're engaged in the process of creating something. While caught in the process of creating or grounding their ideas into reality, *Creative Idealists* will often lose track of time and still forget to care for their physical body. They may go an entire day without eating if they're wrapped up in a creative endeavor.

Creative Idealists embody the playful enthusiasm and wonderment of a child. Their eyes are alive and intense with passion, especially while they're creating or giving voice to their new and exciting ideas. They can still be distracted, detached, and slightly fearful, but not so much so that they dissociate. They're highly intelligent and have the incredible ability to see further, usually finding themselves on the cutting edge of many current subjects. It's not uncommon for them to become targets, as they're often met with opposition from lesser minds who can't expand themselves enough to see their unique vision.

The personal difficulties of a *Creative Idealist* arise when they become stuck in their defense, caught up in the mental realm, and spinning in their thinking. This can happen even if they aren't scared or overwhelmed by a source outside of themselves. *Creative Idealists* can become overwhelmed simply by listening to their own thinking. When they're in their defense they'll have a number of advanced, creative, and abstract ideas, but will have a tough acting on them, and applying the necessary discipline to bring those ideas into reality. However, when they're in their core, working to create their visions is all they want to do.

Physical relationships and worldly affairs may not seem to appeal to *Creative Idealists* quite as much as the inner workings of their own mind, which tends to be far more entertaining and fascinating than any other worldly endeavor. *Creative Idealists* aren't likely to find themselves happily climbing the rungs of a corporate ladder, unless they're deeply inspired by a company's larger vision. To truly gain the courage to engage with the world and share their genius with others, a *Creative Idealist* will generally need to enlist the help of a secondary character structure which can be any of the remaining four, each of which we'll be discussing in the sections that follow.

Root Energetics

Now that we've covered just about everything you need to know relating to your Root System and the consciousness that governs it, along with the character structure associated with it, let's asses the health and function of your own Root System. Again, I'm not asking you to look inside your energy field to discover a spinning disc, I'm suggesting you look to your own life for the answers.

Remember from the chapter on the human energy system that energy behaves in a multitude of different ways—it can be *excessive*, running too much energy; *deficient*, not able to generate enough energy; or *blocked*, meaning no energy is able to transmit through the chakra at all. Chakras can also have both *excessive and deficient* characteristics, so the energetic state of your chakra may also fall somewhere in between any of those three states, depending on the situation. In an ideal world, however, we want our energy to be *balanced* and able to flow freely throughout our system. If a chakra is out of balance, not holding enough or holding too much energy, we will need to either charge, discharge, or otherwise reorganize the energy of that chakra in order to bring it into balance.

Those who carry an *excessive* amount of energy in the Root System might feel heavy, dense, sluggish, and tired. Their bodies tend to be large and solid, but this isn't always the case—as certain eating disorders, like anorexia, are also born out of the excessive need to have dominance and control over the physical body, as is the desire to exercise excessively and manipulate the muscles in the body in order to look a certain way. Conversely, they may not move their bodies much at all. The tendency will be towards *excess* in any given direction, either towards movement or sluggishness.

Characteristics of an excessive root chakra can manifest as an exaggerated need for structure, routine, security, and the need to amass a large amount of material wealth, more than what is necessary for comfort and security. Hoarding is another manifestation of excessive energy carried in the root chakra. These individuals will have a very difficult time making changes in their lives and routines. They may complain about being bored or stuck but feel unable to change.

Those with excessive energy in the roots often characterize themselves as *realists* and focus primarily on the physical world, while scoffing at spiritual concepts. They're often neatly dressed and care a great deal about their physical appearance. Taking pride in one's appearance is never a bad thing, but when its excessive it will take precedence over all else, including the need for an inner state of peace and physical balance.

In order to discharge some of their excessive energy and come into balance, those with excessive root energy will need to release a bit of their need for structure, in favor of adding a little bit of movement and flow into their lives. Simple acts, like deciding to take a new route to work in the morning, can begin to slowly shift the energy of the root; however, physical acts like moving the body, are most recommended. If you think you have *excessive* energy stored in your Root System, try dancing, playing, hiking, swimming, yoga, or anything else that gets your body moving in a gentle way. These are all wonderful ways to get the energy in the root to move and begin to balance out.

A *deficiency* in the energy of the Root System is going to look quite different and will be more commonly seen in creative types who have difficulty grounding themselves to the planet. In stark contrast to the realist whose energy is entirely *too* grounded, a *deficient* person often doesn't feel connected to their body, or grounded to the planet at all.

You might notice *deficient* energy in those who show up physically but don't really seem to take up space within a room—their presence is hardly noticed. They're often meek and timid and generally appear anxious, restless, overwhelmed, and scared. Their body will usually be frail and lacking in density, but may also be otherwise unformed, manifesting as a body that is large and heavy but with no real solid borders. The connection to the physical world and their home within it, *the body*, is never solidly established.

Those with *deficient* Root Systems might struggle to hold down a job, care for their bodies, or meet their own basic survival needs. This is because they don't really recognize the body's needs as relevant. Dreams, ideas, and fantasies will be favored to that of everyday living.

A person lacking in root-energy is most likely going to have a dominance in their higher energy centers like the mind and spirit. In order to bring energy into their *deficient* Root System, their mental energy will need to become grounded in their body. Those with *deficient* energy usually do really well with basic grounding techniques that allow them to connect to their bodies in this space and time. I've also found that those with deficient roots will feel more comfortable coming down and grounding with those of a similar nature to them. Having the support of a like-minded tribe can help establish a sense of safety, enough to come down into the body and onto the planet.

The third state of energy, *blocked-energy*, may manifest in the root as complete and total stuckness, not just sluggish, not just tired—totally stuck, like cement. No energy is flowing, nothing in life is able to move, therefore, nothing is able to manifest or change. If you're overweight, you won't be able to take the weight off; if you're underweight, you won't be able to gain anything. Chronic physical disease is a major indicator of a blocked Root System. It can feel like an insurmountable task to get energy moving through a blocked root, but it's not impossible. If you feel like your root is blocked, start with simply connecting to your body and addressing your physical history. Was there a major trauma or life-threatening situation that may have caused you to block energy from going to the root? How was your root nourished in the early stages of your human-development? How connected are you to your body? And how safe do you currently feel?

In order for you to bring energy into a blocked root, physical movement is always key. Unblocking a chakra isn't always comfortable, though, as it often means we will need to move through the issue that originally caused the block. Having support, especially from a qualified healer, therapist, or support-tribe is very helpful.

Idealistically, we want to achieve a state of *balance* in all our energy systems, as they are equally important to our overall well-being, but bringing balance to the root is imperative for us as humans. An imbalance in our root will have a detrimental effect on all of our other energy centers and will have the most obvious effect on our physical lives. In order to balance the energy in our physical bodies, we need to first claim our physical space as our own. We need to come down from our heads and occupy our own bodies. We'll need to learn, or perhaps re-learn, how to eat, how to move, how to hydrate, how to sleep, how to think, and how to breathe. When we make learning and practicing those things a priority, our lives will reflect the balance.

A *balanced* Root System manifests in a life and a body that is solid but not rigid, firm, but not overly-focused. When balance is achieved in the root, we feel grounded in our humanness but not fearfully attached to our physical form. Our bodies become the vehicle for our spirit to move about this world and life becomes an extension of the energy and consciousness that moves throughout our system.

Just like electricity, our human life-force is a conductive energy; we are electromagnetic beings, after all. When our energy gets out of balance, if we somehow acquire too much of it or don't have enough, *grounding* is always the answer. *Grounding* is an essential to balancing any Root System, whether our systems are *excessive* or *deficient*, we will still need to ground ourselves. *Deficient* systems might need to absorb energy from the ground and into the body, while *excessive* systems might need to discharge some of their energy into the ground.

Grounding is a practice, also referred to as *earthing*, that connects us to the energy of the earth. When we're connected to the earth, our energy just flows better. There was a time when we slept directly on the earth, gardened in her soil, drank of her rivers, and lived in balance with her nature. Now we wear rubber on the bottoms of our feet, build houses on top of concrete foundations, and drive in cars with rubber wheels. We spend very little time connected to the earth and we're more disconnected from her than ever before. The state of the world and our health are an obvious reflection of that disconnection. I highly suggest making it a daily effort to get your bare feet onto the bare earth and reinforce your connection to nature. If you can't get your feet on the earth for whatever reason, purchase a grounding mat. I prefer to sleep on one, and so does my daughter. Grounding our energy is vital to our Root System, especially given how disconnected we are from the natural world.

To sum up the root of our humanity: eat of the earth, drink of the earth, connect to a tribe, move your body, and reawaken your essential nature. It's really that simple—it's just not always that easy.

Questions for Reflection

I've included some extra questions here to help assess the health and function of your Root System, which I will be adding to the end of each subsequent system. I encourage you to select a journal and dedicate some time to answering each of these questions. This will help you tremendously as you begin to analyze the current state of your energy and clear out any debris that may be stuck in your system.

Tribal wounding occurs at the level of the body so look back into your childhood and see how your physical body and your right to exist and take up space within the tribe was supported.

- How connected do you feel to your physical body and what are its characteristics?
- Are you grounded in your body or do you prefer to live in your mind?

- Do you feel solid, safe, and secure in your life now?
- Did you feel safe enough growing up?
- Were your basic needs met when you were a child?
- Was your presence within the tribe honored?
- How did your early childhood experience shape you into being?
- How is your relationship to money and the material world?
- How well do you care for your physical self?
- What is your diet like?
- Are you adequately hydrated?
- How often do you move your physical body?
- What is the current state of your health?
- What belief systems did you inherit from your tribe and do they strengthen or limit you today?

There's a great chance that if we're loving people now, it's because we've been shown love. If we're kind, it's because we've been shown kindness. If we're forgiving, it's because we've been forgiven. If we're cruel, it's because we've been shown cruelty. And if we've evolved beyond any of our tribal inheritance, it's because we've willingly chosen the path of growth.

The real question to ask yourself is this:

- Are you currently being defined by a vision of your future or a version of yourself that was shaped by the past?

Take a close look at the groups you find yourself in, be they your family, your friend circle, your church, your support groups:

- Are they conscious of their own belief systems?
- Do they accept you as you are?
- Do they encourage you to be and discover your most authentic self, whatever that might look like?

- What role did you play within your family, and are you still playing it within the tribes you currently find yourself in today?
- Do your tribal groups inspire you to grow, while simultaneously honoring exactly where you are?
- Do they challenge you to be more like them in order to maintain group coherence?

Remember, we're all in an oscillation process, bouncing between two states of conscious-awareness and unconscious-reactivity.

While you come into consciousness around your body, really start to analyze your tribal programs and begin to purify your unconscious tribal mindset, you may notice qualities of both consciousness and unconsciousness within and around you. This is a wonderful thing, as our growing awareness of our own unconsciousness is exactly what's creating a massive awakening to higher levels of self-realization.

There's more power than we could ever realize in our human collective and when we claim our space physically and dissolve the mental barriers that have separated us from one another energetically, we will witness the emergence of an entirely new earth. This is happening on our planet *RIGHT NOW*, and thanks to the internet, we're more connected than ever, which makes this shift in consciousness a greater possibility than ever before!

THE SECOND CHAKRA—
THE SENSATE SYSTEM

"It takes practice to hear your true desires.
Your passion will often come as a whisper or
serendipitous event that reminds you of what's
important and what makes you happy."
—Eckhart Tolle

When we were born we came into the world perfectly whole, totally and completely ourselves. In our completeness, we came equipped with every faculty and function necessary to express our uniqueness in the world. Our passions and deepest desires came already pre-programmed into the nature of our character. Just as our bodies came stocked with innate wisdom, like the intelligence that keeps all our body's physical processes functioning, this intelligence also gave us an internal system of navigation. We've each been given an emotional blueprint, or code, to help us skillfully maneuver through life. This code affords us the wisdom and ability to *feel* into the richness of our life, to lean into what's pleasant and away from what's painful. It helps us identify the process happening within ourselves and align it with what's happening in our environment. This is also the part of our human-system that urges us to drink in slowly the sweet nectar of life and to experience it completely; to thoughtfully taste the exquisite nature of our food, to embrace the subtle beauty found in the richness of color and texture that exists all around us. This system is what compels our bodies to dance and move to the rhythm of music. An inner intelligence pulls us gravitationally, as if by an invisible magnetic force, towards a life of pleasure and yet simultaneous repels us from anything our system might perceive as offensive. Our *Sensate System* exists to help us *feel* deeply, so we can understand when we are in alignment with our most authentic passions and values, and it's also there to alert us when we're out of sync with our true nature.

Our Sensate System is just coming online between the ages of 6-18 months and is characterized by many psychologists as the *oral* stage of our development. Our primary focus at this stage of life is *taking energy in* through the form of nourishment, and perhaps more importantly, nurturance. We're still heavily reliant upon our caretakers at this stage, as they're completely responsibly for meeting our every need, and at 6 months old, neediness is basically our essential state. Although our awareness is growing, we still can't quite feed ourselves or mobilize ourselves physically; we don't yet understand the workings of the body and have little control over them. Most of our exploration at this time is still done via rooting and sucking; an infant at this stage of development experiences the world through the sense-organ of the mouth, thus, the given name, *oral*.

Right around this time is when we start to realize that we are in fact, separate from our mother. Prior to the oral stage, we're pretty much fused to our primary caregiver. There's essentially no energetic border, boundary, or separation between us and them. We haven't yet become aware of ourselves as an individual and experience a sense of unity, not only with our mother, but with our environment as well. What this means is, prior to 6 months old, there's really no distinct difference between the experience of our inner world and outer environment; everything both inside and outside of us is perceived *as us*. If mom is upset, *we're* upset. If the house around us is noisy or chaotic, we're experiencing the chaos as if, it too, *is us*. We don't yet have a way of energetically defending ourselves from the onslaught of external stimuli and that can be scary for an infant, which makes having attentive caregivers a cornerstone in our development. At that stage, our body is just developing the very basics of human functioning: eating, digesting, eliminating, sitting upright, and beginning to crawl, and all of this is done instinctively, not in accordance with our own desire or directive. But the oral stage of our development changes that; here is where our unconscious instinct begins to shift, ever-so-slightly.

The second chakra stage of development landmarks a major turning-point in our human development. Right around 6 months of age is when we begin to sit up straight, start to gain a slight amount of mobility and just a bit more motor skill. Shortly thereafter, we're granted the experience of solid foods. Some of them, like fruits, are wonderful, sweet, and delicious, while others, like broccoli, are perhaps not so good. The polarity and duality of life now becomes obvious, as some things feel good to us while others feel bad. There's also a budding concept of self, a growing distinction between *me* and *them*. Sometimes mom is warm and comforting, other times she may be upset and withholding. The formerly fused attachment to our primary caregiver begins to diminish as the desire to explore our surroundings intensifies. Life at this stage becomes full of contrast and richness offered to us by new experience. Certain colors come into focus, as do our own hands; we can now reach out and pick something up. Our hands become an extension of our minds and we direct them to grasp and clutch the objects of our desire. We experience various textures and sounds, and of course, put everything into our mouths. This is usually the time when our caretakers provide us with lots of colorful, textured toys that make sounds as a way to help us develop our growing sensitivity. Life's new and added dimension is a *sensational* one. Along with the emerging desire to experience life as it exists apart from and outside of us, a new and added dimension is burgeoning inside of us as well. We're having *feelings!*

Surprisingly, we'll find early on that not every feeling is as welcome as others. And sadly, because of this, our sensual and emotional intelligence system isn't always able to develop fully or appropriately. Prior the personal growth revolution we see taking place today, a full capacity for emotional intelligence wasn't entirely recognized as a necessity, therefore, not enough people got the emotional understanding they needed—especially during formative years when the newly developing emotional system needed to be nurtured the most. Our emotions exist to help us connect our inner world with our outer experience. They help us make sense of who we are, how we feel, and what we need. Severance from this system in early childhood is why so many adults are left confused as to what they really want out of life. Without being able to feel themselves, they can't truly know themselves, therefore they can't come to know their own inborne desires.

In truth, our emotions are our greatest allies, but many of us learned early on that our survival or sense of belonging to our tribe often depended on withholding, denying, or suppressing our feelings. Preceding this stage of development, we experienced the fixed and firm foundation of the root and that one-dimensional state of awareness was really all we knew. We were simply an awareness, although we were completely unconscious as to what we were *aware of.* But with the growing development of the second chakra, earth begins to give way to water, what was once fixed now becomes fluid and with that comes separation, movement, and a natural desire to express ourselves as individuals. We haven't yet developed the faculty for expressing our minds, and thus begin first by expressing our emotions. The emotional environment of our home and family has a tremendous impact on how well we're able to develop our own emotionally intelligent, Sensate Systems.

When we were young, before we'd become domesticated by our tribe, our feelings were genuine and authentic. They would arise and be expressed in the exact moment that they arose. We didn't know how to avoid our feelings or stuff them back down, only to save them for a later, less opportune moment. We only knew that something within us was either painful or pleasant and that it was our job to express whatever that feeling was. As children, we lived in a state of non-resistance to life. Life was a series of moments that quickly passed into the next. If something was joyful, our little bodies would perk up, our cheeks would turn a rosy shade of pink, and giggles and smiles would escape from our lips. If something was upsetting to us, we expressed that also; our bodies became tense, our breathing shallowed, tears would flow, and major emotional melt-downs were likely to follow. There was no judgement on our part in regards to whether these expressions were bad or shameful. They were just feelings, ones that we were being called on to express. This is the way that feelings are designed to move through us and back out of us. When we express what we feel in the moment we feel it, we allow ourselves the full experience of really *feeling* our feelings. If the space is created within us and around us for a feeling to be felt, our bodies don't need to armor themselves against it, they can just feel the feeling and then release any tension that might come along with the feeling. This allows the energy that emotion brings with it to flow freely through us. Remember, emotion is simply energy in motion, and in order to free ourselves from emotions that get stuck, we need to learn to let them move. The freedom to allow emotional expression is why young children are usually quick to forgive and forget; they're not really concerned with hanging on to what's already happened because they're far too busy finding the joy in what's happening *now*. Children are still deeply connected to the bliss of the present moment. But if in childhood, which is sadly the case for many, there was trauma to this energy system and feelings weren't allow to pass through us unrestricted, or worse, we were punished for having them, we learn to defend ourselves against them. That's when we start to see our emotions, our natural, internal messengers, as unwanted visitors that need to be avoided.

For the majority of us, our feelings just weren't honored or nurtured the way we needed them to be or when we needed it most. Our emotions didn't fit into the predictably rigid, controlled, and structured environment that humans have created. Emotions are messy, noisy, explosive, intuitive, vulnerable, unpredictable, and incontrollable. Emotions are the antithesis to everything we've been conditioned to believe we need to be. The healthy and necessary expression of emotion is rarely taught to us by our caregivers at age-appropriate times, if at all. In fact, it's most likely we'll have to learn it for ourselves. But our innate emotional intelligence isn't something we can deny—it's an imperative part of our humanity. It must be nurtured, supported, mirrored, and encouraged, especially during our toddler years, which is when we often receive exactly the opposite. So many of us were taught *not* to cry when we were upset and were actually threatened for doing so. How many people recall hearing the phrase, "I'll give you something to cry about!" If we were excited about something and got too charged up, we were told to chill out and calm down, so we learn to hold back from expressing ourselves when we're joyful. Anger can also be a huge no-no of an emotion. Should we dare to get upset and explode in a fit of rage or wave a tiny fist of fury at our parents, we're likely to be met with a far scarier form of aggression. We're taught to behave, to be *good* little boys and girls. This means we're supposed to *act* the way our parents want us to, rather than the way we *actually* feel. We're taught to follow the powers outside of us and disregard the directives of our internal system of sensate guidance. This creates a major severance between ourselves and our inner world of thoughts and feelings. The denial of our emotions causes us to shut down and mistrust the most sensitive, intuitive, and intelligent parts of ourselves.

When we're young and developing, we need to be held and loved, nourished, and nurtured, and we need to be able to express our emotions. This is fundamental for the growth and development of a healthy human being. When a child isn't allowed to healthfully express the diverse range of his emotions, he will start to mistrust himself, and this mistrust of his essential nature will cause his spirit to splinter from his body. This is the beginning stages of where the fine lines between mind and body, thought, emotion, and action begin to blur. When we were little we learned that certain emotions warranted praise and recognition, while others brought about punishment and rejection. This pain/pleasure dichotomy, epitomizes the characteristics of the second chakra.

Again, I don't bring this up so you can point fingers at your parents and blame them for why you're so screwed up. No one escapes the original program. The suppression of emotion is a *cultural* condition and that means it can only be healed through a cultural conscious awakening to it. Our parents inherited ancestral suppression of emotion from their parents, who in turn had inherited it from their parents, so none of them were capable of holding space for us to fully express our own. The only tool our parents had was to encourage us to curb our displays of emotion so we could fit into a box that they could easier handle. If you have children, I'm sure you probably did the same. The wild, uninhibited, totally intact Sensate System of a child is enough to begin shaking loose some of our own energetic blocks to emotion. If we're not ready to address those emotions in ourselves, or we don't have the tools to do so, we simply can't allow our children to express them. The growing need for our own reintegration becomes all too real. If emotions are too loud or too excited and we've been conditioned into constraint, we will reject them. If feelings are too melancholy, too depressive, or too emotional, we'll shut them down in ourselves or reject another for having them. When our emotions are too something for someone else, they've become a trigger for the unconsciousness within that person, and usually that's when we get shamed for expressing them. What this means for most of us is that we're only comfortable expressing *certain* emotions, usually the emotions that were approved of in our own immediate families. For some, acceptable emotions are anger, aggression, and rage. In other families those emotions are completely denied. Certain families are totally okay with loving displays of physical affection, while this might send other families into an incredibly awkward and anxious state of avoidance. Showing sensitivity to some is strength, while to others it's a sign of weakness and unnecessary vulnerability. Our family conditioning around emotion is a sure indicator of what we've allowed ourselves to express and experience. For some, this conditioning means not trusting or showing our own feelings at all, but only reflecting those approved of by of the family. The cultural suppression of emotional intelligence isn't anyone's *fault*, but it's certainly our *responsibly* to heal from it. We must be willing to look at, understand, and reclaim our rejected emotions—only then will we reclaim the full expression of our humanity.

Masculine and Feminine Energy

This brings us to yet another division that needs to be unified in order for us to fully awaken our full potential, the unification of masculine and feminine energy. The expression of genuine emotion is particularly difficult for men in our culture because we so often teach them as children that *boys don't cry*, because crying is equated with weakness. But crying is an intrinsic part of our feminine energy; it's directly related to acknowledging and releasing our inner hurts, pains, feelings, and emotions. Because men have been conditioned to deny their natural emotional instinct, many have become hardened and insensitive, splintered from the very core of who they really are. While it's generally more accepted for women to be more nurturing and deep feeling than it is for men, there are still countless women who have denied their own emotional intelligence systems, along with their feminine energy. Women have been consistently ridiculed for being too emotional, too weak, too sensitive, or God-forbid, *hysterical*.

No matter what we do or how we act, we're always going to be *too* much something, for someone and encouraged to change ourselves in order to make others more comfortable. But what we need right now can't be denial or suppression of *any* aspect of ourselves, neither our masculine nor our feminine energies. We need both, and we need them to be in balance. Once we're able to integrate both sides of our nature, our logic and our emotion, our intuition and our ability to reason, then and only then, will we come fully alive.

Interestingly enough, what we're seeing now with a genuine display of this level of integration and awakened authenticity, especially when it comes to emotional expression, is that it starts to shine a light on the many unhealed aspects of others. Instead of doing the work to embrace and reclaim them, many tend to drive them further into the unconscious, mostly because we just aren't aware of our own triggers. The goal of this work is to create an atmosphere where people can begin to understand themselves and their awakening journey and become willing and active participants in their own growth process.

The balancing of polarities, of masculine and feminine energy, don't exactly have much to do with our gender, rather what our genders represent. And although achieving balance between men and women isn't exactly the intended goal, balancing the polarities inside of us will inherently balance them outside of us as well. Masculine energy is linear; its strong, direct, disciplined, and focused. Whereas feminine energy is far less rigid; it's watery, fluid, emotional, and intuitive. The masculine likes to learn and know things logically, whereas the feminine is okay with just naturally understanding they know something, even if that means not exactly knowing *how* they know.

In today's modern world, especially the corporate world, we tend to value masculine qualities like logic and reason over our more feminine qualities like intuition and emotion. Women have fought incredibly hard to work alongside men in the workplace, and in doing, so many of them have allowed their masculine energy to override their intuitive feminine nature. This soul fracture has contributed to major imbalance, not just between the physical genders of male and female, but between their energetic counterparts as well. The need for integrating both masculine and feminine energy within the individual and the collective is a vital aspect to creating harmony and balance in our world.

Historically, women needed men for their strength and protection and men needed women for their intuition and nurturance (if men acknowledged the need for women at all). Over the past few decades, however, our world has seen tremendous growth in terms of gender equality. Women are now able to do things never before allowed. We no longer live in an age where men are masculine and women are feminine, where men are thinkers and women are feelers. We are now living in an age where gender has very little to do with our being masculine or feminine. Some men are more feminine than women, and vice versa. Same-sex attraction, bisexuality, and transgender people are now becoming accepted and even celebrated. Women dress in men's clothing and the opposite is also true. Men can now be better at doing hair and makeup than women; women can be carpenters, plumbers, architects, and even have a chair in the boardroom. Men can stay home and take care of the kids while women work to provide for their families. Thankfully, the stigmas and stereotypes of the past are being filtered out of our collective consciousness as people are allowing themselves to feel and express who they really are. The younger generations are rallying to support the emerging changes. Things in our world have been slowly balancing themselves, preparing us for the epic recalibration of what's to come.

Despite our growing equality, our culture has suffered greatly from the past, not only due to the imbalance of power between the sexes, but primarily because of the severance from our emotional centers. We see the results of this suppression in the large numbers of people reliant on antidepressant drugs, excessive alcohol use, self-medicating, over-eating, addiction to narcotics, and a whole host of other physical manifestations that occur when we deny any integral part of who we are. To deny our emotions is to deny a very vital aspect of our human nature. Human beings aren't naturally cruel; we're creatures of empathy, creativity, kindness, and compassion. But without a connection to these fundamental characteristics, what manifests is a world very much like the one we see today, a competitive world where most people struggle for the benefit of a few; a world dominated by a *power-over-others* paradigm ruled by fear, selfishness, and greed; a warring world where we take more than we need and throw away the rest. The world we live in today is dominated by masculine forces and the only way to heal it is for the divine feminine within each of us to rise up and restore ourselves to harmony.

Just as we observed with the breaking of tribal consciousness, we're finally breaking away from the duality consciousness found lurking within the shadow of our Sensate System. It's worth mentioning again that if we're going to restore harmony and balance to our planet, we need to begin by first restoring harmony and balance within ourselves. When we do, our inner balance will inevitably influence the balance of the collective. That means we must learn to harmonize both our masculine (yang) qualities of action, logic, and reason with our feminine (yin) qualities of empathy, emotion, and intuition. That means honoring *all* of our feelings, not just embracing the comfortable ones, but doing the difficult work of reclaiming the rejected ones as well and then being brave enough, and vulnerable enough to express them.

A Brief Lesson in Shadow Work

"The world is a teacher to the wise-man and an enemy to the fool."
—Chinese Proverb

Although it may be full of contrast, and perhaps even store some of our more painful childhood memories, the second chakra is also home to some of humanities most playful and connective features. An open, active, and balanced second chakra is exciting, sensual, and a totally good time! It's where all the juice is at, both literally and figuratively. The second chakra is a place within the human energy field where we learn to construct borders between ourselves and others, and it's also where we can allow those borders to dissolve and truly merge ourselves with another physically, spiritually, and emotionally. It's perhaps the most intimate, exciting, and vulnerable part of us. But difficult to handle emotions aren't the only aspect of the second chakra that we've rejected, and now need to reclaim. In the midst of our tribal and social conditioning, humanity has created an ostensibly separate aspect of its own psyche, what pioneer of modern-psychology, Carl Jung, coined the *collective unconscious.* Others have simply called it *the shadow*, and its home is the second chakra.

The shadow is basically a storehouse for all of humanity's rejected parts. It's like a big, unconscious closet where we stuff away all the parts of ourselves we don't like or don't readily admit we have. As children, we learn the notions of *good* and *bad.* We tend to be punished for being *bad* and rewarded when we're *good.* And so, we learn to praise the parts of ourselves that are deemed acceptable and reject those that are labeled unacceptable by those around us. Through this process, we create our shadow-self. Like the *collective* shadow of our culture, each of us also has a private shadow side, a deeply unconscious place that serves as a repository for all our rejected aspects. We can't just cut away these less-than-desirable parts of ourselves, or kill them off, but still, we find their presence too painful or unpleasant to accept, so we banish them to the shadow where we no longer need to acknowledge them. Casting aspects of ourselves away doesn't mean they cease to exist, it just means we're no longer aware of their presence. But that doesn't stop them from finding their way back into our lives, they're still powerful, and still apart of us, only now, the shadow-self acts without awareness, thus the term *unconscious.*

The only antidote for human-unconsciousness is *awakening* and only by awakening to our shadow can we accomplish the task of healing the senses and finally achieve a state of unified-polarity: a balance between light and dark, masculine and feminine, self and other, inner and outer reality—which is the primary goal of the Sensate System. But if we are to achieve this balance, we must learn to shine the light of awareness onto ourselves and be willing to expose our own darkness. We can no longer pretend it simply doesn't exist. We must become willing to see self *as* other, inner *as* outer; neither can exist as separate from the next, as each is an intimate reflection of the other. This is the evolutionary call of our time, which is basically bellowing for a mass awakening to the collective unconscious. The spirit of humanity wants to awaken to its shadow, it wants to integrate its fragmented parts so it can become whole and we can move forward in our evolution. But that can't take place if we aren't aware of what's happening. The soul's desire for healing, for seeking to reclaim its wholeness, is why there's such a growing interest in personal-growth. It's why more and more are taking refuge in spiritual interests and it's also why we're being drawn to books like this. But real spiritual work isn't always easy and shadow work can be messy, sometimes even terrifying, but it must be done—and I believe that we're strong enough to do it.

When Jung says "until you make the unconscious conscious, it will direct your life and you will call it fate" he was talking about the shadow. The shadow will never go away just because we pretend we don't have one. It will take on many different forms, appearing in almost all our intimate relationships. The shadow sneakily shows us the neglected parts of ourselves by proudly displaying them in the behavior of others. For example, if sexuality is rejected and banished to the shadow, we'll find ourselves critically judgmental of those who indulge in it. Or maybe our sensitive side is the part of us that we disowned, so somehow, we attract every emotionally needy person in the neighborhood. And it's not only negative qualities that get exiled either; we splinter from our powerful parts too. Perhaps you're a talented songwriter, but that wasn't allowed in your family, so into the shadow you tossed the potential and now you're highly critical of those who put their lyrical work out into the world. You might not always condemn your rejected parts either! You might actually love them, just not as they appear in yourself. Remember, the shadow is an aspect of *yourself* you rejected, not necessarily the *quality* that you shunned. You might really want to be a painter, but you rejected your inner artist a long time ago, and instead of reintegrating this part of you, you continually visit art shows, purchase art, and show praise for your favorite artist without ever picking up a paint brush. The term for this is *shadow hugging*. Good news and bad news though—our shadows want to be integrated—that's why they keep showing up all around us.

It's said that the greatest mysteries in life are air to birds, water to fish, and man unto himself. Birds don't know they're soaring through the air when they're flying, in the same way that fish don't realize they're surrounded by water when they swim. Man, by his very nature, is blind unto himself. The great mystery is that he simply cannot see himself unless he's looking at a mirror, so it isn't until he's developed eyes that can see into the looking glass of life that he'll be able to recognize his true reflection. The only way man can really see himself and learn to integrate his shadow is through conscious relationship with others. He can't heal on his own because he can't see his shadow without a mirror. This is exactly why he needs what author and spiritual teacher, Caroline Myss, calls *noble friends* for reflection. These people serve to help him to acknowledge and reclaim the rejected parts of himself—although these relationships aren't always the most pleasant.

Our spouses, children, bosses, coworkers, siblings, friends, and family, will show up for us as our *noble friends* and our greatest teachers. These relationships tend to mirror back to us all the places within us that are yet to be healed. When we enter into these relationships with consciousness and are willing to use them as reflections to look deeply into our own selves, they provide us with the opportunity to witness our most wonderful gifts, along with our most unfortunate shortcomings. Learning to embrace shadow work will help to develop our spiritual sight as well. When we develop this sight, all of life becomes a sacred mirror. When we're ready to see ourselves clearly, we'll begin to observe aspects of ourselves within all people and all things, both what we admire and what we reject. This is the epitome of shadow work.

It's only natural that we align with what we consider to be favorable traits in others because they also exist in us. Unfortunately, the same can be said for negative traits, only we tend to deny these qualities because we've judged them as bad or inadequate. This doesn't mean that we currently *are* what we judge, or even that we currently *are* what we admire; it just means that the *potential* for these traits exist within us or we wouldn't be able to recognize them in others. Most of the time what we judge harshly or reject in another is really a disowned aspect of ourselves, a denied part of us that was tucked away in the shadow and is now yearning to be embraced and reintegrated.

The key to understanding which of these traits are calling to be recognized within you is to be aware of exactly which characteristics you're triggered by. Being triggered by another is an indication that your shadow's been activated—the stronger the reaction, the bigger the shadow. Qualities in others that generate a strong reaction within us are often *our* most powerful qualities. Personality traits that I admire about someone might be the same attributes that you dislike. Neither observation has much to do with the person, but rather how we individually perceive ourselves as reflected through them. When we honor the greatness in another, it's truly an expression of our own greatness. Passing judgement on another is a condemnation of ourselves. When we can look with honesty at the relationships in our lives and clearly observe our own reflection, life becomes our greatest teacher and our relationships our greatest allies. It's not always easy to shine a light on our own shadows, but when we do, we heal the polarity of the second chakra and we welcome ourselves back to wholeness.

Pleasure is our Birthright

"Sexual pleasure, wisely used, and not abused
may prove the stimulus and liberator of our finest
and most exalted activities."
—Havelock Ellis

There are other essential parts of our humanity stuck in the shadow of our unconsciousness that need to be reclaimed if we are to return ourselves to wholeness. But some of these parts carry with them the heavy burdens of the past, and we must be brave enough to heal from the battle wounds and scars that humans have endured throughout history and at the hand of our own unconsciousness. We can no longer look away as the shadow-features of humanity begin to rise into our awareness, which they inevitably will. We definitely can't pretend that some of these things didn't happen or don't exist—like cultural oppression and racial injustice, for example. We must be willing to allow these ancestral pains and hurts to resurface, embracing them in the same way we would embrace a child whose had a traumatic experience. As spiritually and emotionally mature adults, we're responsible for creating a safe space for healing to happen. We must deny the temptation to stuff these pains back into the shadow and out of our awareness. Some of these traumas are extremely difficult to look at—but we must not look away.

Healing in the Sensate System happens when we learn to reintegrate our splintered parts and reclaim our right to wholeness. And a fundamental right to human-wholeness includes our right to experience pleasure—a right that has been most *highly* rejected. As long as we find ourselves tethered to a body, we can't sever ourselves from its nature or its needs. We can only do our best to accept ourselves fully and pleasure is a basic human need, one we simply can't deny any longer. The task of integrating pleasure into our lives has proven most challenging for humans. In an embarrassing display of egoic vanity, we've completely dishonored and downright abused our bodies; we've trained our muscles into submission, sculpted our features to perfection, and suppressed our emotions to a level that could be classified as a global mental illness—all in the name of being *desirable* and wanting to experience pleasure. Desire and pleasure go hand in hand and the majority of us are totally screwed up around what it even means to want pleasure. The unconscious suppression of a most basic instinct, like desiring pleasure, has created such a radical imbalance within the psyche of humanity that a horde of subcultures have been created just to placate the many facets of these rejected, and confused parts of selves. We don't fully understand our desire to feel good, so shadow businesses, like the adult film industry, absolutely *thrive* upon the exploitation of our most sacred selves. All of this is due to the lack of understanding surrounding our own biological instincts and our most basic rights.

It's essential that we start to remember that pleasure is our birthright; it isn't a luxury, nor is it sinful or shameful—its absolutely vital and necessary. It's not our longing for pleasure, but what we choose to do with our desire that determines its moral. Our lives are meant to be pleasurable. We were created to enjoy life, not just to endure it, or even worse, suffer through it. Our bodies were designed for experiencing that which is pleasing to our senses. Do you really believe that we were created with all these sensual pleasure centers if we weren't meant to experience them? The pursuit of pleasure plays an essential role in what motivates the majority of our human-behavior. But because of pleasure's primal origins, along with our lack of understanding, collective suppression *and* exploitation of it, it's also become the cause for tremendous wounding to our culture and to our species.

If we're to ever understand ourselves completely and reclaim our human-wholeness as beings of both flesh and spirit, we first have to start by understanding what motivates our earthly desires. To put it simply, our body and its desires are motivated by our senses. Can you remember the last time you heard your favorite song play through the speakers? I bet you knew all the words by heart and sang along as you bobbed your head to the melody, feeling it move through your body as you danced to the beat. I bet all your stress melted away, even if it was only for a second. Pleasurable experiences like listening to our favorite tunes are designed to usher us into the beauty and bliss of the only thing that's real—the present moment. The same is true for any pleasurable experience that calls us deeply into moments of *being*. Unfortunately, some sensual experiences aren't as simple as listening to our favorite music. Some experiences engage aspects of our shadow that cause us to go unconscious in ways that we don't yet completely understand.

Take eating a slice of chocolate cake, for example. Each bite invites explosions of flavor; the rich decadency of combined ingredients like sugar, butter, and chocolate unleashes a sensual experience in our mouths and unlocks all of the feel-good chemicals in our brains. If we allow it, by surrendering ourselves to a piece of chocolate cake, we can find ourselves totally immersed in the experience of pleasure. But how many times after we've eaten the cake are we left feeling guilty for having had it, and how many are still left wanting afterward? For many of us, we cannot simply eat the chocolate cake and savor the moment because we don't know how to be present with our experience. We don't know how to be present with our pleasure. Most of the time we're either feeling guilty halfway through our dessert or we're already thinking about the next time we'll eat cake again. Some of us are better at receiving pleasure than others, but most of us are still pretty twisted up around it. Because of our conditioning around our right to have pleasure, we're no longer able to utilize the experience of pleasure to bring us into the moment. Often, when we're faced with a pleasurable opportunity, like a delicious meal or a sexual encounter, we're not even totally connected to the sense organs of our bodies, we're stuck in our heads with heaps of our past conditioning. Next time you eat a piece of cake or eat a good meal, ask yourself, are you really *there* with your food or is your body just going through the motions of eating it?

Aside from chocolate cake, nothing motivates the lower self more enthusiastically than sex. That's right, I said it—*sex*. We all think about it, most of us engage in it, but not everybody talks about it. If there was ever a topic more loaded than politics or religion, it's definitely sex. No one in the world escapes scratch-free from the awkward programming around the hot topic of sex. As soon as we're old enough to feel the sensate world on our skin, we begin to explore what pleasure means to our bodies. There was a time when we felt *everything* and there's a good chance feeling *yourself* was a part of that everything. When children begin to explore their own bodies, the adults around them usually have a reaction to it and their first response is generally shock! I guess I was fortunate to have a Mom who didn't humiliate me or send me for an exorcism when I enjoyed the friction of my lady parts against a firm surface, except for the time she pinched me in the grocery store for rubbing myself against the metal divider separating my legs in the shopping cart—but that I can understand. Most times though, she just sent me to my room and left me alone to familiarize myself with . . . myself. Thanks to Mom's equitable approach towards masturbation, I wasn't traumatized by my first sexual explorations. In fact, this freedom allowed me the right to my own pleasure, within the appropriate context for a child, of course. Because of that I was able to understand and create a healthy link between myself and my body's right to feel good. Not enough of us got that and some of us got far worse. The sexual sense organs and our human desire for pleasure, touch, and intimacy often create a recipe primed for disaster. Especially in children, and even adults who don't quite understand their bodies, or the bodies biological urge to experience pleasure. More wounding has occurred in the second chakra than perhaps any other. And so, it is with this center that we must be the most gentle, delicate, and understanding.

In this society, parents are usually very uncomfortable and don't know how to respond to a child's self-exploration because their own right to pleasure was never talked about. Since it's not something we're taught to honor, we're usually shamed for it instead. And so, we absorb the message that sex is naughty, that our bodies are dirty, and that it's shameful or bad to experience pleasure. Thus, we try to hide our desire for it, and in doing so, we create a massive shadow. The majorly rejected, sexual shadow, still active but now totally unconscious, acts out in ways that can be highly damaging, especially to someone who hasn't learned how to construct a healthy boundary around their own sexuality or right to experience pleasure. An agonizing and heartbreaking truth is that children are often the victims to the sexual-shadow of others. When a child, or even an adult, becomes a victim to the second-chakra shadow of another, which happens far more often than any reasonable person cares to admit, they develop very conflicted feelings around their body and their natural desire for the body to feel good. Once a person's physical boundaries have been violated, humans will often have a very difficult time establishing these boundaries later on. They will either become totally rigid, as a means of self-protection, or completely dissolved, without any boundaries whatsoever. A painful divorce between mind and body becomes so polarized within them that they're often paralyzed by it, and sometimes this causes them to dissociate from the body altogether. After a second chakra trauma, it's hard to allow in the experience of pleasure, as pleasure is now intimately interwoven with pain. If they do allow it they're usually met with feelings of guilt and shame for doing so; but if they deny themselves the experience, they're left empty and wanting. They will often develop secondary pleasures like addictions to cope with their pain and compensate for the loss of their sensual nature. Sometimes, they become excessive in the very same way that originally wounded them. It's a very difficult and painful process to heal from a sexually related trauma, but it's not impossible to do so with the help of a qualified professional.

The misunderstanding and misuse of sex and the biological and instinctual desire for it has caused such a great divide among humans, so great, that I sometimes question our ability to reconcile it. The result of this divide is the massive and collective traumas of rape, pornography, prostitution, incest, pedophilia, and many other horrific acts of sexual perversion. Men will clearly carry much of the blame when it comes to inflicted sexual traumas, but this too can be broken down to an unfortunate misunderstanding of our basic needs as humans. I don't care what religion says, humans *need* sex. Not just for the pleasure of it, but for the discharge of energetic tension that orgasm provides. I want you to take a good look at the Catholic church for an idea of what happens when people try to deny their sexual natures and you'll get a clear glimpse of humanity's largest and darkest shadow. Rather than unifying opposites in genuine pleasure, sex has created a great wedge between people. What was created for us as a gift to experience the natural pleasures of being in a body has instead become a primary source of wounding to the people on this planet.

Sex was never meant to be demonized; it was intended to be like the chocolate cake. Other than for procreation, sex is really about the experience of pleasure, unifying opposites, and drawing our consciousness into the present moment. Sexual, or *sensate,* energy is creative energy and it makes creation of all forms possible. Everything we create in this world will move through our second chakra. Our passions, our desires, our hobbies, and interests, are all acts of creation; each one brings with it the experience of pleasure into our lives. Done right, sex, or any other creative act can be a most liberating experience. We can lose all track of time, self, and space. Our ego-identity completely dissolves as we find the ultimate union with another human being, or piece of art, and sometimes with divinity itself.

But for many of us, instead of experiencing the journey through pleasure, like appreciating each bite of a delicious chocolate cake, our minds can easily become focused on the conditioned guilt. Sometimes we feel guilty because simple pleasures and creative endeavors aren't as valued as *hard work*, but most often our guilt around pleasure has been associated with sexual desire. There was once a time in history when sensuality and sexuality were rightfully celebrated and even worshipped. There are entire religions completely devoted to the art of sacred lovemaking. This was a time when humans understood the power of sex, understood the alchemical processes that take place between the combined forces of the divine feminine and the divine masculine. We honored how they come together to create pleasure and to create life. We knew how this sacred act could anchor us to the present moment, connect us to the heavenly, provide us with glimpses of Divinity, and thereby create more harmony, order, and balance in our world. However, it now seems as though pleasure walks hand in hand with her greatest adversaries—guilt and shame—through a darkened alleyway, shrouded in layers of misunderstanding and pain. Because of our collective wounds in regards to sex and intimacy in general, man and woman have learned to fear each other instead of honoring one another. This is something that needs to change if we're going to learn to work together to save our planet. Men may need to heal the relationship they have to the feminine, which often stems from mother, and women may need to heal the relationship they have to the masculine, which is often influenced by father. (We'll address more of this in the fourth chakra, the Compassionate System.) Our human traumas run deep and are deepest within the Sensate System. Healing this area can be quite messy, but entirely possible. I highly encourage you to enlist the help of a qualified therapist before you go stirring up the skeletons you might find hanging in your ancestral sensate closet—especially if you know they're in there.

Character Structure

Emotional Intelligence Specialist
(Poor Me)

| Sweet gentle soft features and muscles, large eyes and have a longing within them, S curve in lower back | Soft unformed body, fat held in lower belly, gentle, loving, sad and sweet, non-threatening |

According to Thomas: The Merging Patter
For more information visit www.4dhealing.com.

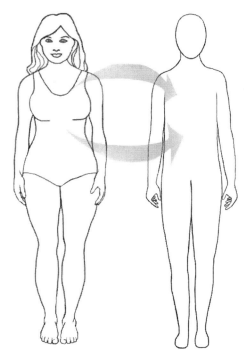

According to Kessler: The Emotional Intelligence Specialist/The Poor Me
Images from The 5 Personality Patterns *by Steven Kessler © 2015. Used with permission.*
For more information visit www.The5PersonalityPatterns.com

The character structure most closely associated with the second chakra is the *Emotional Intelligence Specialist*, or *EIS* for short. The *EIS* describes the highest potential of this character, which is revealed when they're able to release their energetic defense and allow their soul quality to be expressed. We cover both the soul quality, and the defensive-quality of this character in the section on the Sensate System, since this structure has the most difficult time developing a connection to their own feeling centers and establishing boundaries. Kessler has identified its energy pattern as the *Merging* pattern; when threatened, an *EIS* will shift their consciousness energetically away from their core and merge it with another in an attempt to get his or her needs met or in an attempt to meet the needs of another person. Kessler refers to the latter as the *Compensated Merging Pattern.*

When the *Emotional Intelligence Specialist* is under duress or they have a need that isn't being met, they will attempt to hook into others energetically. Their focus becomes fixated on relationships, primarily ones that can satisfy their need for love and affection. They focus on others, because they fear more than anything feeling empty inside and not having enough to nourish themselves, both physically and emotionally. Thomas calls the defensive quality of this character structure the *Poor Me*, because their insatiable appetite for love and affection often leaves them needy and wanting. If those who possess the soul-quality of the *EIS* live within the confines of its defense, they will chronically be experiencing some sort of emotional issue and the answer to that issue will most often be found in the comforts of another person.

The *Poor Me* defensive pattern is thought to have developed during the *oral* stages of childhood, when the primary developmental task is to *take energy in.* As infants, we absorb the energy from our environment and bring it into our inner selves. We do this via the loving and tender care of our mother, and by receiving physical nourishment in the form of breast milk or formula. At this stage of our development, we thrive off touch, love, and affection. An infant's only desire is to be nourished, and to be nurtured. When those primary needs are met with regularity and consistency, and an infant receives adequate amounts of nourishment and love, the child develops a felt sense that they are seen and supported. And they will then come to believe that the world is capable of meeting their needs. Every infant goes through a regular process of having a need, crying out for that need to be met, receiving nourishment, and then relaxing back into contentment. This process is essentially a cycle that needs to be consistently repeated and accomplished for the child to solidify a link between her inner state and outer experience. When this developmental task remains regularly unaccomplished, however, and the child is unable to satisfy her need, she is left feeling empty and wanting. Left with an overwhelming sense of abandonment, the child isn't able to return to a state of content relaxation, and instead becomes focused on others as an attempt to fulfill her unmet needs. This pattern can be created when the need for physical nourishment isn't met and a child is literally left hungry. Perhaps the mother isn't able to produce enough breast milk or she's busy working a demanding job and simply can't provide it. Although, the *Poor Me* defense occurs most often when a child's desire for love and affection isn't met with the tenderness they desperately need from their mom. If the mother is emotionally unavailable, or worse, mentally unwell, deliberately cold, or withholding, the child is never able fully form a solid connection between their inner self and outer relationships. Adults who favor the *Poor Me* defense, will experience a wide range of deep feelings of neediness and a desperate desire to be nurtured, to both love and be loved. This excessive neediness can become so extreme that it overwhelms and repels the ones they love most, who often can't handle it and leave. This abandonment only re-wounds the inner infant and leaves them yet again with an overwhelming sense of emptiness, which perpetuates a cycle of trauma.

The body of an individual who favors the *Poor Me* defense is usually weak and fragile, or otherwise heavy but unformed, with a curved spine and slumped shoulders. Energetically, they lack definite boundaries and can't really tell where they end and you begin. They often feel as though they could collapse at any moment under the weight of life's pressure. They're easily overwhelmed and often appear to be in an emotional agony or experiencing an emotional upheaval of some sort. Their position in life is that of a victim, rather than a creator. At their core, their deepest desire is to share with others in the experience of genuine love; they're quite literally starving for it.

In their defended state, they tend to magnetize highly critical, emotionally unavailable partners. The highly emotional EIS will mirror all their partners rejected qualities, and vice versa. The unemotional partner won't tolerate the neediness of the *Poor Me* and will often struggle to handle their extreme sensitivity. The *Poor Me* won't be able to understand their partner's rigidity and dismissiveness. As long as both partners remain defended, both will struggle in the relationship.

In order to shift out of their defended position and into the core of their profile the *Poor Me* will need to accomplish the unfulfilled tasks of their infant development. They will need to establish a link between how they feel inside and what they need in relation to that feeling. *Poor Me's* have a strong likeliness of developing co-dependent relationships, and other oral fixations like smoking, food, and alcohol addictions. But once they're able to make sense of their own inner needs and desires and show up for themselves, they'll begin to establish some of their own energetic boundaries, drop some of their addictions, and appear less draining to those around them. When a *Poor Me* is living from their core as opposed to their defense, they are free to serve the planet in the way their soul intended.

When a *Poor Me* shifts into their core, they display the soul-quality that Thomas has identified as the *Emotional Intelligence Specialist*. *Emotional Intelligence Specialist* are born to feel deeply and to pave the wave of genuine feeling for others. This can be a painful path at times, as they have a capacity for emotional depth that's beyond what most can understand. *EIS's* are unusually kind and gentle soul's and planet earth can be a very difficult one for them live on.

The body of an *EIS* is most likely going to be soft and flexible and they'll have deeply compassionate and loving eyes. They'll often find themselves in the field of nursing or social service work—anywhere that deeply caring and compassionate souls are needed. *Emotional Intelligence Specialists* are generally labeled as perceptively meek and timid, yet their souls are most innately powerful because they're actually capable of genuine love. An *EIS* understands the pain of loves absence; therefore, they also know the power of loves presence, and they're capable of delivering the goods.

An *EIS* soul is of the more challenging profiles to have, especially for men who are taught that to be masculine is to be insensitive and unemotional. The world can be a really difficult place for the *Emotional Intelligence Specialist* because they're constantly being told that who they are is not okay and probably never will be. If you're an *Emotional Intelligence Specialist,* you're the most undervalued source of true power on our planet. You'll often find yourself drawn to children, plants, elderly, and animals, as you can really feel them and resonate with their deep, loving connectedness to the essence of *all that is.* Your gift of empathy and deep feelings aren't embraced or celebrated as they should be; in fact, they're often rejected and judged. You cry very easily. You may even be crying now. You'll cry both in sadness and in joy, for yourself and for others. In childhood, you may have been told that you were too sensitive and needed to develop a tougher skin. You may also find that you've become rigid with your emotions as a way to deflect and protect yourself from the enormous capacity of your emotional depth. Instinctively, you know that to deny your feelings is to deny who you are, and although this is incredibly painful to you, it's how you've learned to survive and exist in the world. At some point you'll long to reconnect with your feelings, as they're truly your gift to the world.

Sensate Energetics

Now that we've covered just about everything you need to know relating to your second chakra and the consciousness that governs it, along with the character structure associated with it—lets assess the health and function of your own Sensate System. I encourage you to look to the connection you have to your own body and to use your life as a reflection for how well you manage the energy of your Sensate System.

Remember from the chapter on the human energy system, that energy behaves in a multitude of different ways—it can be *excessive*, running too much energy; *deficient*, not able to generate enough energy; or *blocked*, meaning no energy is able to transmit through the chakra at all. Chakras can have both *excessive and deficient* characteristics, so the energetic state of your chakra may also fall somewhere in between any of those three states, depending on the situation. In an ideal world, however, we want our energy to be *balanced* and able to flow freely throughout our system. If a chakra is out of balance, not holding enough or holding too much energy, we will need to either charge, discharge, or otherwise reorganize the energy of that chakra in order to bring it into balance.

Those who carry an *excessive* amount of energy in the Sensate System might feel consistently antsy, excited, or never fully satisfied. They're constantly craving a charge that energizes and excites them. Excessive-sensual types may have a tendency towards hedonism, as they just love to experience pleasure of all kinds. Food, artwork, or fashion—it doesn't matter—they relish in anything that makes their senses come alive. They're fantastic lovers, taking pleasure in both giving and receiving, embracing all of the senses and all things sensual. They have an insatiable desire, which doesn't always work out in their favor. They live to experience pleasure and just can't get enough of it, but also have a hard time applying limits or self-discipline.

If your second chakra is holding too much charge you might have difficulty with stillness. You might favor high energy activities and probably drink a lot of caffeine. You might even be an adrenaline junkie and seek out things that excite you, even if they're dangerous. You may be overly sexual and find amusement in pushing to feel-out someone else's boundaries in regards to sexual matters. No matter the size or shape of their bodies, their energy will tend to be sensual, sexual, and perhaps even seductive. Some people have second chakras that run so much charge and become so excessive that others may actually find the energy offensive, even predatory, and feel the need to get away.

If you're excessive in your Sensate System, you may have an addiction sex, pornography, masturbation, etc. Many excessively-sensate people have disconnected from their emotions but not their need for pleasure, so they will crave sex, as it allows them to momentarily feel something exhilarating. But as soon as the sex is over, they're only temporarily satisfied, and usually left mentally craving more.

Another manifestation of *excessive* second chakra energy occurs in those who are overly emotional or exceedingly needy. Although their second chakra is technically *excessive*, still they want more. The second chakra is literally thirsty, which gives them the unsavory characteristic of the energy vampire. No matter how much attention you give them, it's never really enough, because they are insatiable in their desire for affection and attention. Those with *excessive* energy in this way find it difficult to establish a sense of boundaries between themselves and others, because they're lacking a true connection to their inner self. The line that distinguishes self and other has been blurred in early development, so their energy is often enmeshed with the energy of other people. This makes them really good at sensing the feelings and needs of others, but not so good at feeling their own.

In order to bring an excessive second chakra into balance, one might assume that discharge of energy is the appropriate course of action. But when it comes to the second chakra, the solution isn't always expression, but rather, containment. An excessive second chakra is *always* finding a way to express itself; the problem with excessively-sensual types isn't really an inability to discharge as much as it's an inability to be present to what's happening inside. A person with an excessive Sensate System needs to sit still long enough to feel what their feelings are telling them, so they can decide what they really want to do with the sensation. If the answer to excessive excitability is always to run from it, numb themselves with food, avoid themselves by staying busy *doing* things, or connecting to the needs of another person, a better solution might be to sit with the sensation for a while, track how it feels in the body, and then make a more conscious decision on what to do with the energy.

A *deficiency* in the energy of the Sensate System is going to look quite different than the above and will be more commonly manifest as a rigid personality and a body that is unyielding to movement or flow. Those who don't run enough charge through their senses don't usually trust their feelings, or simply don't understand them, and so don't really listen. They aren't overwhelmed by them in the way that an excessive person might be, they just don't allow themselves to feel. They're more inclined to trust their logic and reason over their emotions, and prefer to keep their choices limited to a this-or-that context. Variety is *not* the spice of life for *deficient* types. They like to keep their emotions in check, that way they don't ever run the risk of being caught off guard by them. Sex for them might be more of a mechanical process, rather than a pleasurable experience. Or they may not be able to generate enough energy required for sexual for arousal at all. Because they're split off from their senses, and prefer to live life ruled by logic, they're highly critical of themselves, and so allowing themselves to become undefended, as often happens during sexual intimacy, is an undesirable idea. If they do allow themselves to dissolve their rigid boundaries and allow intimacy, either physically, or emotionally they're generally quick to judge themselves for doing so.

In order to bring the Sensate System of the second chakra out of deficiency and into balance, one will need to introduce the flow and movement of the water element. Our goal with deficiency is figuring out what part of us is blocking the filling of energy from happening. In the case of a deficiency, it may be a chronic avoidance of that which makes us feel uncomfortable, which many feelings often do. I can be the type that doesn't like to slow down and often keep myself busy and achieving as a way to avoid the feelings that arise in moments of stillness. One technique I've used to connect to my second chakra is to allow myself to be gently guided by that which I find pleasing and then give myself permission to experience the pleasures that those things bring. Whether it's creating a piece of artwork, reading a good book, or even something as simple as relaxing on the couch, I allow myself to fully embrace the experience. I've also found that if we introduce daily movement to our physical bodies, we'll start to shake loose some of our energetic armoring. Then, if we can establish a safe container that allows our emotions to emerge without rejecting them, we can slowly and safely start to harmonize our senses. Dance, particularly ecstatic dance, but really any kind of moment, is a wonderful way to get the second chakra energy flowing in a deficient system.

The third state of energy, *blocked-energy,* may manifest in the second chakra as complete and total rejection of pleasure or an absolute disassociation from the body and emotions. No energy is flowing, nothing about our life is able to move, we've forgotten how to connect to what brings us joy, and we might even find ourselves in a state of depression and desperation. Or we just can't feel anything at all—the only thing we can be sure of is that there is a pervading sense of numbness.

A *block* to the second chakra is generally characterized by some sort of traumatic experience around our right to our feelings, or worse, a victimization of our bodies. Again, be gentle with yourself here as the second chakra is a most delicate area to work on. If you feel as though your second chakra is blocked, begin by addressing your personal history in regards to the second chakra. How was your right to feel supported in childhood? Was the sacredness of your body honored by those closest to you? How is your relationship to pleasure? Do you allow yourself to have it, or do you deny your body's desire for it? If there's a potential for any type of trauma to become triggered by asking these questions, I highly encourage you to enlist the help of a qualified therapist or healer so they can first help you to unpack some of your energetic baggage, and then provide suggestions and exercises that will be helpful to your healing.

Idealistically, we want to achieve a state of *balance* in all our energy systems, but particularly our Sensate System, as this system is intimately linked to our experience of pleasure and who doesn't want a pleasurable life? No matter how much we've denied or suppressed our desire for pleasure, we all deserve to have the experience of a life that is pleasing to us. Having a balanced second chakra is critical to creating that life.

Having a balanced second chakra will manifest as a life and a body that has a healthy structure to it, but not so structured that it becomes rigid. Both the body and life will have a flexible quality, but not so flexible that it becomes spineless either. People with a balanced second chakra are able to feel deeply and allow themselves to express their emotions, but also know how to contain those feelings when needed. There's a definite boundary between self and other, and the ability to reference both is available to them at all times. These people know how they feel and they're also really good at sensing how other people feel as well. They're adept at reading the cues from their inner emotions, as well as their outer environment and although they're highly empathic, they're capable of determining which emotions are theirs and which ones belong to someone else.

A person with a healthy second chakra will have a deep felt sense of connection to themselves and what makes them come alive. They know what they enjoy, need, and want, and they're comfortable asking for those needs to be met by others, or going out and meeting those needs for themselves. These people have a healthy relationship to pleasure and are able to both give and receive energy in a healthy exchange between people. Their lives and relationships will be a beautiful reflection of all the things they're passionate about.

The Sensate System can be one of the more challenging systems to balance because it carries with it so much baggage and so much of our shadow. If you were raised in an uptight or religious environment or if you've experienced any trauma around your sexuality, this system is likely to give you some trouble. In a utopian world, where everyone walked around with balanced Sensate Systems, we would see an appreciation of beauty in all of its forms. Men would honor women, women would honor men, and both would be deeply connected to their own emotions. The people on this planet would be so connected to their own senses that they could clearly feel their passions and desires and allow that connection to pull them towards work that is both fulfilling and purposeful. Addictions would diminish. Sex would be seen as a sacred union between lovers, rather than just an animalistic act to get our primal needs met.

In order to bring this center into balance, we need to reconnect to our inner guidance system, our emotional body, and also do the sometimes-difficult work of reclaiming our shadow. Glance back into your childhood and observe how your parents and caretakers supported emotional expression. Were you allowed to express some emotions but not others? This will give you an indicator as to what feelings you allow yourself to experience and which you resist today. Learn to practice expressing whatever it is that you're feeling—however the emotion arises within you— in the moment that it arises. In order to have healthy Sensate Systems, we need to reconnect our mind to our bodies' sensual nature and understand our need for physical touch. You can begin this by first feeling your connection to your body and observing your relationship to your senses. Do you avoid physical intimacy or do you crave it? Do you allow yourself the experience of pleasure, both sensually and sexually? If you're the type of person who numbs yourself, try to become aware of what feelings you're most likely to try avoiding.

Whereas the Root System is balanced by the energy of earth, the emotions and the Sensate System are balanced by the energy and fluidity of water. Practice fluid movement. Take time to connect to your body and learn how it wants to move and how it likes to experience life. Surround yourself with beauty, color, texture, and fragrance. Nourish your body by doing what pleases your senses. Have good sex with people who honor and respect you. Spend time in water, take a salt tubby, go swimming, *love yourself.* Dance, because life itself is a dance, and all your relationships are your dance partners. Energetic movement practices like tai-chi, bioenergetics, and yoga are also very helpful in bringing balance, not just to the Sensate System, but to all systems.

Another healing modality that's beneficial for restoring harmony and balance to the Sensate System is a practice known as EFT, Emotional Freedom Technique — or *tapping.* EFT asks us to tap on meridian points throughout the body used in conjunction with a specific dialogue to heal whatever issue is arising for you in a moment. Somehow, this tapping process allows trapped emotions to return to their fluid nature so we can experience them, express them, and release them. It looks a bit silly, but it's a very powerful technique.

Questions for Reflection

Here are some additional questions for reflection. I encourage you to sit with each question and really take the time to let honest answers to emerge. I also suggest journaling, as the process of writing your thoughts down on paper helps the brain make sense of what you're feeling.

- How flexible do you feel in your body? Specifically, in the area of your hips, and lower back.
- How connected do you feel to your passions and desires?
- Are you aware of your own needs?
- Do you feel as though you have healthy boundaries in your relationships?
- Are you able to reference your own feelings, as well as tune in to the feelings of others?
- How often do you rely on others to meet your needs?
- Do you feel reliant upon others, overly self-sufficient, or do you have a healthy balance of both?
- How was your right to feel and express emotion supported in your family?
- Are you more comfortable expressing some feelings more than others? And if so, which emotions make you comfortable and which make you uncomfortable?
- Are you aware of your own shadow?
- What shadow qualities do you think you have?
- What triggers you most about others? And can you, perhaps, see this as a reflection of yourself?
- Do you allow yourself the experience of pleasure? Whether that's food, sex, or other luxuries.
- Are you all work and no play?
- When you do allow the experience of pleasure, is it accompanied by guilt?
- What lights you up so much that time stops when you're doing it?

THE THIRD CHAKRA—
THE PERSONAL-POWER SYSTEM

"Personal power is the ability to take action."
—Anthony Robbins

If reclaiming the right to our feelings reignites our passion, then reclaiming our right to *act* on those feelings, reignites our personal power. Power is of primary importance to our lower-selves. We don't just *want* to feel powerful, we *need* to feel powerful. A felt sense of power allows us to act in accordance with our desires and affect change in our own lives. We really need to nurture and develop this understanding of personal power, especially if we hope to inspire change within our evolving collective. Unfortunately, like our feelings, authentic power isn't always something that gets supported in childhood, and therefore it can be difficult to access in our adulthood. Powerful and willful children are usually seen as more of a nuisance than a benefit and are most often suppressed more than they're supported. They present a challenge to our carefully crafted and predictable realities so we treat them as a disturbance when we probably should be celebrating them for their powerful contribution to move and change our world. As a result, we punish natural leaders for being strong. We train them to fall in line, to not ask questions, to quiet themselves, to not stand out too much, and to *definitely* not challenge authority—even though that's the very thing they were born to do.

Not only have we severed ourselves from our connection to our personal power, we've been brainwashed into believing that *real power* looks like forceful action. Humans have learned to see power as masculine, dominant, or violent and we display our personal power by demanding that others bend to our will. We've created a power-hungry world, where our degree of power is measured by how much control we have over *others* and not necessarily how much control we have over *ourselves*. What we consider *power* is actually *force*, and because we've been so badly abused by what has traditionally been called power, many of us have become truly terrified of it.

Our relationship to personal power starts forming at about two or three years old, right around the time we learn to say, "No!", and we become a huge pain in everyone's ass. This is the development of our will and the assertion of our right to act independently from the tribe. This stage of development is characterized by a growing desire for autonomy and the right to act as an individuated-self. In the first chakra stage of our lives we were awakening to our own conscious-awareness; we're conscious, just not sure what we're conscious of. At that stage, we're basically a lump of matter, *a body*, and a consciousness that occupies the matter—that's about it. In the second chakra, we began to establish a growing connection between our awareness, our body, and our inner state of emotions and how they relate to our outer experience. The third chakra, the Personal Power System, is where we claim our right to act on behalf of everything we've gathered up until that point. The first chakra claims the body, the second chakra claims the emotions, and third chakra claims the ego. The ego is basically a combination of all three lower chakras—the body, the desires of the body, and how our emotions motivate our bodies to act. A healthy, well-developed ego is essential for creating a healthy and well-developed human.

The first and second chakras are primal; they aren't motivated with intention, rather, they develop by instinct. But the third

chakra introduces another dimension of consciousness to our natural instinct—*the will.* The ego, and the will that governs it, help to
control our basic instincts and impulses. The ego connects the body
with our emotions and directs our actions in alignment with our
desires. It unifies the consciousness of the lower two chakras, and
also connects it to those that exist above it as well. Leading authority on chakras and human development, Anodea Judith, calls the
ego an *executive identity,* or the *CEO of the Self.* It's the organizing
principle that serves as the interfaces between our primal instincts
and the consciousness that directs those drives. The ego represents
how we want to express ourselves in the world, and the part of
us that's capable of controlling that expression. The ego's job is
both complex and pervasive. It's responsible for allowing our natural instincts to emerge, while simultaneously protecting us from
actions and emotions that might cause rejection or pain. This also
makes the ego the controlling-power behind creating *and* maintaining the shadow. Many new-age circles and spiritual organizations have demonized the ego and advocate the transcend of it, but
a healthy ego is a foundational element to understanding the self.
Although awakening to our true Self is to expand our consciousness beyond the limitations of the ego, a healthy ego is necessary
for genuine human-development.

By the time our ego and our third chakra begin developing,
we should have a decent amount of mobility and motor skill, we
should be able to move ourselves about fairly easily, and probably
have a growing collection of simple words we can use to express
ourselves. I want, I need, I like, I don't like, yes, and definitely no are
usually enough to get our point across. This is about the time that
children want to start doing things on their own, whether they're
capable or not. Children want to dress themselves, feed themselves,
and make choices on their own behalf. They want to feel powerful
and they have a right to that power. But this can also be a very
frustrating age for parents, who are usually stressed out and under

a timeframe to get things done. Waiting around for your toddlers struggled attempt at tying their own shoes, (a task you know is beyond their motor skill), not to mention the meltdown that follows their failed attempt, all while trying to get out the door in the morning, can be incredibly aggravating. But not receiving enough personal autonomy at this stage of our development can severely thwart the development of a healthy personality as well. It's a very delicate time in our child development.

This stage generally landmarks the time in our lives when our parents determine whether we are "easy" or *good* kids, or challenging ones. This is usually decided by whether we comply to their wishes or whether we have our own toddler agenda. I'm not sure about you, but I was an extremely strong-willed kid! Although, I now prefer the term *personally-powerful*. My mother still seems quite surprised that I survived my childhood; not because I was reckless and could've killed myself, but because she thought my father would kill me first! Like most, my dad was the power in the family, and he wielded his power in the way many humans do—with force. I spent a lot of my adult life afraid of being too powerful because I didn't want to be like that. (Sorry, Dad; I still love you.)

A lot of people don't remember the early years of their childhood, not because they can't, but because they're traumatized by them. Not being perceived as powerful is painful and we do the same thing with our power as we do with every other painful thing we can't face, or don't have the tools to process, into the shadow it goes. Most of our power is still hiding out there, lurking around in our shadows, just waiting for the right moment to explode. If someone dares to test our authority, they're probably going to get 30 or 40 years of pent up rage unleashed on them.

I didn't fully grasp the ancestral suppression of personal power until my own little powerhouse of a daughter, Rhythm, came screaming onto the scene. Everything was rainbows and butterflies with my beautiful little girl until she turned two and a half.

That's when my Dad and I really started to see eye to eye. I finally understood the pain he endured by being gifted with a highly spirited child and not having a clue how to manage the power. Right around the time Rhythm hit four, I completely understood why I grew up feeling like my dad hated me so much, because I felt that the same with her. She challenged me in every single way possible. After much struggle, I finally came to the realization that Rhythm was my noble friend. She had come into my life to remind me what authentic power looks like and teach me how to move my own power out of the shadow and into the light. In this way I could become a leader for her, rather than an enforcer.

You see, most of us don't know what it means to own how truly powerful we are, because a lot of our programming around power is so screwed up. What we call power couldn't be further from the truth of what personal power really is. Personal power is the ability to make choices for ourselves, as individuals. But sadly, most of us have been conditioned from an early age to give our power away. We give the power of our health to the doctor, the power of our education to our teachers, the power of authority to our parents and elders, the power of our mental well-being to the psychiatrist, the power of our individuality to the tribal mind, the power of our love to whoever we're in relationship with. We've somehow forgotten all about the innate power that comes from within us. We've learned to see money as power, beauty as power, and brute force as power. We see power as something that's represented by the external world and not our inner core.

So, what *is* true personal power?

Personal power is found in our ability to think, act, reason, accept responsibility, and apply discipline to makes changes for ourselves. In fact, there are incredible numbers of people on our planet today embodying what it means to be personally empowered, although they aren't quite getting the recognition they deserve. These are people doing remarkable work; they're regularly practicing virtuous behaviors like honesty, personal integrity, and humility and they're getting real about what their shortcomings are. Instead of blaming the world for their misfortunes, they're accepting the role they played in creating them and they're taking back the responsibility of creating their own lives—lives that were probably at one time a devastating mess. That's more powerful than what the majority of the world does, which is to look externally for power.

People who identify as being in recovery are surrendering their own will and merging with the will of a higher intelligence. They're discovering purpose and accountability by being of service and making themselves available to others for guidance and support. The altruistic traits of these spiritually based foundations are as close to the truth of power that we can find on our planet today. If we can collectively recognize the authentic power in the work they're doing, these groups will lead our collectives. But in order to awaken the collective to this power, we must bring the power of the addict archetype out of the shadow and into the light of higher awareness.

Certain support groups, especially those founded on healing the wound of addiction, are some of the most powerful groups on the planet. But if we're going to restore a sense of personal power and place it in the hands of our truly most powerful people, we really need to clear up some of the more destructive belief systems that permeate the addiction and recovery culture.

The first destruction occurs by making an identity out of being an addict or having an illness. For example, certain fellowships make a distinction between *real* or *true* addicts and *non-real* addicts. It may be true that some will experience a higher degree of addiction than others, however, this personal ownership associated with the behavior unconsciously encourages a bonding over the wound of addiction. It creates a mental division that feeds the ego and reinforces a need for identification. This becomes an identification that gets nurtured within the group. Being labeled a *real* addict makes some people and their egos feel special, and different from the rest of the world. Author and spiritual teacher, Caroline Myss, calls those who bond over various wounds, *woundmates.* Woundmates are those who share in the same painful experiences we have—and the wound doesn't need to be an addiction either, it can be anything traumatic—cancer, loss, abuse, you name it. If it hurts, humans can bond over it. If the shared wound of addiction, or being labeled a *true* addict provides members the right to exist within a fellowship, why then, would an individual ever willingly let that identity go?

Let's just face it—we're all our own special breed of fucked-up— it's not just addicts. Claiming your disease as an identification can be seen by the ego as an invitation to stay broken and believing that certain diseases are beyond a cure leaves us unwilling to educate ourselves further so we can finally *heal* beyond our wounds. Without the correct knowledge, we feel disempowered and this leads us to a secondary disadvantage—the concept of powerlessness.

Unfortunately, many addicts have collectively accepted the notion of powerlessness in a way that has become detrimental. Powerlessness over addiction seems to gain a stronghold on anyone who claims it, as those who have experienced an addiction truly understand what it means to be disempowered. They know the feeling of helplessness against forces outside of themselves. They know what it means to have their own personal will rendered ineffective, thereby losing the ability to make rational and wise choices. But just because we've experienced addiction doesn't mean that powerlessness must become a way of life. We do have a choice. I've also learned that we'll only surrender to an idea that's equal to our emotional state. So, if we believe that we're powerless, we'll feel powerless, and then we'll be far more likely to behave in a way that resembles our belief. The idea of powerlessness in the realm of recovery reinforces the idea that addiction will forever be an issue and will remain a daily struggle. This might be why relapse is such a common occurrence in recovery.

For many, sanity only returned when they surrendered their will to a higher power. And while it's true that surrendering your will to the divine is totally effective and absolutely necessary, the concept can still be easily misperceived. By relinquishing our power to a higher source, it implies that the source is found outside of us, whether that source is God, an angel, the universe, or our deceased grandmother, it doesn't matter. What matters is that source is not us. If we do get clean and support the ideology that it was at the hand of a higher power, we tend to give full credit to that higher power and deny that we too, played a part in our own recovery. This is essentially a denial of our own Personal Power System.

I know firsthand that active addiction is a state of powerlessness; that the addict has given their power away to something outside of themselves and now that external thing has their power. But that power dynamic doesn't have to be permanent. In fact, an even greater negotiation of power becomes available to addicts who get clean and that's the complete restoration of their Personal Power System. I recognize that overcoming addiction is no easy feat and that those who overcome addictions often do so with undeniable spiritual aid—but the spiritual aid isn't what keeps them sober, they do that for themselves. That's an example of personal power.

When I overcame my addiction, I know that I didn't do it alone, but I most certainly played my part. It wasn't God who made the effort to break my unproductive and hard-wired habits, leave toxic friendships, and create new patterns of belief and behavior. It wasn't God who made the decision to never abuse drugs again. It also wasn't God that dropped each harmful addiction, one by one, until my life was entirely different. I didn't just quit drugs; I quit smoking weed, I quit smoking cigarettes, I quit jobs that didn't serve me, and friendships that didn't propel me forward. I changed my thoughts, I changed my habits, and I changed my life. I became an entirely new person in the process. That was me. That was done through my third chakra, my Personal Power System.

My willingness and determination to change and my commitment to that change is what made transformation possible. Although the inspiration may have come from a source that was higher than me, I did the work. And there may be a time when you too need to call upon the divine to assist in some type of recovery, and surely, the divine will come to your aid. But once it does, and you have your power back, it becomes your responsibly to maintain that through your own Personal Power System.

Aside from addiction, there are plenty more examples of how becoming aligned with our personal power can help us to accomplish our goals and change our lives. To heal a body that suffers from a chronic disease, for example, (even diseases that are deemed incurable like addiction) will require a fusion of powerful energy. As will a weight loss journey, or a goal of running a marathon, or anything else that requires our persistency and discipline.

If someone desperately desires change, enlisting the help of their Personal Power System makes that change possible. One can make any change they desire to happen in their lives by aligning their intentions with their actions and their faith with their emotions. When our Personal Power System is engaged and our actions follow our intentions, all things become possible—even the impossible. Despite any personal resistance to change, persistence of applied personal power can allow a person, *any person*, to redirect their energy and change their behavior. If they work to create new thoughts, new feelings, and new behaviors, the new can replace the old until who they are no longer resembles the person they used to be. In that way, they become an entirely new person, and they can no longer create the same life experiences or physical manifestations in the body as the person they were before. So, oftentimes, the disease, excess weight, or lack of stamina they had before simply disappears. This is a clear example of applied personal power. Given the appropriate understanding of personal power, any individual who accesses it could not only transform and heal themselves, but could in turn help inspire to transform and heal the rest of us. If enough recovering addicts learn to understand their relationship to personal power, I think addicts are capable of changing the world and the world would gain an entirely different perspective as to why we have so many addicts on the planet today.

Understanding the Hidden Power in Addiction

"What the addict is seeking is not to be ashamed of.
The whole spiritual world wants to reach that blissful state
of consciousness. Change your technique, not your aspiration.
The state doesn't have to be sought; it is always within us."
—David Hawkins

Although addiction effects all our chakras, and our reasons for turning to addiction are many and varied, I've chosen to cover the concept of addiction in the Personal Power System because the experience of addiction is truly a detriment to this system. Addiction, by definition, denotes a loss of personal power and it can also produce a significant amount of shame at the loss of that power. No one wants to admit that they've lost power over their choices, and their lives. At the same time, not many people want to experience the shame that comes with accepting that they no longer have control over their own will. This juxtaposed position can make moving beyond the wound of addiction a challenge to those who experience it. But perhaps if we shifted the context around addiction and removed the shame from the experience, we'd have a better chance at delivering ourselves from its grips.

Not everyone identifies as an addict, but every human will experience addiction, or an attachment to *feeling good*. We all want to feel good and avert ourselves from feeling bad. It's part of our human design. But in our attempts to feel good all the time, and never experience a painful feeling, sooner or later, the longing becomes so great that we usually try to alter or escape our realities. Most of the time, it's because we're not comfortable with what's happening around us. Or that whatever life is presenting us with is beyond our capacity to cope. When we don't know how to sit with our discomfort or have the tools to process it, our best option is usually to numb ourselves to it instead. We overeat, drink alcohol, take prescriptions, obsess over love interests, compulsively work out, shop, stay really busy, play video games, or do anything else we can think of to silence our feelings—when we could just as easily learn to sit with what is happening inside of us, listen to what it has to tell us about our inner-state, and do our best to either accept it or change it.

When we rely on things outside of ourselves to get temporary relief from our unhappiness, it changes our physical chemistry. We get a rush of feel-good hormones that lift us into higher states of consciousness, and diminish the stress and anxiety caused by whatever's happening inside of us. And although many of our aversion tactics work temporarily, the power to change the way we feel inside will remain reliant upon sources outside of ourselves. Because of our skewed relationship to power, many of us have forgotten that the power to shift and change our inner state also exists within us. But because we've been conditioned into giving that power away, we often turn to things outside of us as a means to feeling better by utilizing different substances and behaviors help kick in our feel-good chemicals. They change the way we think, feel, and behave dramatically and using them helps us feel better. That's all we really want; it's why we keep repeating certain behaviors even when they become destructive. But in relying upon different habits and substances, we rob ourselves of the opportunity to really understand our feelings and learn what exactly we're avoiding by numbing ourselves.

Be they natural or synthetic, chemicals change the way we feel—and we all want to feel better. But the problem is, a lot of us don't know why exactly we don't feel good to begin with. We've learned from the chapter before this one that most people have become so disconnected from their Sensate System that they're disconnected from their inner selves and no longer know *why* they're doing *what* they're doing. They don't know why they don't feel good because they've long been severed from their feelings. Chemicals produced by avoidant behaviors help people feel better. They'll feel less stressed, more relaxed, energized, or focused. Some behaviors make people who are generally shy or self-conscious a bit more confident. The shifting of our inner state can be as innocent as drinking a cup of coffee in order to wake up on a Monday morning or as destructive as taking party drugs to let loose on a Friday night—it all alters our consciousness. Once the chemicals are experienced by the brain and body, we're more easily able to move beyond our dominant states of mind and shift into lighter, more elevated levels of consciousness. And that usually feels better to us, than not feeling good.

According to David Hawkins, an authority in the field of spirituality and enlightenment who dedicated his life to consciousness research, human consciousness ranges from lower levels of shame, guilt, and fear; moves through to midrange levels of pride, courage, and willingness; and then expands all the way into the highest levels possible of peace, love, joy, and enlightenment. All the world religions since the beginning of time, and all the ascended masters who revealed them, were born from the recognition of these higher states of awareness. Hawkins also declared that drugs themselves are not actually capable of *producing* a specific state of being. Rather, they're merely responsible for *silencing* the energy fields where we interpret lower vibrational feelings like stress, fear and anxiety. Without the experience of these limiting lower frequencies, we're allowed to freely access and explore the more liberated states of consciousness that are always actually available to us. And really, who doesn't want to spend even just a few moments without the nagging presence of fear lurking behind the scenes?

Hawkins' states that drug users aren't actually addicted to the drug itself, but the state of consciousness produced by the mind while under the influence of it. The same can be said for any other avoidant behavior as well. He uses a brilliant analogy to capture the essence of human involvement with substances like drugs, alcohol, and even food. Hawkins compares the sun to the omnipresent energy of the soul within and the clouds to lower vibrational, unwanted states of awareness. Removing the clouds does not cause the sun to shine; the sun is shining all the time, in the same way that the love of the soul is accessible at all times. When clouds move from the sky, like fear being removed from the mind, one gets a glimpse of the love of the soul. This love has been there all along, only our own fear has prevented us from accessing it. A person who has achieved higher states of awareness understands this. Whether that state was achieved by natural or artificial means doesn't change the reality of its existence, nor should either approach be discredited in any way.

So how do we break the stigma around drugs, addiction, and other avoidant behaviors? We do that by accepting people just want to feel good, but most people don't know how to feel good because they've forgotten how to feel—and now they just don't want to feel bad. But it needs to be said, drugs aren't the enemy; in fact, drugs can be quite powerful for delivering us into elevated states of consciousness. Former academic, clinical psychologist, and spiritual guru, the late Ram Dass, speaks heavily of his use of plant medicines and psychedelic hallucinogens, like psilocybin and LSD, as his induction into the elevated states known as enlightenment. Having had the liberating experiences of these higher states of awareness (and the acknowledgement that they exist), he dedicated himself to studying under master yogis and gurus who could teach him to recreate these states through spiritual practice.

Even Bill Wilson, the man responsible for establishing Alcoholics Anonymous, used LSD therapeutically to overcome his addiction to alcohol and credits those psychedelic experiences with his development of the 12 steps. Mind-altering substances aren't bad and our culture could really benefit from them, as long as we can stop demonizing them. Some people use plant medicines and synthetic hallucinogens to escape reality and get high, but that's mostly because they misunderstand the medicine. Healers and shamans have long used planet medicines to deepen their connection to self and to expand their understanding of the universe.

These medicines aren't the problem, how our culture relates to them is what makes them problematic. Hallucinogens are known to expand the mind of the user well beyond its average perception and the effect of this expansion generally lasts long after the substance has worn off. Often these experiences are equally as real, if not more powerful, than our actual waking life experiences and have a permanent effect on our consciousness. These experiences have a profound effect on our Personal Power Systems as they can reorganize the way we process our reality and our sense of self— but to get the best out of these experiences, they need to be integrated in a healthy way.

When medicines like these are used in order to escape yourself and escape reality, they can be detrimental. But when medicines are used appropriately, as *medicine*, to understand yourself and your place within reality, their benefits are unspeakable. With proper support, education, and training, experiences with psychedelics and other forms of plant medicine, used therapeutically, can be life changing. If enough people come to understand that, the effects of these therapies will make a global impact on our collective wellness.

Ram Dass and others like him have also shown us that drugs aren't necessary to experience elevated states of consciousness. It's enough to first be aware that these elevated states are available to us, and then we must have a desire to experience them.

Drugs, for many, have acted as a catalyst, a window that allowed them to glimpse into eternity and to experience first-hand what's possible in terms of thinking and feeling in expanded ways without the presence of fear getting in the way. Once the mind has been opened and exposed to these higher realms of consciousness, it can never be closed off to them again. Many people who have had experiences with such elevated states have also come to understand a level of freedom, ecstasy, and liberation that's foreign to most. Somewhere within, they recognize that these realms are available and achievable. Not only that, but it *feels* better than the hell that many of us have created for ourselves here on planet earth.

Not drugs, but the desire to experience a state of being that is free from fear and pain is what becomes addictive to the user. Problems arise when we continue to chase these states without learning how to recreate them for ourselves without the use of a substance. This isn't solely a drug addiction issue, this is a personal power issue. An addiction is simply the result of becoming reliant upon an external chemical to facilitate an inner state of consciousness. But we have the power to do that ourselves, we just need a strong third chakra to do it. We may enlist the help of a substance or behavior if we need to—but if we become reliant upon those things to feel a certain way, we essentially lose our power to them.

If those who've have had the opportunity to experience these transcendental states of awareness (be they through drugs or spiritual practice), could learn to replicate those experiences on their own—the world as we know it would change. And if those who've experienced elevated states by means of addiction could take their personal power back from those behaviors and apply that power to healthier habits, especially ones that facilitate the same level of freedom, they would shift from a position of powerlessness to becoming the most powerful people on the planet. I believe that if we can stop demonizing altered states of consciousness and the medicines that facilitate them, they can become our greatest tools for transformation. And if we can bring the archetype of the addict out of the shadow and into the light, we can see how reclaiming the loss of power serves only to restore a healthy sense of personal power to the entire human-collective. The tables will turn. Plants will no longer be classified as drugs, and will instead, become medicine. And those in recovery from addiction, will no longer be considered powerless, rather, they will become the greatest examples of personal power and transformation that our world has ever known.

The Empowered Personality

If we took all the people in the world and placed them on a giant scale, the disempowered on one side and a single authentically-empowered person on the other, the mass of those without power would be exponentially greater in volume to the one person of power. However, the magnitude of energy generated by just one authentically empowered person would be more than enough to balance the scale. This is the power of a fully awakened human being. Can you image that for millennia it's been a single few enlightened beings maintaining the balance for the entire human race? Are you ready to level up and finally tip the scales?

The awakening of true and authentic power is a necessary and critical shift that's taking place on our planet today. The forces of good and evil are just as real now as they were in the storybooks that were read to us as children and the movies that we indulge in as adults today. The fear based, power over others paradigm is losing its grip on the collective of humanity, and the darkness is struggling to maintain its stronghold. Fortunately for us, our universe was created with a self-correcting, self-recalibrating intelligence. That's why we have so many healers waking up and why so many of our gifts are being activated; we need them now more than ever. We need to be the light in order to maintain the natural balance, but we must be willing to allow ourselves to be activated. Humanity needs to be willing to participate in our own evolution, and remember that what we do as individuals makes a difference in the collective. This is a time of great awakening on our planet as more and more of us tap into our creative capabilities. We're challenging outdated belief systems, practicing mindfulness, mastering our own wellness, and connecting with others of like mind to make a positive difference. We're remembering who we are and *we're taking our power back*! When we do this, we literally become like superheros. And just like in the comic books, each awakened superhero possesses a force of unspeakable greatness, a power from within that makes them unstoppable elements of change, all dedicated to the betterment of our world.

So, what does it mean to be an empowered person, and how do we become one?

To be empowered means to be real, and to be real means to be *you*. Being your authentic self *is* your superhero's super power. When you remember who you are, being yourself is an act of service—it's the greatest gift you have to offer the world—but you must remember who you really are. Little children understand this, but far too many adults have lost connection to it. For the majority of personally empowered individuals out there living awakened lives, it didn't come effortlessly. It took courage, willingness, strength, and discipline—it required personal power to reach a level of genuine authenticity.

Becoming empowered usually begins with disempowerment. It starts with the desire to be somewhere other than where we find ourselves to be. With willingness and willpower, the empowered personality stands in the heat of their own flame and takes every action necessary to burn away everything that no longer resembles the highest vision they hold for themselves and their lives. Empowerment isn't easy—but it means you believe in yourself more than you believe in someone else's vision for your life.

Sometimes becoming yourself means letting go of long-term friendships and relationships if they're no longer in alignment with who you are; sometimes it means outgrowing a career and embarking on a new path; sometimes it means making a radical change in diet and lifestyle to heal from an illness; sometimes it means letting go of everything you thought you knew in order to start over completely. Becoming real is scary. But it beats trying to be someone you're not.

Discovering your true power is a humbling process. It requires taking a long hard look at the common dominator of all of your life's problems—*you*— and cutting away all that's erroneous. Personal power is an act of surrender just as much as it's an act of will. It's a relinquishment of the need to be in charge and in control, just as much as it means taking back the reins of your life. It's a letting go *and* a moving forward.

Becoming personally empowered is taking responsibility for your own life, your own choices, and your own actions. It's a willingness to learn from the lessons life delivers, even when they're painful. It's a waking up to your true desires and a readiness to make the next necessary moves to make them happen, even if that requires disciplined action. Empowerment is the call to that action, and it usually means change, which is most always scary.

Being you is all about discovering the true essence of your personality and then being that quality unapologetically—even if it's the last thing the world said you should be. It's serving something other than yourself and serving you at the same time! The process of truly becoming our authentic selves can be a demanding task that requires a great deal of personal power, discipline, and relentless self-reflection. Sometimes it can feel like swimming upwards against the current of a river raging downstream. But when you finally become you, there's no better feeling in the entire world. Being you, and being happy with being you, is what it means to be truly empowered.

Everywhere you look there's an ad or infomercial subconsciously convincing you that who you are isn't good enough, and that in order to be happy you need to be more like someone else.

If you're a woman, you need to have great hair, perfect skin, and a perfect body. Or if you're a man, you have to be super macho, have a six pack, and a huge you-know-what. Those things are cool and all, but you really don't need them, and having them might boost your confidence but doesn't add a single thing to your soul. Yet everywhere we look there are endless advertisements with celebrities' faces plastered all over them, creating a message in your mind that you're not good enough.

These marketing giants want to convince you that if you just buy their product, you'll be less like yourself and more like the public figure that everyone admires. If you buy that certain cologne, it'll make you smell manlier and only *then* can you attract beautiful women, like the guy in the commercial. If you buy that shampoo or that product, your hair will be thick, luxurious and beautiful, not thin, damaged or untamed and wild like yours is now. If you buy the fancy makeup and cosmetics, you can paint and contour your face to make it look better than the one you were born with and more people might look at you. Our cultural conditioning towards narcissistic self-absorption and self-gratifying, self-negating behaviors is so outrageous it borders on insanity. The result of this insanity is a world full of people desperately trying to change who they really are.

The unconscious identification with our culture has caused an extreme disassociation from our genuine authenticity as empowered individuals. When we're busy upholding beliefs that aren't ours or vigilantly protecting ourselves against the way that culture has wounded us, it makes it near impossible to discover who we really are in the present moment of our lives. If you've had the pleasure of meeting someone who is genuine, without a doubt, you will know it. There's a quality about them, an air of unshakability to their attitude, a confidence that doesn't feel boastful or arrogant, humility beyond reason, and an energy field that radiates knowingness. Empowered people know exactly who they are—they're the rebels. Behaving in a way that's personally empowered in today's society is a radical form activism.

At this point, you might be wondering who you are, right? What your superpower is or how to discover it? I'll tell you a secret; you can never access your superpower through your analytical mind. The part of you that questions who you are will never be able to provide you with the answer. The part of you that *thinks* can never truly *know*. When you *feel* your superpower, you'll know it. You'll know it because it's who you are! Being who you are feeds your energy rather than draining it. It awakens your passions, it lights you up instead of turning you off, and it excites you and makes you feel good and radiant and alive. It's probably the last thing you ever thought it would be, simply because it feels effortless and natural to you and because you enjoy it. Things that come easily aren't usually valued and so we devalue being ourselves. We're taught to glorify hard work instead. It's no wonder we're all chasing these idealized versions of reality and overlooking the simple truth—to be unapologetically ourselves is to be awakened and to be awakened is to be empowered.

Empowered people are confident people. Their lives are guided by a personal code of values; they're sure of who they are and they're driven by a deeper sense of purpose. Confidence is the natural byproduct of getting to know yourself on a deeper level. It's not the kind of confidence you might observe in someone who is undeniably attractive or exceptionally gifted, or talented. It's certainly not a boastful arrogance or cockiness used to mask a deeper insecurity. It's an energy of knowingness and a solidity of presence that arises from deep within. Genuine confidence arises from doing the things you love, being the type of person you'd admire, and living in alignment with your values. When you've tapped into this kind of personal power, it doesn't matter what you look like, what type of job you have, the amount of money in your bank account, or the material possessions you've acquired. What matters is that you're out there making your own unique impression on the world, living in the truth of who you are, doing what you were meant to do, and being who you were born to be.

Taking Responsibility

"To achieve major success in life—to achieve those things that are most important to you—you must assume 100% responsibility for your life. Nothing else will do."
—Jack Canfield

Before we go any further, I want you to make a commitment—not to me, but to yourself. I want you to promise that you're going to take this information and use it to make the rest of your life the best of your life, because you deserve it. And the whole world is relying on those who are brave enough to wake up fully, take charge of their lives, and show those living in fear the way to greatness. If you want to live the kind of life you've always dreamt of, that means you have to take responsibility for the life that you have now. It also means accepting 100% responsibility for the life you've lived up to this point. If any area of your life feels lacking it's because on some level, you realize that it could be better and that you want it to be better. Taking responsibility means acknowledging that you—and *only* you—are capable of making it better.

You have to relinquish the idea that you're *entitled* to a happy, successful, fulfilling life, and instead accept responsibility for *creating* one. You have to decide that you want more, better, or something different for yourself, and then you have to be willing to put in the work to get it. This might mean that you need to stop blaming your parents for the childhood you wanted but didn't get; stop blaming your spouses for the lack of connection and romance in your relationship; your ex for why you have trust issues; using your boss as an excuse for hating your job; blaming your kids for not pursuing your own dreams; or blaming the doctor for why you're not healing, and start taking responsibly for the role you've played in creating all aspects of your life. We may not have had any control over what's happened to us in life, that's true, but what we have control over is how we react, and that makes all the difference.

If we want change, we have to give up our best excuses that keep us stuck in the same old cycle of thinking and feeling in limited ways and instead start introducing new thoughts that influence new feelings. We then need to take new actions to create new outcomes *now*. As long as we continue to do what we've always done, or respond to life in the same way we always have, we will only continue to get more of what we've already gotten. If we want something different, we have to *become someone different.* We can't just complain and expect things to change, that will never work. We can't shame and blame the people around us into a state of subservience by expecting them to meet our every need. Others cannot be the determining factor to whether we're happy or not. We must choose to make ourselves happy. And we can't wait for tomorrow because it may never arrive. We have to accept 100% responsibility *now*. We're living in a time like no other, an age of infinite possibility. If you're experiencing a problem, you have access to solutions. If you're presently stuck in your life, there is only one reason for it and that's *you*.

In order to reclaim your personal power there's a good chance that you'll need to read some new books, go to therapy to deal with childhood trauma, learn to communicate more effectively, leave a toxic relationship, face your fear of vulnerability, take a risk, drop an addiction, find a new job, go back to school, start an exercise regimen, or change your diet. It might mean waking up early or staying up late to create your dreamlife while you continue to live the life you've created up to this point. Taking responsibility means getting seriously committed to turning your dreams into your reality. It means moving through the comfortable life you've created and pushing yourself beyond your own self-imposed limitations. If you're reading this book, it means that you really want better for yourself and chances are you have a vision of what that *better* might look like. If you don't know what it looks like, I'm sure you at least have an idea of what it *feels* like. I'd be willing to bet it's a feeling of freedom, authentic self-expression, peace of mind, financial security, passion for your relationships, and an overall joy for living. If you aren't yet sure exactly what lights you up in life, that's okay too—I can guarantee that if you begin the search within yourself, you'll find your answers. Your soul already knows exactly what's going to make you wake up every morning filled with passion, enthusiasm, and unlimited excitement simply because you've re-discovered exactly who you really are. The more you let go of fear and the person you're not, the more space you create for who you really are and the essence of your soul will begin to emerge naturally.

There are absolutely going to be things that need to change if you want to experience something new in your life. If you want to move from where you are and get to where you want to be, you'll have to do things you've never done before. That's how you create the life you want, but don't yet have.

In his book, *The Success Principles*, Jack Canfield gives us a wonderful formula for understanding our personal power and accepting responsibility for our lives. The formula is:

$$E+R=O$$
(Event + Response = Outcome)

The equation illustrates that every event in your life, be it your health or lack of it, your happiness or despair, your successful career or your financial ruin, your happy marriage or bitter divorce, or anything in between, has all come about as a result of how you've responded to the events in your life. We only have so much control over the events that take place in our lives, but we *always* have control over how we react to them. Most of us, however, will choose to blame the events in our life for the outcomes we experience, rather than paying attention to how we've reacted. We'll blame the car for breaking down before we blame ourselves for neglecting basic maintenance. We'll blame the economy instead of our lack of ingenuity and determination to succeed. We'll blame our bodies for getting sick when we ignored the warning signs. We'll blame our partners or family for the conflict in our lives and then we'll find a way to minimize or justify our own contributing behaviors. Taking responsibility for the way that we respond to the life we're presently experiencing is paramount if we're going to intentionally create the lives we want.

If you aren't happy with the situations in your life, you can only do one thing; change your response to get a new outcome. It's not always possible to change the events of our lives— some things are simply beyond our control—but we *always* have control over how we *react* to life's circumstance! We always have the power to choose how we respond. We don't become personally powerful by trying to control the people, places, or things outside of us. Personal power arises from *within* us.

The most effective way to change is to first accept the belief that we are worthy of so much more than we've previously allowed ourselves to have. We have to believe that we're capable of more than we could ever imagine and become more open and willing, and then we have to love ourselves enough to make those necessary changes happen. We all deserve meaningful lives, fulfilling relationships, healthy bodies, and purposeful careers, and we're equipped with everything we need to achieve those things. We must learn, however, that we can't criticize ourselves into an abundant life, nor can we simply complain about our current position and expect it to change. We can't fantasize about a new life and just hope we'll miraculously end up where we want to be. We have to take action! We have to make a definite decision that we're worth more than our current position and then we have to dedicate ourselves to going after what we really want. The commitment to ourselves has to be stronger than our commitment to our excuses, our unconscious patterns, and our fear. We have to make a daily effort to become the best versions of ourselves possible. This means doing the work especially when we don't feel like doing it. The ability to act upon our desire for change is what's discovered when we awaken our third chakra, our Personal Power System.

Character Structure

Team Player
(People Pleaser)

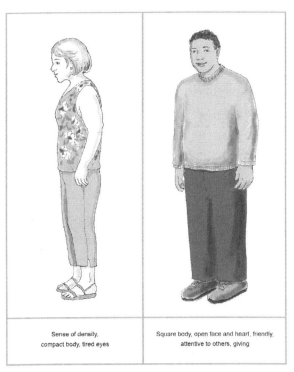

| Sense of density, compact body, tired eyes | Square body, open face and heart, friendly, attentive to others, giving |

According to Thomas: The Team Player/People Pleaser
For more information visit www.4dhealing.com.

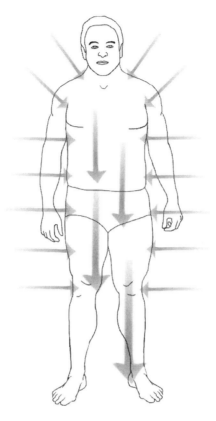

According to Kessler: The Enduring Pattern
Images from The 5 Personality Patterns *by Steven Kessler © 2015. Used with permission.*
For more information visit www.The5PersonalityPatterns.com

The character structure most closely associated with the third chakra is the *Team Player*. The *Team Player* describes the highest potential of this character, which is revealed when they're able to release their energetic defense and allow their soul quality to be expressed. We cover both the soul-quality, and the defensive-quality of this character in the section on the Personal Power System, due to the fact that this structure has the most difficult time developing a connection to their own willpower and sense of autonomy. Kessler has identified its energy pattern as the *Enduring* pattern; when threatened, a *Team Player* doesn't believe they have the inner resources to challenge or change their external circumstance, so they will shift their consciousness energetically away from their core and send it down into the ground in an attempt endure his or her surroundings. The *Team Player* epitomizes a loss of personal power, which is why Thomas has identified the defense of this profile as the *People Pleaser.* A person who lives in the energetic defense of *People Pleaser* will feel like they no longer have a say in their own lives, they've lost their will to the will of another, and are usually left with feelings of shame, unspoken resistance, and defeat.

The *People Pleaser* defense is thought to have been created in childhood, during the very sensitive time of individuation. If a child is allowed to express their autonomy and act separately and willfully during this time, then they're able to accomplish the developmental task of feeling empowered as an individual self. The developmental task required at the age of individuation is to feel confident in *putting energy out* into the world and *People Pleaser* personalities were never allowed to do that.

This particular energetic defense is characteristic of children raised by overly controlling parents. If the parent was too domi-nant and didn't allow the space necessary for the child to express his growing need for autonomy, that task was never able to meet completion. If the need for autonomous action remains unaccom-plished throughout life, the child will grow into an adult with a *People Pleaser* defensive pattern and will continually doubt their right to act independently or without the direction of a more powerful person. The *Enforcer* defense, which we will cover in the fifth chakra, the Creative Communication System, had a similar experience of not being able to express themselves in childhood, however, those who choose the *Enforcer* defense create an entirely different strategy than *People Pleasers.* Enforcers develop the need to feel excessively-powerful and explode their energy field when they're afraid and *People Pleasers,* weighed down by the heavi-ness of defeat and feeling of powerlessness, will send their energy inward and down, anchoring themselves deep into the earth. The difference between the *Enforcer* and the *People Pleaser* is that the *Enforcer* challenges authority and the *People Pleaser* succumbs to it. The *People Pleaser* personality has given up their right to individual power, and instead of fighting for it they forfeit their own needs and learn to endure the constant demands from others. Because they never were able to establish boundaries or develop a felt-sense of autonomy, as adults, they aren't really able to even distinguish between what they want for themselves, and what others want from them. The adult *People Pleaser* was never allowed a connection to their personal power, so they don't really know who they are; the only attempt they make at claiming their power will be unconscious, and they do that by being in a state of passive-resistance. They really don't know what *they* want, so they'll make an attempt at individuating by resisting what they think *you* want. But when standing in opposition doesn't work, they'll cave and conform to the demands of others.

This energetic-defensive pattern is often characterized by a dense, slow-to-move, or highly resistant personality. Their bodies often carry an excessive amount of weight, even if they're consistently dieting. Their weight can manifest as the energetic representation of taking on the needs and burdens of others. They're soft, but mainly because they lack personal boundaries. Because their energy isn't used to fill their own energetic field and is often focused inward and down into the ground as a means of defense, *People Pleasers* are often invaded by opportunistic leaders who take advantage of them to get their own needs met.

People caught in the *People Pleaser* defense don't act of their own volition and will often show up to serve others, but not necessarily because they choose to, rather, because they feel obligated to. Never claiming the right to their own personal power makes it incredibly challenging for *People Pleasers* to say no to others, even when saying no to someone else is really saying yes to themselves. *People Pleasers* will do for others even when they're undeserving and unappreciative. Their deepest desire is to be recognized for their unconditional love and support, and yet, they very rarely get it.

In their core, the *Team Players* own needs are intimately related to supporting and nurturing others but in the *People Pleaser* defense, they can easily be drained by the needs of others. As a result of feeling unacknowledged and unappreciated, they often build up resentments towards those closest to them and can become jaded and bitter. They no longer give to others freely and from the heart, but resentfully and out of obligation.

If *Team Players* are stuck living in the *People Pleaser* defense, they'll tend to do so much for others and so little for themselves, that they usually only reward themselves with food, which adds to the redundant issue of weight gain and the inability to lose it. When they've finally had enough of being taken advantage of, they may choose to withdraw from the world, resulting in depression and disconnection. Those who adopt this defensive pattern must keep in mind that withdrawing will only serve to sabotage their true purpose, which is to be in relationship with others. If a *Team Player* lives in *People Pleaser* defense, they'll experience an intense dichotomy between their individuality and the essence of their soul. They'll experience a deep need to be of service to others and simultaneously feel resentment for not being appreciated for the unconditional love and support that they provide.

In order to shift from the defensive quality of *People Pleaser* into the core profile of a *Team Player*, they'll need to claim their personal space as individuals and establish a healthy sense of boundaries. *People Pleasers* will need to learn to differentiate between their own energy and the energy of others. In the same way that a parent gives a child a variety of options and choices to feel powerful, an adult who is living in *People Pleaser* will need to offer themselves the same options; this way they can begin to develop a sense of who they are and what they like. Remember, *People Pleasers* never got to be individuals in childhood and need to discover themselves in order to come to completion with the task of individuation. Only then can they move forward in their own personal evolution. Once a *People Pleaser* connects to a felt sense of self and develops a clearly defined boundary, they'll be able to consciously choose when they genuinely want to nurture and support others and they'll also be able to identify when they're supporting others because they feel as though they don't have a choice in the matter. In the making of that shift is when a *People Pleaser* shifts into their core soul quality as a *Team Player.*

Nothing in the world makes a *Team Player* happier than caretaking and nurturing others. They're the divine mothers and fathers, the cheerful teachers, everybody's best friend, and the most hilarious comedians. *Team Players* have a way of making everyone they know feel seen, loved, honored and appreciated. They remember your favorite food, your birthday, and everything else that makes you feel special. They're the biggest fans and cheerleaders for everyone they know and love; no matter what those people are doing, a *Team Player* supports it. *Team Players* know how to love and support unconditionally.

Their body is comfortable, supple, and round; their softness is the physical equivalent of the energetic support they offer to those around them. No one gives a better hug than a *Team Player.* Their capacity for empathy and compassion makes everyone around them feel safe, loved, and supported. Because of their energetic defense of sending energy inward and down into the ground, their presence is really solid and grounded, making them really good at holding space for other people.

Team Players have a genuine interest in the lives of others and feel best when they're connected to a lot of people—as long as they're in their core. If they're in their defense, they see people as needy and demanding, but when they're in their core, they see that people have needs so a *Team Player* can help take care of them. *Team Players* and *Charismatic Leaders* (discussed in chakra five, the Creative Communication System) make the ideal partnership. Without *Team Players*, *Charismatic Leaders* would be ineffectual and without *Charismatic Leaders*, *Team Players* would feel a lack of purpose. If you identify as a *Team Player* character structure, you may have been called a follower by other leaders and felt badly about your lack of personal drive or initiative, but that's because you were never meant to go it alone. It's only through being in relationship with others that you'll truly discover your real sense of reason and direction in life.

Personal-Power Energetics

Now that we've covered just about everything you need to know relating to your third chakra and the consciousness that governs it, along with the character structure associated with it—lets assess the health and function of your own Personal Power System. I encourage you to look to the connection you have to your own body and to use your life as a reflection for how well you manage the energy of your Personal Power System.

Remember from the chapter on the human energy system, that energy behaves in a multitude of different ways—it can be *excessive*, running too much energy; *deficient*, not able to generate enough energy; or *blocked*, meaning no energy is able to transmit through the chakra at all. Chakras can have both *excessive and deficient* characteristics, so the energetic state of your chakra may also fall somewhere in between any of those three states, depending on the situation. In an ideal world, however, we want our energy to be balanced and able to flow freely throughout our system. If a chakra is out of balance, not holding enough, or holding too much energy, we will need to either charge, discharge, or otherwise reorganize the energy of that chakra in order to bring it into balance.

Those who carry an *excessive* amount of energy in their Personal Power System might feel like the world is a battle ground and that they need to be in constant control of everything in order to feel safe; but a lot of times their need for control means being in control of other people's lives but not necessarily their own. They can be hypervigilant in controlling everything around them, because often, they feel out of control within themselves.

People with an excessive amount of personal power might be full of passion and enthusiasm; they're usually go-go-go kind of people, but they can also be overbearing and egotistical. Their excessive need for control is usually overcompensation for unrecognized power. They usually have big goals, or big visions, try to force others into doing what they want them to do, and don't really give others the free will to make things happen in their own time.

People with excessive energy in this system are usually really strong leaders, but they can come across as aggressive. They like to be in charge, but don't always manage their energy in a way that makes others want to follow them. They tend to enforce the rules, and demand others follow, rather than live by them honestly and invite others to join. They may have a lot of pent-up anger as a result of not knowing how to manage their power, and sometimes that energy manifests itself physically in the stomach area. In energy medicine, we call that the *bully-belly*.

In order to bring an excessive third chakra into balance, one might need to discharge a bit of energy through physical activities that release charge, however, excessive third chakras often need to do less, rather than do more. These people are already human-doings, and could use a little time simply *being*. Although this is challenging for them, as is learning to contain emotion challenging for the excessively-sensual person, those who can resist the temptation to act may find that underlying their excessive need to be busy, and constantly feel in control are feelings of stifled power, inadequacy, or exaggerated importance. Strengthening their connection to their emotions, their heart, and their ground will help to improve the balance of their personal power in a way that is healthy and inspiring.

In contrast to an *excessively* charged third chakra, those with a *deficient* amount of energy in their Personal Power System will lack the confidence to act at all. They don't have enough self-esteem to make choices and will often take on the role as a passive participant in life, preferring to follow orders rather than make decisions. This also absolves them of needing to take any responsibility, and thereby leaves them free from the consequence of making a poor choice. These people were often shamed in childhood or never allowed to take action or make mistakes. Or, they may have made a series of poor choices later in life and that too, diminished their confidence to act.

Those who have a deficiency in the third chakra lack the power and motivation to make changes in their lives and their bodies. They have a difficult time sticking to goals, and seeing them through. They avoid the responsibility that comes with taking action, and so remain in a state of inertia—never making moves, but never seeing changes. This perpetuates the cycle of being stuck in their lives.

In order to bring energy into a *deficient* system, one needs to connect to the things that energize them. Once a person understands what they value and what they want, they can establish a plan to accomplish their goals. But one can't establish a plan of action without first being clear on what they actually want. If I didn't have a vision of this book 10 years ago, I wouldn't have known I even wanted to write it and could have never applied the discipline it takes to make that goal a reality. I had to know what I wanted before I could ever carve out the path of realizing my dream. If you think you have a deficiency in your third chakra, try connecting to your Sensate System, your passions and desires and ask yourself what truly lights you up. Then ask yourself how you might need to act in alignment with those desires to bring about a goal you might like to achieve for your life. Maybe you want to start a weight-loss journey, a creative project, or get into a new relationship. If you want to lose weight, you might need to watch what you're eating or hire a coach. If you want to create a piece of art you may need to purchase some supplies. Or if you want to start a new relationship you might need to create a dating profile. If we want something out of life, we're going to need to enlist the help of our Personal Power System to make that wish a reality.

If you're Personal Power System is *blocked*, nothing in your life will be changing and honestly, you might not even care. You might be totally okay with your stuck-ness because you don't have the energy or desire to really change. Usually if you have a block like this in your system, it's because something really painful is stuck in your energy and staying stuck in your life means you never need to disrupt that pain or do anything that might encourage it to rise up to be healed.

To remove a *block* to your Personal Power System begin to analyze your relationship to power. How was your personal power supported in childhood? Were you allowed to act willfully and independently? Or was your right to act stifled by an overly controlling parent? How healthy is your ego and sense of self? Did you have trouble expressing your uniqueness growing up, and if not, how was that expression met by those closest to you? You can start to heal this center first, by connecting to it. Explore some of the following *questions for reflection* and journal your answers. Once we bring our attention to this center with the intention of healing it, energy will begin to flow to and through this center again.

Ideally, we want all our systems to be *balanced*. A *balanced* Personal Power System looks like an even flow of both passion and charisma, of goals and action. A person with a balanced third chakra is strong and solid in themselves, but not overbearing or forceful. They have a deep sense of connection to who they are in their core and the work they're here to do in the world. They're disciplined but not rigid, and they have no problem taking action on their goals and turning their dreams into a reality.

People with a balanced sense of personal power radiate genuine confidence. That confidence is born from a great dedication to their own self-exploration and to areas of personal interest. Even when their will is tested, they're able to apply the self-discipline necessary to remain true to their personal ideals and to stay dedicated to their goals, regardless of outside influence. These people know how powerful they are, but they don't need to boast about it, because their lives already reflect it—and usually, they're busy helping to empower others.

The Personal Power System is connected to the energy of fire and action. If you want to activate this system, you'll have to connect to something in your life worth moving on. Take some time to write down your passions, and then create a short list of future goals that are connected to your passions and within your reach. Don't go crazy with this; start small and build from there. You have to ignite the flame before you can stoke the fire. The power center is about remembering the essence of who you are, so try to remember what you did as a child that made time disappear and do that. If you enjoy art, set a goal to paint at least once a week. If you're a writer, set a goal to write for at least 5 minutes a day no matter what. If you want to lose ten pounds, start exercising for at least 10 minutes a day and build up to 20, then 30. If you're a mom who gives all her power to her children, you might really need time to reconnect with your core, so make alone time a priority and stick to it. If you're overworked and just need time to play, make consistent time for that. The power center thrives when discipline is applied, so find an area of your life that could use some discipline and take action! Action is the name of the game in the Personal Power System.

We tend to house a lot of unexpressed anger and rage in our Personal Power System. Sometimes, in order to get that energy flowing we need to express the pent-up emotion that's been stored in there. A great way to do this is to get a punching bag or a whiffle ball bat and a pillow and go nuts. It might seem strange at first, but you'll be amazed at how much energy gets released once you allow those gates to reopen. Anger and rage can be scary, so they're not exactly emotions we're comfortable allowing into our experience. It's incredible how many times in life we've been angry and have not been able to move that energy up and out of us, so we stuffed it down instead. That repressed energy doesn't go away, it just goes dormant, and it'll erupt as soon as the conditions allow it to. Exercises like these allow that energy to move through us in a way that's safe. Martial arts, boxing and other forms of physical discipline are other great ways of helping to move energy that's been stagnant or stuck in the Personal Power System.

Questions for Reflection

I suggest setting aside some time to sit with each of these questions and journaling on the answers that arise for each.

- How was your right to act autonomously supported in childhood?
- Do you feel confident in your ability to make decisions for yourself?
- How connected do you feel to your core self?
- Are you able to set goals for yourself and meet them?
- How good are you at applying discipline to your life?
- Do you feel the need to control others so you can be happy?
- Do you feel empowered in your personality?
- Do you tend to people please for others?
- Do you enjoy responsibility or do you pass-the-buck to others?
- How much discipline do you have over your diet and exercise?
- How well do you manage your own anger?
- Are you strong in your decisions or are you easily swayed by the opinions of others?
- How good are you at establishing boundaries with others?

- Are you clear on what you want?
- How confident do you feel in yourself?
- Do you experience addictions or times when you give your power away to things outside of yourself?
- Do you get to choose what you give your power to or is it chosen for you?

THE FOURTH CHAKRA—
THE COMPASSIONATE SYSTEM

*"Only when compassion is present will
people allow themselves to see the truth."*
—A.H Almaas

The first three energy systems are truly the driving force behind the lower self, and we need them to help us move about the world. Without powerful lower chakras, it's really difficult to connect to a personal sense of power and capability. Without the solid container they provide for the spirit to anchor itself, we may find ourselves struggling to accomplish worldly tasks—even simple ones, like receiving nourishment and maintaining basic survival needs, nevermind understanding our feelings, accomplishing personal goals, or achieving worldly success. The lower chakras, and the lower self serve our individuality, representing an aspect of our humanity that truly does experience itself as separate; separate from the planet, separate from one another, and sometimes, separate even from God. Although we *perceive* this separation as reality, we can never truly *be* separate, and that truth is revealed as we begin our ascent upward and expand further into our spiritual nature.

The lower three power centers are where the majority of our life-force energy remains stuck due to the traumas of the past. Until these centers are analyzed and cleared out, they function as the storage room where we hide away all of our childhood programs and rejected parts. Until we awaken to our lower selves, these programs run behind the scenes and will become the operating system of our lives.

St. Ignatius, founder of the Jesuits, once said, "Give me a child until he is seven and I will show you the man." This is how hypnotic our childhood is to our state of consciousness. As children our brainwaves are in theta state which is the doorway to the subconscious mind. From birth until about seven years old, we're literally in a state of hypnosis. We're little sponges that unconsciously absorb everything around us until we form our own opinions about life and our place within it. Once we reach seven, we basically just hit the repeat button, replaying the same tape over, and over, and over again.

After that, we learn our lessons through hardship. We usually grow through painful experience, not necessarily through awareness, and that's *if* we grow at all. But it doesn't have to be that way anymore. If we awaken the heart, we can choose to journey into the depths of our lower self, expose all our shadowy parts to the light of consciousness, retrieve our broken pieces and allow ourselves the gift of healing. Once we begin to analyze and process our programs and we liberate the energy that was stored in our lower self, we begin to merge with higher levels of consciousness—places within us where separation doesn't exist, where there are no borders or boundaries, no countries or religions, no polarity and no judgement. That's when we enter into union with what Christ called *The Kingdom of Heaven*—our heart.

To awaken the Compassionate System is to experience a homecoming; it's a return to the true-self—the *soul-self*. The soul lives in the heart and to come into the heart is to come into harmony with all life everywhere. The Compassionate System is an evolution beyond the polarity of our animal natures; it is an integration of our spirits and our souls. It's the space within where light and shadow meet and dissolve into one another; where higher and lower become symbiotic; where self and other become one; where inner and outer join to meet in the middle; where the masculine and feminine energies within merge and become lovers.

The heart is our most powerful ally. It's the epicenter of our being. It's the center of human balance. The heart chakra—our Compassionate System—is the bridge point, the median between our lower nature and the gateway to our higher-self. To live your life through the heart is to evolve beyond the ego-driven program of separation and the power-over-others paradigm. The wisdom in the heart understands that what we do to another, we do to ourselves, what we do to ourselves, we do to the planet, and what we do to the planet, we do to the universe. To live in the heart is to evolve beyond our individuality and to see our connectedness with *all* of life *everywhere*. The heart whispers to us one thing and one thing only, and that's to *be love*.

Love and Relationships

"The fundamental thing that happened, and the greatest calamity, is not that there was no love or support. The greater calamity, which is caused by the first calamity, is that you lost connection to your essence. That is much more important than whether your mother or father loved you or not."
—A.H. Almaas

The heart elevates us into a space of relationship that's far evolved from what we know in the Sensate System—the energy of duality and exchange, give and take, pleasure and pain, self and other. The heart is where all these polarities melt into *Oneness*. The heart brings us into a space of love that's needless, a love that's unconditional. This is a love that many of us can barely remember, a love that many of us never got to consciously experience.

Where senses are the motivators for the lower self, love is the motivating force of the higher-self. Love, not money, is the energy that makes the world go 'round. What would the quality of our lives be without the relationships we have? What would our experience be worth if it wasn't for the people, the pets, the children, and the great loves that give our lives meaning and reason? How would we even navigate if it weren't for the silent magnetism that pulls us in the direction of our heart's desires?

Love is everything that's real to the soul. It's what we're truly after. Love is the very breath that sustains us, the ineffable force that drives us, the glue that holds our families in place, and the essence that draws us into not just our relationships, but into life itself. Love is the ultimate power. It's the only force known to man that holds the potential to bring about a spiritual ecstasy, and in its absence, produce an indescribable despair.

Humans don't really understand love. Sure, many of us have felt it, but really, we have no idea what it is. Even though we don't quite know what love is, there's something we can be sure of, and that's what love is *not*. Love is *not at all* what we've been told it is. Love is not attachment. It's not jealousy. It's not control. And love most certainly isn't abuse. Love is truly beyond what can be expressed through words, but if I was to try, I would define love as the raw material we're made of. It's what emerges from within when we've allowed our hearts to open. True Love is alchemical magic. It's made of stars and galaxies and universes. Love is born of the spirit, not necessarily of the flesh. It comes through the body, but from a source far greater. True love is the way humans feel the presence of the divine and the way they connect to their own divinity. It's the very fabric of our reality and it's the underlying reason for everything we do. Every action we take is an attempt to either reveal love, or to shield ourselves from the pain of loves absence. Love is, literally, who we are. It's the most abundant force in our universe and it's the very fabric of our existence. It is ever-present, and always available. Humans have just become so traumatized by the absence of love, they've accepted the lesser energies of the lower self as a replacement for love and forgotten what true love really feels like.

As Hawkins once stated, love is like the sun—it's always shining. It's human-emotion, like fear, guilt, shame, grief, and despair that act as clouds, preventing us from basking in the golden rays of love's light. Genuine love has no opposite. It's the most powerful, sought-after force on our planet, and yet, the most widely misunderstood. Love isn't something that we get from or give to another person; that's *passion*. Passion is the fun stuff happening down there in the Sensate System, but passion is *not* love.

We humans have convinced entire generations that love is an exchange of energy between two people, so it's no wonder that we confuse sex with love. But love is not a possession to be owned or commodity to be exploited. It's not a Hallmark card or a box of chocolate. Love can't be bought in a store and given to your lover. Love is not a thing; it's an *experience*.

Einstein was talking about awakening to love when he told us to read our children fairytales. Tales of greatness, of magic, of slaying the darkness in order to overcome struggle all speaks to the heart and awaken the hero's journey lying dormant within each and every one of us, especially in children. Fairytales reconnect us to the energy and magic of love that lives in our hearts.

Growing up, we obsess over fairytales and we absorb the idea that perfect love is experienced through finding a perfect lover. When we're young and inexperienced, we fantasize about romance, we daydream about love, and wonder what it's going to be like when we finally experience it for ourselves. But far too many of us didn't witness a loving fairytale-romance growing up, what many of us bore witness to was actually a horrific tragedy. After witnessing fights, divorces, custody battles, affairs, and addictions, love for many is no longer perceived as fairytale romance, rather, love has become equal to suffering, and many vow against love completely. Or maybe our parents did have genuine love for one another, but we ourselves experienced a painful heartbreak at the hands of another that left us completely traumatized. That was my experience.

In truth, love is all there is, and for a time, it's all we knew. If we received the care we needed in our infancy to accomplish embodiment, that was an act of love. If we were held, nurtured, and nourished and attuned to, we grew into ourselves with our loving nature intact. The amount of time we spent connected to the essence of love depended entirely on how receptive and loving our own parents and family members were. Before the mind of the ego, and the illusion of separation took over, love was our primary language. And if we were fortunate enough to be born into a family that was peaceful and loving, we were able to maintain our connection to love. If our family was non-existent, dysfunctional, or abusive, we were left with the painful sting of love's absence. As children, we're so full of love that the only thing we want to do is express is our love—and then to be loved in return.

When we're little and still full of love, we haven't yet fully formed the armor, the blocks, the ego, or the protective barriers needed to keep ourselves from being hurt. We didn't even know that *being hurt* was a thing until we experienced it. We had no choice but to love because love was our essential state. That was until we experienced our first traumas, when our love was rejected and we felt the excruciating pain of loves absence. Human beings are genuinely such sensitive creatures that an abuse doesn't necessarily need be experienced to create a trauma to the heart, although that's often the case. All that's needed to create a wound to our Compassionate System is to feel as though our need for love has gone unnoticed. Once we experience the painful severance from our hearts, our entire lives become an *unconscious* attempt to return to love.

Once we disconnect from our own hearts, we crave love, just like power, from sources outside of ourselves. We all want to heal our hearts, but we don't really know how. And all our hearts are in desperate need of healing, mostly because they've been so badly wounded. For the majority, the vulnerable, sensitive space within us—the human heart—has known so much pain, so much sadness, and so much suffering that we've closed it down completely, forgetting entirely what it feels like for it to be open. To re-open the heart would mean exposing ourselves to vulnerability and addressing some of our repressed pains and traumas that caused us to close our heart to begin with. For this reason, many humans will resist the desires of the heart and actually go to great lengths to avoid opening them again.

The primary wounding of the heart occurs at the hands of our most loving relationships. Let's all just take a moment to, again, blame our parents—just kidding—well . . . kind of. The only way we can awaken and heal is to heal our hearts and to heal our hearts, we have to return ourselves to love. The way in is usually the best way out, so the most effective way to heal our hearts is in the same way they were wounded—through relationship.

When we're young, our budding egos are just beginning to develop and it isn't until we've reached a certain age that we even realize that our behavior has an impact on the people around us. Prior to that time, our energy is focused on strengthening and developing the lower self. Our primary goal is learning how to get our own wants and needs met. Before children have learned basic impulse-control they can be impatient, demanding, and impetuous, driven by the wants, desires, and instincts of their lower selves. They're still connected to love, but in a way that is very unconscious, and now that love becomes skewed by the presence of an ego and a growing sense of self-importance. Before the age of seven, children exist in state of oscillation, bouncing back and forth between the energy of their hearts' loving nature, while also learning to navigate the primal instincts and needs of being in a body. This can be a challenging time for a spirit integrating into the physical world and we need sane adults around to help us make the transition. I'm not sure if you've glanced around the planet lately, but sane adults are a bit hard to come by.

As children, our only desire is to give love and to be loved for being exactly who we are. We inherently understand that we're an original, that there's no other person who experiences the world in the way that we do or who can express it the way that we can. We want to share ourselves with the people around us. We want them to acknowledge the greatness that we know we are. But the average adult human doesn't remember their connection to the unconditional love we're begging for—they only remember conditional love—they only know a love that's based on approval. This form of conditional love is very confusing to children who understand innately that they're deserving of love simply because they exist.

A child's passionate, enthusiastic energy can be overwhelming, irritating, or downright frustrating to parents who are often bogged down by the weight of life's pressures. In their frustration, they often dismiss, reject, or shame a child's behavior, and subsequently withhold their love. Children feel the pain of that rejection in every ounce of their souls and over time, rejection will slowly close the heart of the child—the saddest thing to have ever happened.

Now, parents, there's no need to beat yourself up unnecessarily. No matter how perfect you try to be as a parent, there comes a time when you must accept that *you will* unconsciously wound your children. It's basically your job to do so. Children are little need nmachines, in constant need of recognition and attention, and it's truly impossible to satiate them all the time. That said, it's very important that we not intentionally reject our children's attempts at establishing a loving connection. No matter how frustrating it can be, we must try our best to really see and honor them, to attune to their needs, and to nurture the love in their hearts. Maintaining that connection is the only hope we have for the future.

No matter how much we're loved by our parents and the other adults around us, we're greatly influenced by our relationships with them and the early experience of relational love sets the foundation for all other relationships that follow. Sadly, no one escapes the experience of *conditional* love. It's just a part of being human and learning to navigate the lesser consciousness of the world we are born into.

When we're old enough, usually around age four, our Compassionate System starts to develop and we begin to understand that these relationships and the approval of our caretakers are the foundation of our happiness. In order to get our needs for love met we have to control our behavior, we have to learn the art of giving and receiving energy, and we have to learn how to be in relationship with others. We no longer see ourselves as inherently *worthy* of love. Now we have to *earn* it. So rather than *creating* our own world, we instead try to *fit* into theirs.

When we're young, we have two basic needs—to attach and to be independent. We need and desire love and closeness, but at the same level that we want to act powerfully and autonomously. This can place us in a polarized position as we grow and develop. At this stage in our development, we still rely on our parents or primary caretakers for love, so our personalities are molded by our relationships with them, as well as by our siblings if we have them, and other close family members as well. Basically, as children, we learn about ourselves and about the foundation of relationship through the approval or disapproval of others.

Our families, primarily our mother and father, teach us how to be in relationship with them by either accepting or rejecting us, by sanctioning our behavior or condemning it. And later in life we project that programming unconsciously into the world, and onto every one of our relationships. This sets the foundation for what Harville Hendrix, in his best-selling book *Getting the Love You Want*, calls the *Imago,* or the internalized relationship we have to our mother and father.

We learn to view all people and relationships through the lens of our inherited family program, until we awaken a higher level of consciousness within ourselves. We learn how to relate to women and what it means to be a woman based on the matriarchal energy that we observed in our own mother or mother figures. If our mothers were highly critical of us, then we'll expect all women to be judgmental. If our mothers were nurturing and supportive, then we'll assume all women are also that way and may even become critical of them if they aren't. Through the lens of our programming, we'll project onto women our ideas of what feminine energy is and what it should look like. Whether we ourselves are men or women, we will see all women, and the concept of femininity, through the lens of our own female role models. If our mother took care of our every need, we'll expect that from the women around us. If our mothers were driven and highly successful, we'll expect that from the other women in our lives. If our moms were unable to love us for whatever reason, we'll most likely have trouble in our relationships with women, expecting the same from them as we received from our moms. What our mother was to us becomes what femininity represents to the child-psyche within us.

We also inherit what it means to be a man, or how to relate to men, based on the masculine energy of our fathers or other male figures we grow up around. If we had a powerful, aggressive male figure in our lives growing up, the child in us will probably still be attracted to that quality in men as adults. If our fathers really saw us, attended to our needs, and made us feel special, then that's what we will expect from the men in our lives later on. But if we had an absentee father or one who abused us, then we may also attract men who abandon us or abuse us, or we might struggle to establish any solid and lasting relationships with men because deep down we don't trust the masculine. What our dad was to us, we project onto the masculine energy outside of us and this entire dynamic will continue to play itself out energetically as a way for us to come into consciousness so we can heal ourselves.

I remember a time when my husband, Mike, and I first got together, and I woke up to a flat tire. If I had lived at home, my dad would have fixed it. Probably before I even noticed it was flat. I most likely wouldn't have even had to ask my dad to fix the tire, because my dad was *that* Dad. He always knew if a headlight was out or if something was leaking, and he fixed it for me, usually without my asking, because that's just who my dad was. But Mike, is *not* my dad. Mike is very much like me, he's an artist and his thoughts are occupied by his own ideas and imaginings; they're not focused on tires, or cars, or fixing things. But when I realized my tire was flat, the part of me that had internalized my own dad projected that image onto Mike and I got upset with *him* for not fixing *my* tire! I learned very quickly that if I was going to be fully present in my relationship with Mike, and not my idea of what a man should be based on what kind of man my dad was, then I was going to need to stop projecting my own daddy images onto him.

We project onto our love relationships what we originally receive from our parents. This is totally an energetic attraction. It's why a lot of the time we somehow magnetize partners that have similar qualities to our own parents. It becomes an unconscious part of our energetic relationship signature. Many women try to emulate the positive qualities they inherit from their mothers or search for men who embody the characteristics of the father they admired. They judge themselves if they can't live up, or God forbid, are totally different. We also try to avoid the distasteful qualities that we absorbed from our parents. But try as we might, both the good and bad aspects of our parents get engrained into our psyches. Mommy and daddy issues are a real thing and until we allow them into our consciousness, we will continue to recreate them as a way to heal. The relationships we have today reflect the relationships we had back then. If you have relationship issues in your life, remember that the only way out is through. Be willing to use your mirrors, to look within and see what these relationships may be reflecting about your own inner child. Be willing to see how they're also helping you heal your relationship to love.

The Never-Ending Search for Love

"Romantic love delivers us into the passionate arms of someone who will ultimately trigger the same frustrations we had with our parents, but for the best possible reason! Doing so brings our childhood wounds to the surface so they can be healed."
—Harville Hendrix

As youngsters, we desperately longed for the love and approval of those closest to us and we'd choose the love of our parent or caretakers above all others. Unknowingly, we began to shape our own characters around the sanction or rejection of our parents' love. We learned to keep what was praised and reject what was rejected. Unfortunately, we became fragmented in the process. This fragmentation, or splintering of our spirit, is the beginning of separation, and separation from our true selves is the primary cause of dis-ease within us. The characteristics that we embody early on and the roles we learn to play within our families, become the roles we play throughout our entire lives until we begin the awakening process of coming into higher consciousness. These early relationship dynamics between us and our primary caretakers sets the foundation for our social-identities and all our relationships that follow.

Many of us absorbed the message early in life that we can either be ourselves, or we can be loved. By choosing love from others, we forgot the love of our own perfection. We bought into the story that who we are, as we are, is insufficient. We closed ourselves off to the love that arises as an inevitable result of being comfortable simply being ourselves. Thus begins the search for love—an endless, external quest to find the piece of us we feel is missing. As adults, we naturally find ourselves seeking completion in partnerships, friendships, and in our careers. We tend to avoid the gnawing sense of inner deficiency either by chronic avoidance or through endless searching. We try to perfect ourselves physically and if we can't do that then we judge others on their imperfections. We develop many other coping strategies as we ceaselessly look outside ourselves for a sense of fulfilment that can only be found by going within and reclaiming our hearts. For the most part, we don't even realize that we're unconsciously searching because the world tells us that it's normal to feel unfulfilled. Hollywood movies and romance novels have programmed our psyches into believing that we'll only be complete when we find *love*, and that love is *out there*. The problem is that it's not. Love can only be found *inside* of us. What we aren't taught is that the quest for happiness can't be found in the outside world as it stems from a lack of satisfaction within ourselves.

If our parents didn't know how to love us in the way we needed to be loved, our child mind sees love as equal to pain. But we know now that love is *not* pain, pain is only present when love is lost. We don't trust love so we turn our back on it. Love has never, and will never, turn its back on us. The great Creator has gifted us with love relationships as a way to heal our hearts and to reclaim our wholeness, yet we've used them to destroy ourselves even further. All our love relationships are here to serve as a reminder to return to our hearts. The areas that give us trouble are just the areas that need a little more love. Love heals all.

Want to know exactly how we screw love up? Good, because I'm going to tell you. Most of us closed our hearts off sometime during our childhoods and we only allowed them to open again when adolescent romance arrived. Have you cringed yet? I know I did. The first heartbreak is so bad, that even if we're totally armored up and pretend like it didn't hurt, we're lying. It fucking crushed us and we know it. Opening your heart for the first time after having it closed for so many years is like post orgasmic bliss! Your heart pops open and all of the restricted love force energy comes flowing into your life. The sky seems brighter, the sound of birds chirping is glorious, and you no longer want to strangle your little sister. You've finally reached humanity's most coveted achievement. You sit back and smile. *This Is Love.*

And then you find out your new boyfriend Billy just left you for your best friend Sally. The pain is excruciating. You can't breathe. You can't think. Depression sets in. You quit school. Your life is over.

What happened? Your ego screams out, "It was that asshole, Billy! He broke my fucking heart! I'LL NEVER LOVE AGAIN!" Your soul whispers, *"No, sweetheart, your heart is just temporarily closed."* You pause for a moment, ignore your soul, and continue plotting how to kill both Billy and your now *ex*-best friend.

That's what people do—it's what we all do—only we don't know that we've done it. We open our hearts, we allow our own love to flow through us, and we feel ecstatic. Then, just as we do with all our power, we place it in someone else's hands. In this case, it was Billy's. The love you felt when you opened your heart was yours. It was all you, baby! That's how good *you* really feel. But the moment we give the power of our love away to someone else, we make them responsible for our happiness. That's a lot of pressure to put on a person, don't you think? In the instant of opening our hearts, we're willing to place the source of our most creative force right into the hands of another human being. That's a vulnerable thought, right?

If we make someone else responsible for our love, we've essentially given them the power to hurt us, but if we know that the source of our love comes from within us, we will never *fall* in love again. In fact, we will *rise*, and all of our lovers will rise with us. When two people come together who truly understand the power generated from within the very center of their own chests, they have activated an unstoppable force. True love can happen at any time, with anyone. We just have to keep our hearts open, no matter what. If only it were that easy.

There's a reason marriage counselors are making a living by helping couples and families get their shit together—we clearly have no friggin' clue what we're doing when it comes to relationship—especially marital ones. Fortunately, we're entering into a new paradigm of relationship on our planet. The old paradigm of masculine/feminine, two separate parts coming together to form a whole, is fading while spiritual unity of individuals that has nothing to do with gender is emerging. *Spiritual Unity* is the marriage of the New Earth. A spiritual union is an empowered relationship, it isn't individual puzzle pieces coming together to make a whole. It's a spiritual union made by two individuals that are both doing the inner work of completing themselves, being responsible for their own hearts, and then joining forces to create something far greater than they could have ever made alone. It's only through our relationships with others that we can truly come to rediscover and know the truth of who we are. When relationship is done consciously, we discover the truthful, deep fulfillment of genuine healing and of becoming whole. It's how we get honest, real, and clear on who we are and why we're here. When it's done unconsciously, it's how we continue to play out the ancestral wounding of the heart. In an unconscious relationship, the wounded child within us automatically reacts to the circumstances of life in order to protect themselves from the pain that's felt when love is not present. Healing the heart is using our external relationships as tools to rediscover the most important relationship we have; the relationship to our own hearts.

When we discover people who we can be genuine and authentic with, the ones who accept us for who we are, blemishes and all, the ones willing to see us through our ups and downs and see both our light and shadow, our humanness and our soul, without judgement is when we learn the real value of relationship. These noble friends are diamonds in a sea of rough and unpolished rock. These relationships hold an energetic space for us, allowing us to reclaim our fragmented selves and grow into the people we were always meant to be. When we can remember how to love ourselves and let ourselves be loved by others, we are able to step fully into the emergence of the higher self.

No matter how many personal growth books we read, no matter how highly we've developed our intellect, no matter how spiritual we are or how much we understand life and its processes, nothing can teach us more than our relationships can. It's only through the willingness to open ourselves completely to others that we will uncover the truth of who we are. Do you think there would be 7.5 billion people on the planet if we didn't need one another for something? Anyone can reach a self-actualized state on their own, but not everyone can anchor that into their daily interactions with others. Not everyone can bring their inner enlightenment or self-realization into relationship. It can be incredibly challenging to remain peaceful and loving, open and communicative, clear and kind, when we're being faced with opposition from those closest to us and yet this is when the most opportunity for growth is present. Conflicts in our lives and relationships often reveal the deepest, most unconscious patterns of reaction in us, illuminating many of our childhood programs. How many times have you had a knee-jerk reaction to a situation in life and thought to yourself, "Oh my God, I've become my mother!" or, "My Dad used to say the same thing!" Meanwhile, you know that you could surely respond better than that. The moment we become aware of our defensive patterns is the moment we gain the power to evolve beyond them.

Harnessing the art of conscious relationship is using the conflict in our lives as initiations to transcend the limitations of our past conditioning. It means observing our behavior, reflecting on where we can improve, and then making corrections when they're necessary. These relationships are our greatest teachers. It's through conscious relating that we learn to move through the discomforts that we usually avoid and to maneuver through conflicts that cause us to become defensive. Conscious relationships are the foundation for both inner and outer alchemical growth. Self-observation through conscious relationship is the key to global transformation.

Affairs of the heart—the balancing of self-love and relational-love, inner-child and internalized parents, inner experience and outer expression, human-nature and the nature of the soul—can draw us into union with our highest potential. It can fully awaken our Compassionate System. It's through both love *and* heartache, conflict *and* peace, that we discover the truth of who we are. In love, we open, expand, and allow. We trust and accept our own vulnerability. We let our guard down ever so slightly and allow others into the most highly guarded and secret spaces of our soul. In love, we embrace the unknown with a willingness to be revealed in the process. We soften and we welcome transformation. In heartache, we search for answers. Tormented, we examine our broken pieces, bringing them to the light of consciousness to be analyzed, healed, and transformed. We reflect on our faults, our shortcomings, and our shadows. We review how we may have behaved differently to spare ourselves the burdensome grief that the absence of love presents.

You see, life is made of intelligent love. It has a brilliant way of teaching us through the vehicle of experiences, be they pleasant or painful (and we're sure to experience the pair), that if we allow our hearts to remain open, we'll gain equal wisdom from both. The heart beats in rhythmic pulsations just like life with its continuous expansions and contractions, reminding us that nothing stays static very long. Life is in a constant state of transition and so are we. The heart may break, but it will also break open, and when the heart is open, healing is able to flow through.

Forgiveness

"To forgive is to set a prisoner free and discover the prisoner was you."
—Lewis B. Smedes

Forgiveness is the superpower of the illuminated heart. Even the word *forgiveness* has the power to invoke strong feelings and intense emotion in a lot of people. More often than not, these feelings aren't totally pleasant. They're usually linked to a time in our lives when we feel we've been wronged or taken advantage of. Maybe they remind us of a time that we've been hurt or victimized by the behavior of another, or even by life itself. We hold on to past moments of betrayal in our minds and we keep them alive with our thoughts to reaffirm how others have wronged us and how we have done wrong by others. We judge and we condemn. We criticize and we crucify. We think thoughts of attack and victimization. We make ourselves right and others wrong and vise-versa. In doing so, we close the door on compassion and a willingness to understand others as well as ourselves. The soul within is silenced as the ego takes over and reinforces the illusion of our separateness.

The word forgiveness has the power to stir and awaken within us a deep humility, a calling to acknowledge our own faults as well as the faults of others. We can reflect on the painful moments in our lives that we're still holding onto—memories that we haven't been able to let go of—and we can recognize how these moments still exist in our hearts. These unforgiven memories may still be affecting us today. We now understand how painful events that had a negative effect on us caused us to close our hearts, and in response we built a type of armor around ourselves to protect us from similar events in the future. As a result, we now live in a way that's more connected to our past than to our present reality. To heal is to become whole and we can't be whole if our energy is invested in protecting ourselves from the pain of the past. Therefore, we must find forgiveness if we want to move forward.

We call upon the term *forgiveness* to find a willingness to accept our past and to let it go. But what if there's more to the word forgiveness than just finding mercy for the people who've hurt us, or for ourselves because we've hurt others? What if sparing ourselves from a lifetime of resentment, grudges, and bitterness is just barely scratching the surface of what true forgiveness is? *True* forgiveness is an action of the soul. It's an act of unshakable faith and has the power to move mountains, heal nations, mend broken hearts, and repair broken families. True forgiveness has the power to raise humanity above the current consciousness of division and competition. It has the power to restore us all to sanity and shift us from the chaotic paradigm of fear, ushering us gracefully into the union of universal love.

True forgiveness requires a radical shift in our perspective, a quantum leap from the divisive realms of the lower self, and into the Compassionate System of the heart. True forgiveness is the willingness to accept what *is*, to look at what *was* with the clarity of an opened mind, and to welcome what *will be* from a place of total non-resistance. I'm going to present you with a radical concept, and a somewhat controversial approach, that really shakes the foundation of what we've been taught about forgiveness. If it challenges you, that's okay—it's meant to. For obvious reasons, true forgiveness is going to sound like a lofty concept, and that's because it is. It's lofty in the way that it speaks to a level of consciousness much different than the one that occupies the average human mind, which is still heavily identified with the ego. We've all become so hardened and conditioned by egoic patterns, conflict from the past, and the need to defend ourselves that many of our hearts and minds have become closed to the spiritual growth that forgiveness brings. In order to transcend the present limitations of our lower selves, we must first acknowledge that another way exists—true forgiveness is the way. I'm asking you to expand your consciousness by presenting you with a truth that challenges your ego, a truth that only the heart can truly grasp.

The story of Jesus Christ on the cross is the most epic demonstration of the radical nature of *true forgiveness*. Even in the midst of his crucifixion, Christ is said to have proclaimed "Forgive them, for they know not what they do." True forgiveness presents the idea that the unconsciousness in humanity is worthy of forgiveness *because* it's unconscious! If someone is aware of something they've done, but unaware of *why* they've done it, can we really condemn them for it? Most of humanity is so severed from themselves that we're completely unaware of the suffering we've caused for ourselves, others, and our planet. Presently, we're facing our own extinction! We don't need any more judgement right now. What we need is radical forgiveness.

True forgiveness, although incredibly challenging to the ego, also supposes that there's nothing necessitating forgiveness because the lower self, the part of us that falls prey to deception, dishonesty, abuse, or betrayal, is not in fact *real*. It's not eternal, and therefore, not who we really are. The part of us that experiences pain, suffering, and separation is the egoic-aspect of ourselves that came into this sensory experience to learn and grow from it. The ego is not real in the eyes of the spirit, but that doesn't mean it's not without purpose. The ego that *believes in separation* is harmful before we come into higher consciousness. After awakening however, ego serves the soul.

Once we become aware of our ego and its function here on our planet, the ego can be used to serve creation in a powerful way. Isnt it ironic, it's the part of us we're *not* that helps us to remember who we really *are*? The part of us that's subject to death—the flesh and the ego—is not the whole truth of who we are. To become conscious of the ego is to align the ego with the power of the heart. That's what it means to die before you die. When the ego becomes conscious, it loses its power, and that power is recycled and utilized by the something greater than the ego.

The painful moments in life that create a need for forgiveness are the very catalysts that come to wake us up. They can harden us, or they can move us beyond the limited perceptions of the ego and open our hearts to a more compassionate understanding. The choice is entirely our own. To understand this fully is the very essence of the awakened heart, unconditional love, and true forgiveness. This is the level of consciousness that Christ embodied and it's the very same consciousness that's being reawakened on our planet today.

This kind of forgiveness isn't the place we start awakening from, it's our end goal. It's the enlightenment, the nirvana, and the salvation that we all seek. It's indeed a radical approach and it takes a serious amount of surrender to reach it. For some, it simply cannot be reached and that's ok. Sometimes it's enough just to know that this kind of forgiveness exists, even if we ourselves can't identify with it yet. Don't be discouraged if you find yourself in a place of resistance, anger, judgement, and non-forgiveness of another's actions. This has been the natural response for centuries. Many of us have been deeply hurt and our lives have been greatly affected by the choices of another. Sometimes we have to sit in that place for quite a while. If we're diligent with our inner work, *sometimes* that may lead us to understanding, to empathy, and to forgiveness. I'm in no way justifying or condoning the selfish, cruel, unjust, or downright malicious behavior that humans inflict on one another, nor am I condoning what's been done to our beautiful planet. I'm simply pointing towards a higher path of understanding and a freedom from the suffering it causes. Betrayal, abuse, and neglect can deeply scar us. They leave their mark on our spirits and change how we relate to others, to life, and to the world around us. However, these things can also awaken the true power of the heart—compassion for our suffering.

It's an enormous spiritual feat to bear witness to the frailties of the human condition without judgement. It takes an evolved mind to understand the nature of the lower self, in both ourselves and others. Judgement is easy. It's effortless to project blame onto someone else and neglect our own ability to respond with compassion. It takes kindness and grace to try to understand and find compassion for others, the wounded human condition, and the desires of the ego that cause us to behave in ways that are harmful. This can be especially difficult when we're the midst of conflict, and yet that's also where our greatest opportunities for growth and transcendence arise.

True forgiveness goes beyond the interpersonal conflicts and gives us a glimpse into a much greater design, one that allows us to see ourselves not as separate, but as individual pieces to an already complete and perfect puzzle. With this perspective, we can use each disruption in our lives to invite us more deeply into the understanding. We can see that the higher purpose of separation exists only to bring us closer to one another; that division has only served to return us to unity.

While we appear to be at different places on our individual journeys, we're really all walking on the same path back to Oneness. Once we begin to practice true forgiveness regularly, we begin to realize that humanity at large has been under a spell, amnesia, forgetfulness as to our true nature. It's only through our growing awareness that we can begin to break the spell that's caused us to go to war against each other. We can stop staking our claim and defending our positions, and we can start to acknowledge each other as brothers and sisters working together to *overcome* our adversities. Together we can create a more peaceful world.

Character Structure

Knowledgable Achiever
(Rule Keeper)

| Every hair in place, pelvis tucked under, tight muscles, "perfectly balanced" body, strong chin | Very neat, washboard stomach, can appear rigid, alert and thoughtful, detached |

According to Thomas: The Knowledgeable Achiever/Rule Keeper

For more information visit www.4dhealing.com.

According to Kessler: The Rigid

The character structure most closely associated with the fourth chakra is the *Knowledgeable Achiever*. The *Knowledgeable Achiever* describes the highest potential of this character, which is revealed when they're able to release their energetic defense and allow their soul quality to be expressed. We cover both the soul quality, and the defensive-quality of this character in the section on the Compassionate System, due to the fact that this structure has the most difficult time opening their heart and developing compassion for themselves and others. Kessler has identified its energy-pattern as the *Rigid* pattern; when threatened, a *Knowledgeable Achiever* will shut off all connection to their emotional centers, and although they become highly driven and disciplined externally, energetically they restrict and repress the inner world of feeling and emotion. The *Knowledgeable Achiever* epitomizes the closing off from their own heart, which is why Thomas has identified the defense of this profile as the *Rule Keeper*. A person who lives in the energetic defense of *Rule Keeper* will no longer follow the urges and impulses of their inner selves; they don't remember how to follow their heart because deep down they feel as though their heart betrayed them. Instead of following their heart, they follow the strict orders dictated by the rules they have established for themselves.

Those stuck in the defense of *Rule Keeper* will have a critical personality, strong feelings of judgement, and a lack of emotionality. They can have a very difficult time owning that their actions and behaviors effect the way other people feel, because they have defended themselves against feeling. They act in the way they *think* is right, not the way they *feel* is right.

This defensive pattern is thought to have been created when the Compassionate System was developing, and the task of *trusting self* was never fully accomplished. Children who grow into adults that favor this particular defense didn't have their inner world of thoughts and feelings validated, so their focus was shifted away from the inner realm and onto the material world. Those who display the *Rule Keeper* defense question their own self-worth; they don't trust that they themselves are inherently worthy of love and will discover a sense of worth in something challenging they can accomplish or through a goal they can complete. They'll look to discover their value in status, performance, and achievement and measure their self-worth by their ability to achieve excellence.

The most difficult characteristic of this pattern is that their extreme rigidity and perfectionism often prevents them from allowing themselves, or others, to simply be human, both flawed and imperfect. They have a very difficult time with emotion, not just their own, but everyone else's too. If someone is too emotional for a *Rule Keeper*, they will simply dismiss them, rejecting others often in the same way they were rejected, which lead to their need for defense.

Their body will be hard, inflexible, and rigid. They might even find that they condition their body into submission, the same way that they energetically deny and control any emotional expression. Instead of allowing life energy to flow through them and intuitively guide them, they see life as one big list of rules and guidelines to follow and feel personally responsible to see to it that they and everyone around them follows the rules to precision.

Life for a *Rule Keeper* is full of to-do lists and tasks to accomplish. Everything they do eventually becomes a job that needs to be done perfectly, and their rigidity about turning everything into work restricts the flow of genuine pleasure into their life. Those who favor the defense of *Rule Keeper* are most likely to develop a secret addiction or have an affair, as over time the denial and suppression of feelings generates a secondary need for sensation and pleasure that they'll feel guilty for having. They know they need to let their rigid walls down at some point, but can't give themselves permission, so they need to act out in ways that allow the emotions to escape. If and when they let their emotions out (which usually happens if they've been drinking) they're left feeling deeply ashamed, and that's why they keep these secondary pleasures a secret.

In order to shift out of The *Rule Keeper* defense and into the core soul quality of their *Knowledgeable Achiever*, they'll have to learn to reconnect to their own hearts. Their high level of intellect can actually only take them so far. In order for them to open their heart, they will need to reclaim the inner realm of feeling and emotion that they denied in their early years. This requires them to allow others back into their experience, so that they can be shown the way back to their own emotions. Remember, the only way out of pain is through the window of what created it, and in the case of a *Rule Keeper,* the wound was created in relationship to others. When a *Rule Keeper* feels safe enough in relationship, and becomes willing to let their guard down, they will lessen their need for defense and eventually stop seeing others as a source of criticism. They may eventually come to trust that other people actually have something to offer them and will become willing to learn about themselves from those they're close with.

Authentic relationship is vital; it becomes the life-blood for someone stuck in the defensive pattern of the *Rule Keeper*. Lovers and friends can show the *Rule Keeper* the way back to their hearts, and in turn, the *Rule Keeper* can show others the benefit of consistency, structure, and personal discipline. When a *Rule Keeper* opens their heart, they can really see life's larger framework and understand how everyone has an equally important role to play, and they're highly efficient at helping to organizing large structures. That's when they move into their core soul profile of the *Knowledgeable Achiever.*

Those who embody the profile of *Knowledgeable Achiever* were born to push the limits of what is humanly possible. They're perfectionists and live for the art of mastery in whatever it is that they do. They show others how to strive for greatness. Their body is strong, fit, and lean. They're goal setters and goal smashers. They're intellectually gifted and possess the ability to execute their genius impeccably. They're incredibly driven and self-disciplined, which makes them able to accomplish just about any task set before them with grace and ease, often to the point that it can make others jealous.

When a *Knowledgeable Achiever* is connected to their core, they're able to clearly see the larger perspective and know exactly how they fit into the grand scheme of things. They're organized and well-coordinated and could easily run businesses or manage large projects. They also have an uncanny ability to push their physical body far beyond what the average human is capable of, even when they're injured. They excel in in academia like no other profile. Even if they aren't a scholar, they'll effortlessly reach a level of mastery simply through their own research. In whatever subject they're interested in, they're likely to become more advanced than most experts with a degree. Because they're so logical and intellectually oriented, they're likely to attract an *Emotional Intelligence Specialist* as a partner; the *EIS* reminds them that it's important to make space for their feelings. To embody the *Knowledgeable Achiever*, is to reclaim the heart, and to reclaim the heart is to heal the child within.

Compassionate Energetics

Now that we've covered just about everything you need to know relating to your fourth chakra and the consciousness that governs it, along with the character structure associated with it—lets assess the health and function of your own Compassionate System. I encourage you to look to the connection you have to your own body and to use your life as a reflection for how well you manage the energy of your Compassionate System.

Remember from the chapter on the human energy system that energy behaves in a multitude of different ways—it can be *excessive*, running too much energy; *deficient*, not able to generate enough energy; or *blocked*, meaning no energy is able to transmit through the chakra at all. Chakras can have both *excessive and deficient* characteristics, so the energetic state of your chakra may also fall somewhere in between any of those three states, depending on the situation. In an ideal world, however, we want our energy to be *balanced* and able to flow freely throughout our system. If a chakra is out of balance, not holding enough or holding too much energy, we will need to either charge, discharge, or otherwise reorganize the energy of that chakra in order to bring it into balance.

Can one really have an *excessive* amount of energy in the heart? It seems an impossibility, especially now when the earth and her children are desperately crying out for love. However, it is possible to have too much compassion for others, to the detriment of self. A person with an excessive amount of love in their heart is an over giver, and can drain themselves of energy in an attempt to shower others with love. They often find themselves in co-dependent relationships or might even have an addiction to love. Those with excessive energy in the heart may consistently find themselves craving the high of *new relationship energy*.

I also notice this energetic tendency present in motherly or grandmotherly types, or those whose capacity for compassion can override another's need for growth. They will try to do the work for others or protect them from any painful experience they might encounter. Although the act is born from love, it can deny others the opportunity of doing the work themselves. Excessive hearts don't do this out of obligation like a *People Pleaser* would, but out of the *excessive* desire to express love. The *excessive* heart can't stand to see anyone in pain, for any reason at all.

In order to bring balance to an excessive Compassionate System, one will need to strengthen the balancing quality of the heart. Those who have an abundance of love will sometimes have to expand their hearts capacity to feel painful things as well as those that produce positive feelings—the balanced heart is capable of handling both. Those with relationship addiction may need to feel the emptiness they avoid through being in relationships, and learn how to develop love for themselves first before attempting to love another.

The heart is able to integrate the qualities of the lower self with those of the higher; self-containment and establishing healthy boundaries is a skill developed in the lower chakras that can be applied to balancing an excessive heart. When a person has healthy boundaries, they can love themselves as much as they love another and they'll also be able to feel when their acts of love are genuine, as well as when they're out of balance.

In contrast, those with *deficient* Compassionate Systems won't be able to access feelings of love very much at all. In fact, they're afraid of love. They're afraid of opening their hearts, most likely because they've felt the agonizing pain of heartbreak and aren't so willing to go there again. *Deficient* hearts want the experience of love, but don't necessarily want the risk associated with it. They're not comfortable with vulnerability or letting their guard down in relationship. Because they doubt their own lovability, they usually play games with love, to test out whether a person really cares. Deep down they want others to care, but not enough to ask for it or risk being exposed for caring themselves.

In order to bring balance to a *deficient* heart, one needs to rediscover their own innate lovability. Those with deficient hearts don't trust love, so they'll usually need to go back into their past and see where love became painful to them, which is most always through relationship. They may need to do a decent amount of work integrating the *imago,* their internalized parental figures and see where their most innocent love was rejected. These are the moments that close the heart and often require an act of true forgiveness to reawaken it. The more a person with a *deficient* heart is able to forgive others for the pain they inflicted, the more they reclaim their own self-worth, the more they'll love themselves and the more willing they'll become to accept love from others.

In a heart that is blocked, life loses its *aliveness* and becomes rigid and mechanical. People aren't seen as people anymore, they become more like inanimate objects. It won't matter to the person with a closed heart if they cause pain to another or hurt their feelings, because they're so disconnected from their own emotions. There's a tremendous amount of pain trapped inside a blocked heart, and opening it often requires the willingness to forgive others for the pain they inflicted, knowingly or unknowingly, as well as the support of a loving community or qualified therapist. If you feel as though your heart is blocked begin by assessing your early childhood experience of relationship. How well were you loved? Were you criticized for having certain behaviors or emotions? Which parent did you attach to most and how did their parenting style impact your personality? As soon as you begin placing your awareness on your heart with the intent to heal it, whatever is blocking it will begin to surface. Try to allow the process and avoid the temptation to prevent your feelings from arising, even when they're painful.

Ideally, we want the energy of our hearts to be *balanced*. Those who embody an awakened and balanced Compassionate System are truly warriors of love. They know how to forgive others because they understand what it means to be imperfect and infallibly human, but they're also deeply connected to the soul of humanity as well. They're empathic, understanding, and deeply caring. They aren't afraid of love and they don't shy away from darkness or pain either. Their balanced heart is capable of holding space for both powerful ecstasy as well as deep grief; they know how to handle an extreme range of human emotion with elegance and grace. Balanced hearts are often tuned to the frequency of children, animals, and the elderly, as they're usually the closest to genuine love. They can look deeply into the eyes of another and see into their soul; they feel their joy and their sorrow, they truly feel it all. They know where they're needed in the world and they show up as servants of love, no matter what.

Air is the element associated with the heart chakra, so to stimulate the Compassionate System of the heart, one simply needs to breathe. Controlling the breath can help us handle a variety of emotion without the need to close our hearts. Pain often causes us to restrict our breathing and close ourselves to what we're feeling; this creates all sorts of blocks and imbalances to the heart chakra. To reawaken and redistribute adequate energy to the heart, one can practice a variety of *pranayama,* or *breathing exercises.* These practices are helpful for both charging and discharging energy and moving through blocks created by painful events. *Pranayama* is completely free and you can do it anytime. I highly suggest an active breath practice like *Holotropic Breathwork* to get not just your heart, but all body systems flowing. You can do a simple internet search and you will find a variety of different breathing practices as well (just never do breathwork while driving). And as always, I suggest yoga as a daily practice to restore order to your entire energetic system.

Questions for Reflection

I suggest setting aside some time to sit with each of these questions and journaling on the answers that arise for each.

- How connected do you feel to loves presence?
- Do you feel as though your heart is open, closed, or somewhere in between?
- How open do you allow yourself to be in relationship to others?
- How comfortable are you with your own imperfections?
- Do you feel as though you can love all of yourself?
- Which parts are easier to love than others?
- Do you feel as though you need to restrict certain parts of yourself in order to be accepted by others?
- Are you able to forgive yourself and others for mistakes of the past?
- Do you judge yourself harshly and critically?
- How comfortable are you letting your guard down emotionally?
- Do you feel as though you need to achieve in order to be worthy of love?
- What are your internalized programs in relation to feminine energy/mother?

- What are you internalized programs in relation to masculine energy/father?
- How do your love relationships reflect your early childhood program?
- If you had never felt the sharp pain of loves absence, how deeply could you love?

THE FIFTH CHAKRA—
THE CREATIVE
COMMUNICATION SYSTEM

"Be yourself. Everyone else is already taken."
—Oscar Wilde

As we ascend into higher levels of consciousness, the ability to truly experience them becomes less and less assessable. Their borders are not quite as defined as the solid parameters of the lower chakras. We can't see them like we can our bodies or experience them like we do our emotions. We have to *perceive* them with our consciousness, and this requires training. But a great majority of human consciousness isn't concerned with this type of training, because our focus is still down there on the battlefield of the lower self—fighting over who owns what land and who screwed whose wife, or they're busy hoarding toilet paper or engaging in some other form of utter nonsense. To get the mortals to stop fighting amongst themselves over things that don't much matter, the gods might just send a major catastrophe our way, like Moses and the flood, or maybe a pandemic? Perhaps it has nothing to do with the gods. Maybe humans have actually *become* the catastrophe and the only way we're going to stop ourselves from self-destructing is by directing our energy inward (toward the heart) and upward (toward spirit), instead of outward (toward each other.)

We have to remember that everything in our universe is made up of energy—*including us*—and so we must become more conscious of how we direct this powerful, invisible force of ours. In the upper energy centers, we move far beyond the limitations experienced by the lower self; our experience becomes less *physical* and more *subtle*. As we move away from the material world of bodies and objects, our consciousness expands into fields of vibration, sound, and light. The Creative Communication System operates within a field of energy and vibration that the average human has barely glimpsed, but no one is excluded from its accessibility. There are aspects of this system that everyone perceives, but aren't entirely conscious of.

In order for us to catch a clear glimpse of this level of consciousness naturally, the body must be *vishuddha,* or *especially pure*—the Sanskrit name for the fifth chakra. This can be challenging. It takes a great deal of discipline over the impulses of the lower self, especially given our addictions to the tantalizing nature of the senses. To reach a level of consciousness where we're able to perceive the realm of *subtle* vibration is why the masters and devout seekers practiced fasting and spent extended amounts of time in prayer and meditation. It's also why shamans use plant medicines and other psychedelics. The less density we have grounding us to the earth, the higher our energy can get. I kind of happened upon this state of consciousness accidentally. Remember the raw vegan diet that catapulted me into a state of enlightenment? What I didn't realize at the time was that by drinking just green juice and smoothies and eating only salads, I was actually starving my body of any real source of grounding, so up I flew into the blissful oblivion known as the ethers. I quite enjoy it up there, actually, as it feels more like home to me than planet earth does. But this is not a place one can live in indefinitely unless you're a yogi, ascended master, or breatharian living on light and air alone, which sadly, I am not. I'm the kind of girl who needs to eat a potato from time to time. Anyway, when I was all blissed out on living foods, I was able to perceive the world of vibration clearer than ever before. Everything had its own frequency, its own energy, and its own *pulse*. Life really was *alive*. I know that sounds silly, but really, how many of us actually take the time to pay attention to stuff like that?

When the body reaches that level of purity, I think the brain starts firing different cylinders and making connections that the average human eating a standard American diet of French fries and Pop-Tarts can't really understand. It was like an acid trip, except it was completely clean, untainted by the stigma associated with mind altering substances. What I realized, over and over again throughout that experience, was that Einstein was right. We really are just energy! We each have our very own vibrational frequency, and it gets expressed directly through the vehicle of our Creative Communication System.

A more perceptible aspect of our Creative Communication System would be our voice and our hands, as they're a direct connection to our creative vibrational essence and the primary means of sharing ourselves with the world around us. It's the Creative Communication System that grants us the ability to bring what's happening inside of us and share it with the world outside of us in a way that we're in control of. It's one of our greatest tools for conscious self-creation. Most people who are fluent in the language of chakra consider the second chakra the most creative center, because it's from that area where humans create life. But second chakra creativity happens without our awareness; we don't direct that kind of creativity with our consciousness, rather the innate intelligence of our body creates life for us. In the fifth chakra, however, our conscious intention is very much a part of the creative process; here, we merge our minds with our body, our thoughts with our emotions, our hearts with our will, and then we share all of that through the creative power of our voice.

Our Creative Communication System, our fifth chakra, is what forms our *creative identity*. It's how we create ourselves in the world. The upper chakras don't necessarily adhere to a specific developmental time frame as the lower chakras do, but our Creative Communication System generally comes online between 7-12 years of age, when we're trying to figure out how we want to consciously create ourselves as individuals. At this stage, our social identity extends beyond the immediate family and grows to include a larger network. Now our identity is influenced by school friends, teachers, sports teammates, and various coaches as well.

If we've been able to establish and maintain a solid connection between our bodies, our emotions, our will, and our heart, then finding our voice and expressing ourselves within these new groups shouldn't be much of an issue. But if we disconnected from our feelings or had to restrict ourselves in order to gain acceptance in our family, then expressing ourselves with authenticity might prove to be a bit of a challenge. We have to have a felt sense of who we are, and what we feel before we know what we want to say. This is usually the age when kids start trying on all sorts of new identities and figuring out which ones fit, and which ones feel like them. Although communication is fundamental to this center, its power isn't restricted to verbal communication; this system is about all forms of creative expression. Wounding generally occurs at this level, when our right to self-expression isn't fully supported during this stage of our lives.

Can you imagine a world where everyone was capable of sharing themselves clearly, openly, and honestly without fear of judgement, rejection, ridicule, or annihilation? A world where people were completely in touch with their own inner voice and were able to connect it to the words that they spoke into the existence? A place where people could say what they mean without *being* mean? Where people felt safe speaking a truth that was their own, and not the truth that they thought others wanted to hear? A world where a difference of perspective and opinion was honored and respected? Where the art of active listening was practiced more, rather than simply listening with the intent to respond? We would surely be experiencing a world entirely different from the one that we presently live in. I personally think *we* are here at this time, to *create* that world.

So, what exactly is it that enables some of us to share our voice freely and without apprehension, when just the thought of speaking aloud is cause for extreme anxiety in others? How is it that some of us have no problem speaking up for ourselves, even yelling or screaming and using the power of voice to talk over or dominate a conversation, when others of us can barely muster the energy to tell a person what our name is? How come some of us can create art and share it freely, while others are terrified to show a single soul their work? Why does communication make some people shy away, shrink down, or shut off completely, yet make others become dominant, tyrannical, loud, and overbearing? And what would conscious communication between people actually look like if they realized their voices were created for the purpose of expressing their souls, not their bullshit?

Much like our ego and our social identity, our communication skills are behaviors that are learned and developed early on. And like everything else, they become part of an unconscious program within us. However, just like any other program in our lives, with conscious awareness and diligent practice we can learn a new way—a more effective way to communicate. This isn't to say that through the awareness of self our entire personality will change, although this can certainly be the case with the flowering of higher consciousness. What *can* be expected when learning our signature style of communication, however, is the emergence of a more mature, balanced, directed, and informed expression of the self. If you're naturally soft spoken, there's a good chance you'll remain that way. Your voice isn't going to change simply because you become aware of how you're using it. But the energy that *directs* your voice will change, and that makes all the difference.

In order to understand our communication style, we first have to look back into our childhoods and reflect on whether the right to use our voices and to express ourselves was either supported or stifled. If the basic right to self-expression through speech wasn't supported in early childhood, then it's highly likely it will be difficult for us to find and use our voices effectively today. I think I was the kind of kid who never shut up, and I must have gotten yelled at for it *a lot*, because for some reason I became terrified of speaking as an adult. I remember being in the energy medicine school, and we'd go around the circle each weekend for a check-in. There would still be 15 people speaking before it would even be my turn, but I struggled to hear a word any of them said. My anxiety at the thought of speaking in front them was so bad, it often made my head feel fuzzy and my hands sweat. My heart would pound out of my chest to the point that I thought I might pass out. I had to really work hard at learning to share myself with the group through the power of my voice. I was much better at sharing myself through art or expressive dance than I was through speaking. But now that I've rediscovered the frequency of my soul and I know what I'm here to say, you can't shut me up!

If we want to understand how our Creative Communication System got programmed, we needn't look further than our own childhoods. Alas, the dreaded childhood program again. (By the end of the book, we'll be thanking our parents for screwing us up so badly. We might even remember how our souls picked them to specifically screw us up in just the right way, so we could be right here, right now, doing this work and healing the planet.) We can probably just look to the communication styles that were mirrored for us growing up to discover our own. If our parents were fighting, did they shout at one another aggressively while they tried to defend their own position? Or did they detach, disassociate, and passively dismiss each other? Did one parent keep secrets from the other, afraid how the other might react if they were told the truth? When our parents were faced with challenges in life and in relationship, did we witness appropriate conflict resolution and problem-solving skills, or did we observe childish gossip, passive aggressive cross-talking, blaming, and finger pointing with no real aim at a solution? All of this absorbed information becomes a part of our own internal program that then gets played out in our adult relationships. As children we don't learn from what we're told, we learn from what we witness and experience. If our parents had messed up communication skills, so do we. (I think I hit the motherlode in that department!)

Learning to break the habit of dysfunctional communication can be one of the more challenging habits to break. It calls for a significant amount of self-awareness and a willingness to listen to others without judgment or the need to correct them. It takes an enormous amount of effort to break the habit of placing blame on others, and to instead focus on how we might be able to improve our reactions to them. It also takes an energetic commitment to move through the inevitable discomfort that's caused by not reacting to life in the same way that we're used to and changing a pattern of behavior that has become engrained. It's a humbling process, but the positive results produced from learning the art of conscious communication are undeniably worth the effort.

The Art of Communication

*"People fail to get along because they fear each other;
they fear each other because they don't know each other;
they don't know each other because they have failed
to communicate with each other."*
—Martin Luther King, Jr.

Everyone has their own signature style of communication, varying greatly depending on programming, personality, individual characteristics, and one's overall level of screwed-up-ness. Some of the more commonly recognized styles of communication are passive, aggressive, passive-aggressive, and the ideal style to strive for, which is seldom heard yet much more effective, clear and assertive.

Those who display a passive communication style are more inclined to stay quiet and less likely to express their authentic selves. This is especially true in times of conflict. Passive communicators will often fall into the categories of caretakers and thinkers. These more passive personality types are more apt to yield to a stronger personality than they are to challenge one. These people would rather stay quiet in order to keep the peace than to speak their mind and potentially create conflict. They are the softies and the world sort of beats up on them, which can lead them to harboring unconscious resentment as a result of their many unexpressed, "No!" and "Fuck you!" feelings they've stuffed down. These people have a really hard time setting personal boundaries and saying no to others.

Aggressive communicators are entirely the opposite. They are the jerks. Where passive communicators lack outward expression, aggressive communicators thrive on it. This communication style is common for the Challenger/Enforcer personality because they live for the fight! They're intimidating, loud, intense, and demanding. They use their words to control others through direct criticism, threats, and other verbal abuse. They hardly ever listen to the concerns or opinions of others because they're more focused on pointing fingers and placing blame. It's pretty rare to get them to accept responsibility for their reactions.

A pretty common style of communication used by all personality types is a combination of both passive and aggressive. Passive-aggressive communicators have a difficult time expressing how they feel to you directly. They're still jerks, they're just snide about it. Instead of yelling in your face, they'll just mutter under their breath and use physical gestures like rolling their eyes to piss you off. These people use indirect messages, like the cold shoulder or the silent treatment, to get their point across. Passive-aggressive communicators usually know how they feel and what they need, but they can't find the voice to express it, so it comes out sideways through cruel remarks, muffled complaining, gossip and other jerkish tendencies.

All of these communication styles will work to get a point across, but they also leave a lot of room for miscommunication and unnecessary conflict. Remember, our voice is our most powerful tool for creating ourselves in the world. The voice is the sword of our intellect and only we can decide how to wield it. We can use it destructively to cut others down, or we can use it constructively to cut ourselves free.

In an idealistic world, we'd all be spiritually mature adults about the way we use our voices, and we'd be moving in the direction of clear and assertive communication. Assertive communicators take ownership of their feelings and express themselves with clarity and certainty. These people know what their needs are and speak them aloud, while also being alert to the needs of others. Their skill for active listening is equally as cultivated as their own self-expression. They've harnessed the art of conscious conversation and use both their voice and body language for enhancing the connections they have with others. This doesn't mean they don't experience conflict in their relationships—they do—it just means they're not dicks about it. They navigate conflict without the need to silence their own voices in the way that a passive communicator would. They don't become overly combative or unnecessarily argumentative like the aggressive types do. And they don't make passive aggressive remarks in the hope that someone will pick up on their underlying attitude and change the behavior that's pissing them off. A clear and assertive communicator says exactly what they mean and expresses themselves in a clear and direct way, without avoidance and without being overly emotional or confrontational. They're aware of how they've positioned themselves and they consciously choose the tone and volume of their voice. These people understand that *how* their words are spoken is equally as important as *what* is being said.

Some tips for shifting into a more assertive approach include using *I* statements instead of *you* statements. Communicators using *I* statements accept ownership of their voice instead of being accusatory. Basically, they stop blaming everyone else and take some responsibility for themselves. If you're always blaming the person you're arguing with, they're going to feel the need to defend themselves. If you're using *you* statements against them, they're going to feel attacked. If you turn it around on yourself, they might be able to listen. Most people don't even argue with the intent to actually solve problems, they just fight to discharge displaced energy. Ask yourself honestly, what's the end goal of your conflict? If it's not to find peace, don't even engage. If you're really just pissed off and need someone to fight with, go hit a punching bag or take a run. Find another way to move your energy. When a conflict arises, if both people are in the position of defending themselves, a resolution will never come to be. But if we can take ownership for how we feel instead of placing blame on the people around us, if we can ask for our needs to be met instead of pointing out what others are doing wrong, we are making the space to focus on a solution instead of creating a bigger problem.

People with a healthy communication system know how to hold strong boundaries for themselves. They're aware of how they feel and they're clear about what their needs are so people are less likely to take advantage of them. If you have a tendency towards passive or passive-aggressive communication, you might find that people take advantage of your submissiveness and use it to get their own needs met. Saying no can be really hard for passives because they feel they have no choices and other personality types rely on that. Passive-aggressive communicators might say *yes* even when they want to say *no*. This builds resentment. Changing this pattern and learning to speak up for yourself can be difficult at first, but once a boundary has been established, others will learn to listen to you and respect you. The more you practice tuning into yourself and listening to your inner guidance, the easier it will be for you to speak up and the less people will take advantage of you.

Learning to manage your emotions can also play a huge role in achieving a clear and assertive communication style. During conflict, it's easy to become upset or angry, but allowing our emotions to overwhelm us can inhibit our ability to express ourselves clearly. If we're feeling too upset, it's better if we wait until we're calmer to have a conversation, otherwise our Creative Communication System gets thrown off balance. The next thing you know, we're all droppin' F bombs on each other and a resolution becomes next to impossible!

It's important to take it slowly when you're shifting up the energy of your Creative Communication System—it takes a bit of time and practice—and it usually gets worse before it gets better. It's taken years for you to memorize the program that messed you up, so it'll probably take a while to un-screw yourself. Give thanks to your noble friends for helping you figure your self out. If you've been an aggressive communicator, the people around you are going to expect that from you. You're probably their go-to target for feeding their need for conflict. Get ready to turn down an argument. If you've always said *yes* to helping others, the people who have taken advantage of that are still going to come to you with all their neediness. Just because you've decided that you want to behave differently or have made an internal decision to change, doesn't mean that others are going to respect that.

If all of a sudden you decide that you're going to speak up for yourself and you're no longer going to engage in aggressive arguments or help the people who are used to using you, you're bound to get a little push back. The people in our lives are relying on us to behave the way we usually do, and unconsciously want *us* to stay the same so *they* don't have to change. This isn't because these people don't care about you or your needs, it's because as humans we get comfortable with what's familiar and change is hard for us. It takes a bit of time and consistency to retrain the people in our lives and to establish a proper relationship, but when we stay committed to clear communication about our needs and set healthy boundaries for ourselves it creates a ripple effect, and we'll find that all of the Creative Communication Systems around us will come into balance as well.

Communication in Relationships

One of my favorite viral images that I see shared all over various social media platforms reads, "I hate small talk. I want to talk about atoms, aliens, death, sex, magic, intellect, the meaning of life, faraway galaxies, the lies you've told, your flaws, what keeps you up at night, your insecurity and fears. I don't want to know *what's up.*"

I love this quote not because of what it says, but because it illustrates the desire for honest and intimate relationships, for the real and meaningful conversations that deep down we all strive for even if we're unaware that's actually what we want. If our only purpose in life is to be who we are and to share that with others, it might make sense for us to learn what authentic communication looks and feels like. What makes this kind of intimate communication difficult is that a majority of people find the truth of who they are terrifying. Either that, or they really just don't know who they are. Even with their most significant others they'll use all sorts of strategies for keeping their vulnerable and authentic selves protected. They'll gossip, discuss the weather, or worse, they'll talk *politics.*

I know people that have been married more than forty years and they *still* don't know each another. I also have friends who have more intimate relationships than some married couples. The need for intimacy isn't just for lovers, it's a deep desire within all human beings. It's why we have best friends. It's the desire for genuine companionship and connection. The desire for intimacy stems from the basic need to be seen, heard, and understood for who we really are, for what makes us, *us*. Without intimacy, our relationships barely skim the surface of the truth of who we are. As a result, our lives feel shallow and devoid of deeper fulfillment.

If we're friends, I don't want to know what you ate for dinner last night (unless you're Anna; *then* I want the recipe), but I want to know *who you are*. I want to know what your dreams are, what your soul is made of. I want to know what makes you tick, what turns you on, what sets your soul on fire. I want to know what you're most afraid of, what your craziest fantasy is. I don't want the pulp, I want the juice, baby! I want to get real with you, because the deeper you go with me, the deeper I can go with you and the more rooted we get in our relationship. The more solid the roots are in our relationship, the higher we can reach into the heavens of our Spirit.

But we can't get deep if we're afraid to really see ourselves and each other. We have to be willing to be vulnerable so people feel okay to be vulnerable with us. That's how our Creative Communication System works in relationship. Just as we can use our words to cut people down or cut them free, we can use our Creative Communication System as a way to let people in or to keep people out.

How much time do you spend in communication really letting people into your inner world, and how much time do you spend keeping them out?

When we gossip, report the facts about the weather, talk about what celebrity sex scandal is happening this week, or whose dating who, we're really just avoiding what's real most of the time. We're afraid to give voice to what's really happening inside of us, so we use our voices to talk about a bunch of meaningless shit. I hate to burst your bubble, but most people don't really care about those things anyway. And if they do, they should read this book and then get on with the business of creating a life worth talking about! If your goal is intimate conversation with the people closest to you, make the first move. Get vulnerable with them, and I'd bet they'll follow your lead. It might turn out to be the best communication you've ever had.

Character Structure

Charismatic Leader
(Enforcer)

| Head forward, archetypal beauty, intense energy in eyes, extended solar plexus, seductive energy | Aggresssive, large shoulders, wedge shape, bully belly in solar plexus, stare you down 0-100 in second, dangerous |

According to Thomas: The Charismatic Leader/Enforcer
For more information visit www.4dhealing.com.

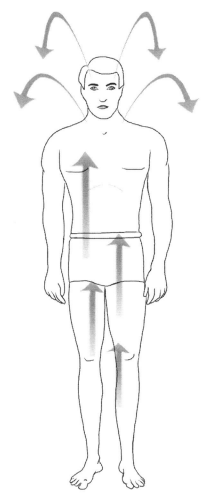

According to Kessler: The Aggressive

Images from The 5 Personality Patterns *by Steven Kessler © 2015. Used with permission.*
For more information visit www.The5PersonalityPatterns.com

The character structure most closely associated with the fifth chakra is the *Charismatic Leader*. The *Charismatic Leader* describes the highest potential of this character, which is revealed when they're able to release their energetic defense and allow their soul quality to be expressed. We cover both the soul quality, and the defensive-quality of this character in the section on the Creative Communication System, due to the fact that this structure has the most difficult time connecting to their voice and clearly and assertively communicating their intentions and their will with others. Kessler has identified its energy-pattern as the *Aggressive* pattern. When threatened, an *Aggressive* person will use their voice and their Personal Power System to become larger and louder than the perceived threat; energetically they feel the need to be bigger and more powerful as a means of gaining control over the situation. Deep down they fear losing control, which is why Thomas has identified the defense of this profile as the *Enforcer*. An *Enforcer* doesn't necessarily need a set of rules to *follow* like the *Rule Keeper*, in fact, they don't really follow anything, but they will make sure to *enforce* that you do.

An *Enforcer's* body will be strong and solid, usually with broad shoulders. They're built for battle and battling is what they're good at. Sometimes the massive energy they carry for movement, motivation, and action balls up in their Personal Power System as a result of unexpressed power and creates what's known as a *bully-belly*. Because an *Enforcer* often doesn't direct their power with conscious awareness, it builds up inside of them and escapes unintentionally in the form of aggression. If that energy doesn't have an expressive outlet like physical exercise or a personal mission, it will build up and get projected onto others. An *Enforcer's* energy will tend towards anger and irritation, arguing with others over differences of opinion rather than channeling their energy for a worthy mission.

Enforcer's will naturally be dominant and masculine, even if they're women. They tend to be *do-as-I say, not-as-I-do* kind of people. They'll easily point out fault in others, even for qualities they themselves possess but don't readily accept. They'll likely spend a lot of their time complaining about others, or telling them exactly how they should be living, and not leading by example. *Enforcers* are likely to be driven by the underlying emotion of anger, which is really there to motivate them to move towards a personal mission or some other form of inspired living. Deep down they know they're powerful and should be fighting for something, but if they aren't connected to a deeper mission in life, they'll channel their energy by fighting people instead.

The real issue for those stuck in the pattern of *Enforcer* is that they were never allowed to be as big and powerful as they know they are. They didn't have a safe container growing up that allowed them to harness their power, and so, they never really learned to trust the adults around them. The *Enforcer* defense is thought to have developed during the time in childhood when the task of *trusting others* wasn't accomplished. Those who favor the *Enforcer* defense were usually very mighty little children, with big, explosive emotions and if they didn't have a parent that could hold space for those larger-than-life feelings, the child never got to express them. Most often, they we're rejected for having them, and sometimes, they got much worse than rejection; their personal power was abused out of them.

All children need to experience a felt sense of safety around the right to express themselves, but they need guidance in learning to navigate their individual will and personal power. This also means they need a safe space for learning how to do that in an appropriate context. They need to be able to feel powerful and also feel safe in expressing that power. Power can be a scary feeling for a child because power and rage are very similar sensations. Unexpressed power in a *Charismatic Leader* turns into the rage of an *Enforcer*. Many of our parents are full of unexpressed power; they couldn't allow us to be powerful as children because they themselves weren't allowed to be powerful, and so, our power threatens them. Expressions of personal power as children are often met with years of the suppressed rage from our parents. In order to protect ourselves from that rage, we create a variety of defenses, and the *Enforcer* is just one them. *Enforcer* children don't *leave* like the *Thinker*, or *merge* like the *EIS*, they don't *endure* like the *People Pleaser*, or become *rigid* like the *Rule Keeper*, they challenge authority, often becoming *aggressive* themselves.

If *Charismatic Leader* children didn't feel that their caregivers were kind and supportive, while simultaneously holding firm but loving boundaries, they never learned to trust anything outside of themselves that was bigger and safer than they were. An example might be in the case of parent who is too aggressive or controlling, never allowing the child to explore their own felt sense of independence and power. When a child naturally expresses their personal power and a more hostile or dominant personality squashes their attempt to be powerful, the child personality creates a defensive pattern out of fear and the need for safety. The child never learned to trust the parents, and therefore, they had to become the biggest energy in the room in order to feel safe.

The same pattern can occur in a child whose caregiver was too lenient and never established appropriate boundaries. The child personality feels the pressure of having *too* much power and will create an *Enforcer* defense to feel in control. Later in life when a *Charismatic Leader* feels afraid, anxious, or unsafe the pattern of needing to be bigger, stronger, or scarier than others will tend to re-appear.

In order for an *Enforcer* to shift out of their defended state and into their core soul quality they will need to reconnect with their personal power. They'll need to realize what truly motivates them and channel their energy into living in alignment with what inspires them. They'll also need to relax their defense enough to trust others, as learning to harmoniously navigate their relationships with others is a vital piece to their mission. When an *Enforcer* realizes that not every disagreement or challenge is an invitation to battle, and they finally stop waging a war *against* others, and instead get clear on a mission worth fighting *for*, they will move from the *Enforcer* into the *Charismatic Leader*.

When a *Charismatic Leader* is living from their core they are focused on a personal mission, their lives will be so inspiring that others will happily follow the example set before them. *Charismatic*

Leaders were born to lead. They're the warriors, fighters, competitors, athletes, and champions! They're the ones that would be willing to die for whatever it is that they truly believe in. They can also be the actors and the actresses of the world, the seducers and seductresses, the people who know that life is a stage and they're in the starring role.

They have an uncanny ability to entice and persuade the people around them. *Charismatic Leaders* don't fit one specific body type, they come in all different shapes and sizes, and they're built precisely for their unique purpose. Generally speaking, *Charismatic Leaders* have a relatively athletic build, strong and stocky, or sultry and seductive. Depending on what their secondary character structure is, they may find that their form differs slightly from the standard *Charismatic Leader's* body structure, but one thing will be certain—they claim the physical space they live within, and their presence is almost always known.

When a *Charismatic Leader* accesses their core and discovers what they are truly passionate about, they will pave a path in that direction and encourage others to follow, but they will always lead by example, never by force. They *show* people what it means to live in alignment with passion and to be driven by a deeper sense of purpose, rather than simply telling them. They have massive and expansive energy, and they might even overwhelm people with the immensity of their presence. Those who can handle their intensity will naturally gravitate towards them and get behind their mission. Their purpose driven lives are greatly inspiring. Martin Luther King was a *Charismatic Leader* who influenced millions with his dreams of freedom and equality. He was never outwardly forceful because he didn't need to be—his true power came from living in alignment with the natural quality of his soul—as will all true *Charismatic Leaders.*

Creative Communication Energetics

Now that we've covered just about everything you need to know relating to your fifth chakra and the consciousness that governs it, along with the character structure associated with it—lets assess the health and function of your own Creative Communication System. I encourage you to look to the connection you have to your own body and to use your life as a reflection for how well you manage the energy of your Creative Communication System.

Remember from the chapter on the human energy system, that energy behaves in a multitude of different ways—it can be *excessive*, running too much energy; *deficient*, not able to generate enough energy; or *blocked*, meaning no energy is able to transmit through the chakra at all. Chakras can have both *excessive and deficient* characteristics, so the energetic state of your chakra may also fall somewhere in between any of those three states, depending on the situation. In an ideal world, however, we want our energy to be balanced and able to flow freely throughout our system. If a chakra is out of balance, not holding enough, or holding too much energy, we will need to either charge, discharge, or otherwise reorganize the energy of that chakra in order to bring it into balance.

An *excessive* amount of energy running through the Creative Communication System will manifest as a voice that is strong and loud, sometimes overbearing. These people tend to interrupt or talk over others, and they won't actually take the time to really hear what another is saying. Sometimes they'll resort to yelling and screaming to get their point across. They're often *Charismatic Leaders* with an aggressive communication style. There's so much energy behind their voice that it leaves little room to take anything else in, and listening is an act of taking energy in. Those who carry this kind of abundance of energy will have no problem speaking their mind or projecting their voice, but often what they have to say comes across as an argument, a complaint, or a demand.

Another type of person that manifests an *excessive* Creative Communication System that isn't an aggressive might be more like a thinker, who chatters as a way of discharging the excessive amounts of energy swirling around in their thoughts. I'll tend to do this when I'm nervous or if I'm meeting new people and I'm trying to establish a connection with them.

In order to discharge some of that excessive energy, one first needs to establish a connection to the true meaning and reason for their voice—which is to share their soul. Strengthening the chakras above and below the throat will also help to bring the throat into balance. Once a person becomes really clear on *why* they want to say, *what* they want to say, their delivery will change. The *why* is of the heart, the *what* is of the head, and once a person is able to connect those power centers with the power of their voice, the message that comes out is usually clear and direct, rather than dominating or anxious.

In contrast to an *excessive* fifth chakra, those with a *deficiency* in their Creative Communication System will struggle to share themselves authentically, both in voice and other forms of expression as well. They might even be afraid to speak altogether. Their voice will be weak and timid, or otherwise quiet. They're usually shy, and if they do allow themselves to speak, it might be done fearfully. Sometimes these people know what they want to say, but they just have a difficult time saying it. Other times they don't know what they want to say, because they don't really feel connected to who they are. If an individual doesn't really know their truth, how can they speak that truth into reality?

Clear communication for a person with a *deficient* throat chakra can be challenging; they might not think to speak at all. Often there is an excessive amount of energy in the head and it just never makes its way down into the vocal chords. And if it does, it's not always clearly expressed.

To balance a *deficient* fifth chakra is to bring energy into the system. Where the excessive has too much, the deficient has too little, however, both will benefit from strengthening the throats connection between the head and the heart. Chanting, singing, drumming, toning, and any other activity that uses the power of vibration and the voice is a fantastic way to get the energy in this chakra moving.

If the energy in the throat chakra is *blocked*, a person won't be able to access the power of their voice. They'll have great difficulty expressing their truth and have a hard time speaking up for themselves. They're usually passive, or passive-aggressive communicators. They also tend to be lie-tellers and will lie to themselves and to everyone else. Many of them have lost connection to who they are and how they feel so they'll say whatever they think another person wants to hear. A block in the throat can manifest from the inability to speak our truth when we were younger that grows into the fear of speaking or expressing when we're older.

If you feel as though your throat chakra is *blocked*, begin by assessing your early childhood experience of creative communication. Were you allowed to speak your truth? Was your truth heard, understood, and validated? Were you allowed to express yourself in a variety of ways until you felt a connection between who you are inside and how you expressed that outwardly? To release a block, one needs to begin reconnecting to the power of their Creative Communication System. This can be done by journaling, blogging, or making videos—any outlet that allows a person to share their truth. Screaming also helps. When energy has been stuck or stagnant in the Creative Communication System for a while, it can take a bit of effort to get things flowing again. Most will find it helpful to get out all of those No's! and Fuck You's! that've been stifled over the years. I like to move this energy by screaming obscenities, mostly in my car while driving. You might risk looking insane to passersby—but it works. Combining this exercise with the exercise from the Personal Power System is a potent practice. So, get out your punching bag or plastic bat and beat something up while getting out all of the things you wish you said. Your communication system will thank you for it. As soon as you begin to place your awareness on your Creative Communication System with the intent to heal it, energy will begin to flow into that area—especially if you give it permission to let out the junk it's been holding onto.

Ideally, we all want a *balanced* Creative Communication System. We want to know who we are, and we want what we say to be meaningful. A personal with balanced energy in the throat can do just that. Their very lives resemble a work of art. These people understand that everything they think, speak, feel, and act is a creative process. They've come to understand the inner territory of their own soul, and they use the tools they've been given to express themselves, be that through writing, art, music—whatever brings them joy. They will be clear and assertive communicators; they know how they feel inside, and by communicating their own truth they can help others gain access to theirs. There's a balanced tone to their voice and they speak effectively with ease and grace. They also listen intently and hold space for others to share their truth as well. You'll be able to recognize a balanced throat chakra in your favorite motivational speaker, podcast personality, talk-show host, author, musician, or anyone else in the world who is powerfully expressing their soul through a variety of creative works.

Sound is the element associated with the Creative Communication System so listening to music, chanting, singing, and sound healing are all wonderful ways to support this system energetically. Remember, your Creative Communication System is made for you to creatively express your unique vibration into the world. Do you do this with your *voice*? Through your *art*? By *writing*? *Cooking*? There are an infinite number of ways we can express our frequency that will benefit the collective. Find your souls frequency, and then figure out a way to bring it forth into creation!

Questions for Reflection

I suggest setting aside some time to sit with each of these questions and journaling on the answers that arise for each.

- How was your right to speak supported in childhood?
- Do you feel a connection to what you want to express in the world?
- What is your communication style?
- How powerful do you think your voice is?
- Do you use it constructively or destructively, to help or to harm?
- How much time do you spend in surface level conversation, avoiding being seen and expressing who you really are?
- How deep are you willing to go in your relationships to get to the level of intimate communication?
- Can you listen as well as you speak?
- Do you say one thing, but secretly mean another?
- Do you lie? If so, what about and to whom?
- How might you be a better communicator?
- Do you trust people?
- Do you feel the need to control everything and everyone around you?
- What do you really want to say to the world?
- What are your favorite outlets of self-expression?

THE SIXTH CHAKRA—
THE PSYCHIC INTUITIVE
SYSTEM

"Focused mind power is one of the strongest forces on earth."
—Mark Victor Hansen

Once we move our consciousness up and beyond the sound spectrum, what do we really have left of real human connection? Not a whole lot. The once solid world of form becomes less and less tangible the higher our consciousness expands. And once we reach the Psychic Intuitive System, the third eye chakra, there's little room left for the experiences of the physical body. In the psychic centers, we no longer experience the need for food or grounding, for sex or power, here we understand the language of dreams, archetypes, symbols, and psychic visions. We see life through the lens of a different eye and we explore the inner dimension of the psyche—the mind.

Sight is the birthright of those born with capable eyes; unfortunately, as we have observed in many other realms of human consciousness, we've also forgotten what clear sight really means. What we do now isn't *really seeing*—it's basically just looking through our eyes. We scan our environment for patterns that look familiar to us, so we recognize things, but we don't actually *see* anything. We don't see things as *they* are, we see things as *we* are. Our perceptions of the world aren't necessarily *reality*, which is why many spiritualists refer to reality as *illusion*. What we call our reality is really the projection of the thoughts that are held in our minds; whether those thoughts are conscious or not, doesn't matter. The experience of reality is really the projection of our collective consciousness as well as our collective unconsciousness. It's a combination of our hopes, dreams, fears, and even nightmares. But no matter how scary the collective manifestation might appear, we mustn't forget; we hold the power to create reality within us.

Human beings are very smart, we're a very clever species. But we lack *insight*. Insight, by definition, is *inward sight*. Sadly, like we did with our love and power, we lost connection to our insight as well. Instead of looking inward for answers to life's questions, we look outside of ourselves for a knowingness that can only come from within. We look and we look, but still we don't *see*. Still, we remain relatively blind. We look at each other's bodies, and we see what the world has programmed us to believe is beautiful or not. We might be presented with a crystal, but only see a rock. Too many humans look at the world around them and don't really *see* it. They see inanimate matter, they don't see *life*. And we're killing our beautiful planet due to our own psychic blindness.

What we don't realize when we're so busy looking at what's happening on the world stage is that we're not actually seeing what's *out there*, we're seeing a reflection of what's *inside of us—all of us*. We don't see with our eyes. Our eyes are the interpreters of what our minds allow into our consciousness—that's how our Psychic Intuitive System works.

When the intuitive system is activated, we've entered into the realm of light. This is what Jesus meant when he said, "The light of the body is the eye, therefore if thine eye be single, thy whole body shall be full of light." The Psychic Intuitive System is where that truth becomes realized through us. Jung also said, "He who looks outside, dreams; he who looks inside, awakens." To look inside, to analyze ourselves, is to awaken our own higher consciousness. We can't keep searching outside of ourselves for answers, we have to direct our sight inwardly as well, especially if we want to see things clearly. We must be willing to see what's inside of us before we can ever hope to understand what's happening around us. This inner sight is why most people are terrified by the thought of psychedelics; they're not actually afraid of the medicines, they're afraid of what they might see. They're afraid of awakening to their own shadows, the parts of themselves they're scared to look at. But the mind can never show us anything that isn't already there. Therefore, to fully awaken, we must make the unconscious mind a conscious mind.

Master Your Mind

The mind is the person in the driver's seat of our Psychic Intuitive System. Whether we know it or not, the mind is the master. The mind controls the body. The mind creates our life. What's hidden in our minds will reveals itself in our lives. Just as each system we've covered so far has its own hidden dimensions, what's hidden inside our Psychic Intuitive System wants to come into the light of consciousness so it can be healed. The soul wants to awaken, and the mind is where we allow that awakening to take place.

Once we've grown into adults and our thoughts and beliefs about reality are pretty fixed, we don't generally accept thoughts that challenge our belief systems into our minds without examination. We have to think, question, and analyze an idea before we're willing to accept the new idea; we must be willing to entertain the idea before we can really let it into our minds, right? Humans entertain a lot of ideas, we do so much thinking, but most of the time we're thinking, we're not thinking about anything productive. Or worse, we're thinking about nonsense! We squander the power of our minds. We waste it on things that don't mean a thing to the betterment of humanity when that's the real reason we're here! To fully awaken our souls and to contribute to the betterment of mankind.

We're here to be powerful creators. There isn't a single facet of the human being that isn't, in some way, powerful. Each of our energy systems carry equal power, they just wield it in different ways. To the Root System, the tribe is what's powerful. To the Personal Power System the body and the will are used to enact power. The voice and vibration are what's powerful to the Creative Communication System. Desire and pleasure are the motivating powers of the senses. To the heart, love is the ultimate power. And to the Psychic Intuitive System, the vehicle of mind is the most influential form of power.

Our minds are incredible tools. We can literally use our own minds to plant a seed in someone else's. If we plant the seed of an idea in someone's mind and they water that seed, we've just influenced a change in their life. If we make someone think we're smarter than them and they believe it, we've influenced the way they feel about themselves. The power of the mind is crazy scary if you think about it. It's basically the power to brainwash. Like the voice can be used to cut people down or cut people free, the mind can be used to break people out of the prisons of their own thinking, or it can be used to enslave them. And there are some very power hungry people in our world, those who understand the power of the mind and wish to use it against us.

What do you think is happening every time you sit down to watch the news and your mind gets bombarded by the horrific things happening all over the world? Then all of a sudden there's a commercial, asking, "Do you suffer from anxiety, depression, general feelings of sadness, and despair? Is your energy consistently running low, and you can't seem to find the motivation to change your life?" *Duh!* You just heard that a bomb was dropped on a bunch of innocent people! Your nervous system is crippled by the subconscious fear of death, and your Compassionate System is probably having a heart attack! The next bomb dropped is an assault *on you.* "We have your solution! Take this pill . . . just don't pay attention to the side effects." You don't need a new pill, what you need is to turn off the damn television and take back the power of your mind!

You have two choices when it comes to your mind. You can master it, or you can let it master you. Your mind is like a puppy, and it's a very busy little puppy that can't quite sit still. It jumps from one thing to the next. Give it a laser pointer and you've lost it for hours. You need to train your mind the same way you would a puppy. You wouldn't let a brand new puppy run loose in your house all day when you aren't home without training him first, would you? He'd pee and poop everywhere! But that's what the uncontrolled, fear based thoughts do to your mind, they make a stinkin' mess that no one cleans up.

We're rarely ever told how powerful our minds are. Our minds are arguably the most powerful function of our consciousness; the mind controls what we think, what we say, how we feel and how we behave—the mind creates our lives! So, we need to be very conscious of what we allow into our minds and which thoughts we allow our minds to entertain. Once we really begin to understand the power of the mind, the Psychic Intuitive system, we won't squander its energy on senseless thoughts. Instead, we'll wield the power of our minds with awareness and direct its powerful force towards what we desire out of life, rather than on what we don't want, or worse, what we're afraid of.

Humans have been brainwashed into believing that there's something to fear lurking around every corner and that we need to be afraid. But the more we hold fearful thoughts in our minds, the more we create things to be afraid of. "Protect your children, guard your wives! War is coming! There's an enemy out there, and there's not enough for everyone! Everyone is sick, you need to be afraid of them!" That's basically the mantra of the collective unconscious right now and it's really damaging to our quality of life. Our fear disconnects us from the truth; humans are genuinely loving creatures, especially when we realize we already have everything we need. We're being brainwashed to fear each other and to fear God. We've forgotten that we live on an abundant planet, and that mother earth and father sun work together in magnificent, unspeakable harmony to give us everything we ever need. Food, shelter, water—all of our survival needs can be met by them, just not our gluttony and not our greed.

The humans of the planet have become the traumatized children of a broken home. We no longer sense the connection between our mother and father, our siblings are at war with one another, and the Government has become our controlling step-parent. We no longer rely on nature to care for us and we stopped recognizing the tribe as a sense of strength. Instead we've learned to rely on powerful sources outside of ourselves for advice and support. Meanwhile, those sources benefit greatly from our reliance upon them. Human beings must take their power back and that begins with the harnessing the power of our minds.

From Newton to Quantum

"At the subatomic level, energy responds to
your mindful attention and becomes matter."
—Dr. Joe Dispenza

The accepted world view of today operates under the Newtonian model of physics, a materialistic belief that *reality* is what's happening outside of us and we are in some way separate from it. This world view is exactly why we see our problems as happening somewhere *out there* and never take a moment to consider that perhaps our *thinking* has something to do with the problems we're experiencing today.

The Newtonian paradigm tells us that everything is predictable. The universe and everything in it operates mechanistically; everything we experience can be understood logically and mathematically, and the world is made of matter as well as forces that move that matter around. Reality is believed to be what you can perceive through your five senses and anything experienced beyond the five senses simply doesn't exist. Scientists don't readily admit that there's a lot we don't quite understand, but instead of questioning things, we've chosen to accept the neat cookie cutter picture of reality they've given us. Unfortunately, this theory is seriously lacking. There's no room in this model of thinking for spirit, soul, energy, intuition, or a creative intelligence that's greater than the human mind. Things of a spiritual nature had once been considered separate from science and assigned to the category of religion. When we separated science from religion, we severed mind from matter and lost sight of the complete picture of our reality and also our place within it. When we collectively accepted science as the ultimate truth and categorized religion and faith as secondary to scientific discovery, we disconnected from the wisdom of our souls. As a result, we've created a world that reflects a major dichotomy.

What we may not realize is that our modern science is limited in its ability to provide answers to life's greater mysteries, like why we are conscious, where does our consciousness arise if it's not local to the brain, and to what extent does this consciousness effect our reality? Despite our best technology, science cannot measure the power of the human mind. The question remains,

Could what's happening within the minds of the people on our planet be shaping the collective reality we're experiencing? And could the solution to today's problems also be found within us?

Despite what classical physics tells us about the nature of reality, the science of Quantum Physics tells a different story, a story in which each and every one of us plays a vital part. In the most basic sense, quantum theory tells us that *nothing* is solid, that at the smallest level everything in our universe is made up of energy, including us.

Classical physics tells us that we are bodies of matter and that our consciousness is simply a product of the brain. This would mean that our thoughts have no influence over our reality because they're contained within, and limited to, our own individual bodies. Quantum theory, however, tells an entirely different story. Not only are we conscious, but our consciousness expands far beyond the limits of our physical brains and has a definite impact on the material world around us. Quantum physics tells us that we can't even observe the material world without altering it in some way on a subatomic level. Quantum theory also postulates that reality exists simply *because* we are observing it and that our observance of our reality is ultimately what is shaping it into form. The current model of science tells us that consciousness only exists within the human brain, while quantum theory suggests that the entire universe is made up of consciousness. I'm by no means a physicist, but from what I've learned, quantum theory flies in the face of mainstream science. It's this shift in perspective, from a *classical* to a *quantum* paradigm, that's pivotal to our evolution as a human race.

If we are to evolve as a species, which I believe we are, then a revolution must take place within our own minds. A shift needs to happen within our consciousness, from a belief in separation and materialism into a Quantum view of reality in which everything is connected by energy, consciousness, and love. If we are to make this shift we all have to become responsible not just for our feelings and actions, but also for our mind! We must awaken to the fact that our consciousness is having a powerful influence on the architecture of the world that we collectively experience.

Changing Your Mind

"The moment you change your perception
is the moment you change the chemistry of your body."
—Bruce Lipton

The mind is all there is—it directs energy and energy creates matter—that's how this whole creation thing works down here. Humans like to think that genetics are responsible for determining our fate, but it's not, it's really the power of our minds. That's why every new drug introduced on the market is first tested against a placebo to determine its efficacy. What does that really mean? It means we have to make sure the drug is stronger than the mind! For those who don't know, the *placebo effect* is a beneficial outcome produced by a pseudo drug or treatment. Take for example, a sugar pill, saline injection, or psychic surgery. The positive effects can't be linked to a drug or actual surgery, but only to the patient's *belief* in the treatment. Crazy, right? Psychic surgery is actually a thing, and what's even crazier is that it often works! Science has done experiments on people in which they show them a video of someone else having surgery. They then make a small incision in the subject's body to simulate an actual surgery, but they don't actually perform a procedure. And guess what? People still heal. If we're performing fake surgeries on people and testing our medication against the power of the mind, then why the hell aren't we just being taught to use our minds in the first place?

The mind is our most powerful ally, but in the same way it can work on our behalf, it can also work to our detriment. The power hungry forces on our planet that control the media consistently broadcast fear into our consciousness, because massive fear in humans creates more terrifying conditions in our world. When we're all afraid, we're easier to control. It's kind of the opposite of the placebo effect—it's more like the *nocebo* effect. A nocebo effect is when there's a measurable *negative* effect produced by a fearful expectation. If we expect the worst, we'll often get the worst. Both our brains and our bodies respond to the stimuli of our minds, regardless of what that stimuli is. Basically, this means that our mind affects the cells in our bodies; therefore, our mind can make us sick and it can also make us well. It all depends on what thoughts we choose to entertain. Change in our lives begins with change in our minds, but changing our mind isn't always as easy as it sounds. That's because our minds *condition* the body, and so, if we plan on changing our minds, we might want to be prepared for the body's rebellion.

On average, each one of us has about 70,000 thoughts a day, and out of those 70,000 thoughts, 90% of them are exactly the same as they were the day before. For the majority of the world, at least 70% of those programmed thoughts are conditioned by fear, negativity, and stress. Over time, our predominant thought patterns become a hardwired program into our brains, and then the program plays on repeat behind the scenes without our ever realizing it. Basically, our thoughts become automatic and unconscious.

Through the process of repetitive thinking, the same hardwiring process takes place and the brain becomes a record of our past thinking. When new thought forms try to come into our mind, they're likely to follow the channels of neural networks already in place from our previous thought patterns—and for many, those patterns were conditioned by fear and stress. Even if there aren't any pressing threats in our immediate environment, our conditioned thinking often leads us to believe there are. If our experience of reality is filtered through the lens of our thinking and the bulk of our thoughts are just a repeat of yesterday's experiences, that means we're no longer processing reality *as it is*. Rather, we're using our minds to recreate the mental conditions of yesterday, based off the stories that are stored in our minds.

Once our thoughts are hardwired into our psyche, we're no

longer consciously aware that we're thinking them, we're just automatically reacting to them. With 98% of the world walking around thinking yesterday's thoughts, it's really no wonder that most of us go from day to day experiencing very little change in our lives. If we're going to transform ourselves, our lives, and our world, we're going to have to move beyond our outdated thought patterns and start to evolve the way we've been conditioned to think.

It's important for us to understand that our thoughts don't just impact the way we feel and behave, they don't just affect what happens in our minds; our thoughts have a physiological effect on our bodies as well. Remember, mind and body are not independent entities having isolated experiences; mind and body are a synergistic organism, each having a direct influence over the other. If we can change our minds, we have the power to change everything about ourselves.

Science tells us that each time our mind generates a thought, our body responds by immediately manufacturing a chemical response so that we're actually *feeling* the equivalent of how we're *thinking*. In other words, our thoughts don't just stay in our heads. In less than a fraction of a second, we're actually *embodying* the thoughts passing through our minds. Have you ever noticed that when you're having negative thoughts, you instantaneously experience negative feelings? And those negative feelings tend to inspire more negative thoughts, creating a feedback loop of negativity in your head. As soon as you've flooded your mind with negative thoughts, the body responds by creating corresponding chemicals of negative emotion and you'll experience a change in your energy. Now that you're really feeling the emotional signature of what you've been thinking, you'll subconsciously start scanning your inner environment, the storehouse of memories and past experiences, for all the things that reinforce that feeling. This process is almost always entirely unconscious.

By the time we're midway through life, we pretty much have our entire lives mapped out and memorized in our brains default mode network. The chemical signature created by our routines, habitual thoughts, and feelings becomes the personality we know to be our *self*. Once we reach this stage, we're no longer living in a state of conscious awareness. We're not *responding* to life or creating ourselves anew in each moment, we've lost touch with life *as it is*, and instead begin *reacting* to life from an unconscious, automatic program based on what we've come to *believe life is*. Once we recreate the habit of *being ourselves* a certain number of times, the body will memorize the familiar feeling of *me*. The body is a recording of the past, of who we've been, how we've thought, and how we've felt. Therefore, our body begins to rely on our specific chemical signature in order to feel *normal*. It even rearranges our cells and receptor sites to better assimilate these specific chemical messengers that remind us of who we are. As long as we keep thinking, feeling, and behaving the same way we did the day before, the body will lean towards predictable experiences for better or worse—just the way our ego likes it—comfortable and predictable.

This is exactly why people have such a hard time truly changing themselves. Transformation is about so much more than just taking new actions or creating new habits and behaviors. Genuine transformation is the process of literally *becoming* somebody entirely new. It's about un-memorizing the old self and creating the internal conditions needed for your future self, the higher self version of you that has been lost to you. As we mentioned earlier, who you think you are is memorized as a chemical signature in your brain and body. The alchemical transformation we're talking about here involves leaving that version of you in the past and replacing it with an upgraded version of yourself from the future instead. It's the chemical death of the old self in order to make space for an entirely new signature to emerge—and let's face it—that's not exactly a comfortable experience.

In order to maintain this change, we have to be willing to go through a temporary withdrawal period while the body disengages from its dependency on the old self. That's the most challenging part. The body has become chemically conditioned to yesterday's mindset, and when you start to change your mind, your body will actually crave the old self, much like an addict craves drugs. This craving isn't a process that we're aware of, however. Most people don't even know it's happening. They just feel an unconscious desire to return to what's familiar. It's not actually change that we're afraid of, we're afraid of letting go of who we *think* we are. We're afraid of the discomfort that comes from not knowing ourselves both emotionally and chemically.

We're terrified to step into the unknown because we've invested a lot of energy into creating and maintaining a life of predictability. As soon as we initiate the process of change and begin to think differently or try to change ourselves even slightly, we might start to feel a pervading sense of anxiety or underlying unease. The body doesn't feel the same when it doesn't receive its daily dose of fear, frustration, stress, anxiety, or whatever it routinely receives the most of and desperately wants to return to its normal state. It's as if as soon as we make a commitment to change ourselves, suddenly, we can't stop thinking about returning to our normal programs.

When you begin to initiate change in your mind, you'll undoubtedly be tempted to return to your old habits as you experience a temporary withdrawal period, or a time of uncertainty and discomfort. The body is desperately craving the predictability of its old chemical environment and it's during that time that many often find themselves unconsciously reverting back to old patterns of behavior, not because they're *better*, but because they're *familiar*. And because old patterns are unconscious and automatic, they require far less effort to uphold, thus making them easier to maintain.

Humans are creatures of habit. We love our routines and our rituals. We use them as a way to reinforce the ego, which is forever trying to keep us safe by convincing us that we know who we are and what we're doing. But if we're going to truly transform ourselves, it means being willing to let go of who we think we are. We have to be willing to withstand temporary periods of discomfort, forfeit some of our normal customs, and go through the uncertainty of *not* knowing who we are in order to discover who we're actually capable of becoming.

We have to be willing to learn new things and take in new information. We have to introduce new thoughts to create new emotional-chemical responses in the body. We have to take different actions to create new patterns of behavior. And then we have to repeat this process over and over and over again until we actually begin to embody a new version of ourselves.

If you've been thinking negatively for years or have habits that are really hard to break, changing your mind isn't going to happen overnight. It's taken years to develop the patterns of thought and emotion that are now hardwired into your brain and body, so it's going to take some time and effort on your part to unlearn your old energy habits so your authentic self can emerge. Have patience with yourself and trust the process.

Remember, your transformation won't just affect you on a personal level, it will affect everything and everyone around you, and to some extent, the entire human collective. There's a lot of unconscious resistance behind that, but if we're going to witness a widespread awakening, we must keep moving forward. Awakening is a lot like throwing a pebble into a pond—the ripples are easily seen as they reverberate across the water's surface—but in truth, the entire pond is affected by the pebble's vibration. You're the pebble and humanity's the pond. Go ahead and make some waves! The best way to break our addictions to our old chemical signature is through the practice of meditation.

Kristin Johnston

Meditation for Creation

*"Meditation means dissolving the invisible walls
that unawareness has built."*
—Sadhguru

The practice of meditation removes our consciousness from the outside world and places it on our inner selves; the inner world, then, becomes more real than our outer experience. When we spend time in mediation, especially lengthy amounts of time, we move beyond the known self, away from our identification with the body and our senses, and merge with a consciousness that is greater than our own. Meditation changes the hardwired patterns stored in our brain and alters our physiology as well. When our minds are aligned with this greater mind, there's nothing we can't create. When we're spending time in meditation, we're merging with the quantum field. The quantum field is a field of infinite potential that exists beyond time and space. Nothing is impossible in the quantum field. If we can think it in our minds, we can hold it in our hands. And meditation makes this process a lot easier.

Everything that's been laid out for you so far is designed to help you liberate your energy, but you must be able to apply that energy towards a vision of the future in order to create with it. All of our energy systems need to be active and online to make a New Earth a reality. That means we can't have our energy stuck in survival mode. We can't feel guilty about our desire for a pleasurable life, and we can't be afraid of the power we have to make that life happen! We have to access the power of our hearts and use our creative frequency to speak this reality into existence. But most importantly, we need to have a clear vision of what we want to create. Sitting down in meditation helps us get clear on what we really want. It removes us from the stimulation and input from the outside world and connects us with our inner world of hopes, dreams, and visions. Daily meditation removes us from the limitation stored in our bodies and utilizes the power of our minds to make our inner vision an outer reality.

Here's the missing link to the secret of meditation for creation—the power of the mind is amplified when we enlist the help of our heart. When the heart and the mind are working in unison, our creative potential is at its peak. If our intentions are clear and backed by emotions that support them, there's nothing we can't do, be, or have. But we have to be able to feel the reality in our hearts, just as powerfully as we see it in our minds. There's a trick to doing this; we must emotionally embrace the intention as though it's taking place right now. When we slow our breathing and focus our attention on our hearts while embracing an elevated emotion (think of something that makes you feel good), our bodies enter into a state known as *coherence.*

Coherence is a state of balance within the body. It can be measured instrumentally when our brains and hearts are in sync. When we're thinking and feeling in harmony, our heart starts to beat in a rhythmic pattern which produces an energetic frequency, or a field of information, within and around us. In a state of coherence, our respiration, heart rate, blood pressure, and other bodily functions, both psychological and physiological, become more orderly and consistent. Coherence is the body's state of optimal functionality.

Think of your thoughts as the electrical current and your feelings as the magnetic current of the body. When they fuse together, they create an electromagnetic charge around you; that charge is like a telegraphic code used to communicate your desires to the quantum field. The universe doesn't speak English—it speaks *frequency*—so keep your thoughts positive and your vibration high. When we think and feel in harmony, we broadcast a very concise and coherent frequency out to the universe. Contained within that wave are our intentions and heart's desires. When our intent is clear and consistent and our signal is strong, the universe can easily respond by organizing the events in our lives to help us achieve our desires.

By contrast, when our bodies are out of coherence, when our thoughts and feelings are out of sync, when we're feeling stress, anxiety, and chaos, the universe responds by giving us whatever situations match that frequency. The quantum field doesn't judge what our minds and bodies send out, it simply responds to it. Maintaining a regular state of coherence is the key to unlocking quantum creation; this is, quite literally, the definition of magic. This type of reality creation is best developed through the practice of meditation, but it's also possible to do just by being in alignment with who you are as a soul. We all have the power of creation within us, the question is, how have we been using it?

Consciousness and Unconsciousness

"Normal waking consciousness feels perfectly transparent,
and yet it is less a window on reality than the product of
our imaginations—a kind of controlled hallucination."
—Michael Pollan

By now, you should understand that consciousness is the ultimate force in our universe; the mind is greater than matter and everything we perceive to be real is actually just vibrating fields of energy. Once we really accept that the mind—*our consciousness*—is the driving force behind this energy, we regain the ability to consciously and magically create our lives.

Many people reading this may have already been introduced to the concept that we have the power within us to change the material world by simply by focusing our own consciousness—but if this is true why then aren't we witnessing miracles all around us? Why aren't we all happy, healthy, and ridiculously abundant? Why is the world still in such an obvious state of chaos? The reason we can understand this concept intellectually and not experience the tangible result is because of the nature of our minds.

The human mind has many functions, but primarily it operates in one of two ways—*consciously,* or *unconsciously.* If you can learn about what's stored in your *subconscious*, and reclaim it, then you've awakened your consciousness. I'm sure just by reading, you've had glimpses of insight or gained some awareness as to how you've been programmed or why you do the things you do, but if you *really* want to change your life, you'll need to reprogram your subconscious mind.

The conscious mind, the part of you that learns intellectually and the part of you that's reading this book, isn't capable of changing your life—it's just not powerful enough. The reason why people can read a million and one self-help books and never see a change in their life is because the material they've read never makes it into their subconscious mind. Our conscious mind is only responsible for creating 5% of our reality, the subconscious mind is responsible for the other 95%. This means the subconscious mind is infinitely more powerful than the conscious mind. If we don't do the work to rewrite our subconscious programs, our life is destined to stay the same.

The conscious mind is like our *thinking* mind, and the subconscious is more of our *emotional* mind. We like to think that our conscious/thinking mind is the captain of our ship and our subconscious/feeling mind is the crew, but it's actually the other way around. It doesn't matter what the captain orders, without the crew to back it, the ship of our life goes nowhere new. This means if we want a new subconscious program, we need a new crew, not necessarily a new captain. We need new emotions and not just new thoughts. That means we need to move beyond the emotions already stored in our subconscious if we want to captain a yacht instead of a dingy.

If you inherited a limiting belief about money, it doesn't matter how wealthy your conscious mind believes you're going to be; if you feel weird about wealth, your subconscious mind won't allow abundance into your life. If you don't *feel* worthy of love, it doesn't matter how bad you desire it, you just won't be able to attract it.

So how do we do it? How do we get beyond ourselves?

There are many techniques to get us there, but there is only one way to really make it happen—and that's to get beyond the conscious mind. If we're going to change our reality, we need to hijack ourselves, and get into the operating system of our brain so we can rewrite the programs that keep our lives limited.

Meditation, self-hypnosis, and psychedelics are the three of most effective ways I've found. Many have heard of meditation for stress reduction, but fewer people are familiar with the practice for rewriting the limiting beliefs in the subconscious mind. Meditation, hypnosis, and psychedelics change the physiological structure of the brain. It's science, and here's how it works—the brain is a receiver for the mind; what the mind thinks the brain interprets. Our regular thoughts create measurable, hardwired patterns in the physiology of our brain. In his book *How to Change Your Mind: What the New Science of Psychedelics Teaches Us About Consciousness, Dying, Addiction, Depression and Transcendence,* Michael Pollan uses a brilliant analogy, comparing the brain to a snow covered hill. Our thoughts become the tracks left behind when we sled down the hill and the more we think our regular thoughts, the more ingrained the tracks become. Overtime, the sled doesn't carve any new tracks, it simply falls in line with the tracks that are already laid down. What that means is that our brains go on autopilot, we're no longer conscious, we're just slaves to our subconscious program. He calls this the *default mode network* or *DMN* of the brain.

Meditation, hypnosis, and psychedelics are major pattern interrupters to the *DMN*. These things help us clear the mountain so we can create new tracks. Psychedelics are clearly a more intense shift than meditation, as they do instantly what meditation may take weeks, months, or years to accomplish. Either way, all of these practices can produce the same effects—a change of *mind*, therefore a change of brain.

The brain is like a very complex supercomputer and it functions within a series of vibrational frequency known as *brainwaves*. Along with the influences of chemicals, hormones, and microbes, brainwaves are basically responsible for our varying degrees of consciousness. Our brainwaves range from higher to lower in frequency, from beta, to alpha, to theta, to delta, moving us along a spectrum of alert wakefulness (beta), all the way down into dreamless sleep(delta).

- *Beta* is the highest brainwave frequency. It represents our conscious, thinking brain. When our brains are in beta brainwave frequency, our mind and body is alert and our senses are focused on the material world around us. The majority of the world spends their time in beta brainwaves of high beta, or *mild stress* to be exact. This state of consciousness is what has caused us all to become materialists. It's why we care so much about what we drive and what we wear; we'd rather *look* good than *feel* good because all of our energy and attention is focused on the material world.

- *Alpha* is our analytical mind and is responsible for our relaxed and creative thought process. We achieve this state of consciousness when we're creating or reading a book, for example; our body is in a state of relaxation but our mind is alert. Alpha is an ideal place to be.

- *Theta* brainwave is the hypnotic sweet spot that we're looking for. When our brains are in a state of theta, our minds are most susceptible to autosuggestion, meaning the mind is fertile soil for planting seeds of our choosing. I mentioned earlier that we spend our childhood years, 0-7, in theta brainwaves. Essentially what that means is we spent our childhood being hypnotized by the world around us. The garden of our mind was planted in childhood, and unless we do the work now to uproot the weeds of our inheritance, those weeds will continue to strangle all the flowers we're currently trying to plant. If we want to rewire ourselves, we need to get back into the theta brainwave frequency we experienced as children—and that's where the benefits of meditation, hypnosis, and when necessary, psychedelic medicine, comes in.

- *Delta*, is the slowest brainwave frequency and occurs when we are in a state of deep dreamless sleep. Basically, that's when nothing is happening behind our eyes, we are out of the way, and the body is able to repair itself.

The average person spends the majority of their time in beta, completely engaged in the material world, and a very short amount of time in the states of alpha and theta daily. Alpha and theta are the only states capable of shifting our subconscious minds and we experience these states only briefly as we're rising in the morning and when we're falling asleep at night. Meditation practice gives us the opportunity of learning to maintain extended states of alpha and theta. When we make it an effort to access these states of consciousness every day, with the intention of overcoming our old selves, we are doing the work we need to literally rewire our brains and create new subconscious programs. Because of the inner chemistry of the brain, the subconscious mind is most susceptible to change when the brainwaves are slower, in the early hours of the morning and the later hours of the evening. So, the best times to meditate are immediately upon rising or just before retiring to bed at night. A great way to practice making autosuggestions to your brain that have been incredibly effective in helping me to rewire my subconscious mind is to use a software program called *Mind Movies*. *Mind Movies* allow you to create your own video, uploading music, photos, and phrases that you can watch throughout the day, especially in the early morning and later in the evening. Watching these videos regularly when your brainwaves are just right helps implant new images and emotions into your subconscious mind that will create the inner environment of a future you are excited to live. Remember, what you think about and emotionally embrace, you create—that is the unlimited creative power of your mind.

Everyone's a Psychic

"Psychic Power is the ability to download information directly from the Universe."
—Lada Ray

A book on awakening wouldn't be complete if we didn't discuss the psychic power of your third eye. Your third eye exists in your Psychic Intuitive System and it's the storehouse for all of your *clairs*. Your clairs are basically the parts of you that can perceive beyond your five senses. They are our psychic powers, and they're not just reserved for special people—we all have them, just some of our clairs are more highly developed than others.

Good ol' Hollywood has plastered into our minds what it means to be a psychic and to have a clair. Our imagination drums up an image of a gypsy woman in dark robes wearing a head scarf, tarot cards spread out across the table, incense burning all around her as she gazes into a crystal ball and reads your palm or predicts your future. Or we hear the Long Island Medium's thick New York accent practically yelling in our ear, "Hey! I've got your grandmother on the line! She's got a message for you!" Those are cool tricks that psychics do, but psychic sight is the birthright of your Psychic Intuitive System. Psychic insight comes in the form of our clairs. We have six primary clairs: clairvoyance, clairaudience, clairsentience, clairalience, clairgustance, and claircognizance.

- *Clairvoyance* is the ability to see clearly; visual psychics have this clair. This is the kind of psychic that sees visions. This is the clair everyone wants, but those that have it sometimes wish they didn't.

- *Clairaudience* is the ability to hear clearly. It's common for audible psychics to hear words or phrases from sources outside themselves.

- *Clairsentience* is the ability to feel clearly. These psychics will be able to feel whether something's right or wrong, even if they don't know how.

- *Clairalience* is the ability to smell clearly. This is kind of a strange superpower, but I know someone who has it and it's actually pretty cool. These psychics will smell things like cigarette smoke or roses when deceased loved ones are around them.

- *Clairgustance* is the ability to clearly taste. People with this psychic ability might randomly experience the taste their grandmother's cooking or their favorite meal, only to come home and have it waiting for them.

- *Claircognizance* is the ability to clearly know. Those who have this kind of clair will simply know things, they might not always know how they know—but they will know.

We all have psychic powers. We all have a clair behind the scenes, hooking us up in one way or another. Some of us are just more in touch with ours. *Psychic* actually means *of the soul.* The closer to your soul you are, the more your intuitive system is activated. A lot of natural lightworkers are drawn to psychic work and intuitive development. Why do you think that is? Well, I'll tell you. Psychics work at the level of light. That's why their symbol is the all-seeing eye. Psychics don't rely on their two eyes to see, they use the *eye* of the Psychic Intuitive System, their *third eye.*

We can all see beyond the veil of this illusion if we choose to, but we have to activate our intuitive center. We have to learn to see with our single eye. The eye in the center of our head is called the pineal gland and it's pretty damn awesome. The pineal does all sorts of things, but mainly it connects us to light. In his book, *Becoming Supernatural*, Dr. Joe Dispenza quotes an article that defines the pineal gland as, "a neuroendocrine transducer, capable of receiving and converting signals within the brain. When the pineal gland acts as a transducer, it can pick up frequencies above our three-dimensional space-time, sensory based reality. Once the pineal gland is activated, it can tune into higher dimensions of space and time."

We actually have a gland inside our heads that's capable of receiving information from somewhere beyond this sensory world, from somewhere beyond this space and time! Not only that, this little gland has the ability to take that information from somewhere beyond and translate it into pictures in our minds that we can understand. How crazy is that?! But more importantly, why don't we know about it? Why haven't we been taught how to activate it? Why have all of these incredible superpowers been hidden from us? Maybe because some power hungry people would prefer that we don't know about it.

When I was getting really deep into this work (I'm never not deep into this work), I was doing a lot of fasting, meditating, and breathing practices. I was reading a ton of Dr. Joe's material (I love you, Dr. Joe!), and I was asking the Divine for a mystical moment. I'd had tons of mystical moments in the past, but most of them had been induced by various medicines. I'd experienced all sorts of synchronicity and I knew the universe had my back, but I wanted something that was going to blow my socks off, something that I couldn't deny.

I started doing Dr. Joe's pineal gland meditation at four every morning, when the chemicals of the body are just right. One morning as I was doing the meditation—specifically the breath-work portion—I felt something in my brain change. I felt *ecstasy*. (Trust me, I've done the drug before so I know what it feels like.) My brain waves changed and my body was vibrating like crazy. This new energy was taking over, and before I knew it, I was gone. My awareness was still there, but the *I* behind my eyes was not. I had become pure consciousness. I was one with the observer. What I witnessed take shape in my mind's eye was a television screen which soon became flooded with images of molecules. Chains of chemical structures were forming in front of me. When the pineal gland is activated, it releases an array of different chemicals, and I think I was seeing some of them. Then the chains of molecules disappeared, and these entities showed up on the screen. They were formlessness, and somehow, I just knew they were extraterrestrial and they were family. I couldn't exactly see them the way we see things in this world, but still, I saw them. They delivered a hopeful message to me, "Don't worry about anything. We're sending help-ers." As suddenly as I had left myself, I was being pulled back into my body. When I came out of that experience, I tried to pretend it didn't happen. My rational mind just couldn't accept it. I told myself it was a dream, that I had fallen asleep while I was meditat-ing, but the events that transpired throughout the day let me know that this was no hallucination. It really happened, and it altered the matter of my reality.

The entire day seemed synchronistic. Events flowed like water. I dropped my little one off at preschool, and when I got home, my mother-in-law was waiting at my house. She's really awesome, and spiritual too, so we talked at length about the Blessed Mother and the Holy Spirit; not in a religious way, but in a truthful way. My heart was illuminated, and my soul was totally lit up. As soon as she left, it was time to pick up my daughter. On the way, I stopped at a local shop to pick up some supplements. The lady behind the counter asked me what ever happened to my dream of opening a wellness center. Years prior, when I was going through my raw vegan awakening, I was ranting about my dream of healing people to anyone who would listen. She, apparently, had been one of them. Feeling a bit disheartened, I told her sheepishly, "I'm not sure when that is going to happen. If it's meant for me, it will come to me, and I won't have to force my will onto it." She smiled, we exchanged goodbyes, and I left. I made a quick call to a restaurant up the street and ordered my daughter's favorite chicken soup for lunch.

Along my route to pick her up, I drove by the little art store, the one that once wore rainbow colors. The windows had been boarded up, and the once brightly colored building had been painted over in a drab shade of muted purple. Someone was out front excavating plants and doing some landscaping. I glanced over at my mother riding in my passenger seat and said half-jokingly, "Look, they're getting it ready for us." As I picked my daughter up from school, it suddenly dawned on me! The owner of *that* building also owned the restaurant I was driving to, and I was on my way there to pick up lunch! In an instant, I realized this day was being divinely orchestrated. When I got to the restaurant, I asked to speak to the owner. When he came out, I asked him about the little art store. Do you know what this man said to me? In his thick Greek accent, *he* asked *me*, "Why, you want it or something?" Hell, yeah, I wanted it!

Later that day, I met with his brother and business partner. I poured my heart out to him. I shared my vision and my passion with him. I told him about my dream to help people heal them-selves and, in turn, heal the world. I got *deep* with a man who I had only met just moments before, and you know what this man did? He put the key to that building right in the palm of my hand. There was no lease, there was no *For Rent* sign, there was no strategy or plan. There was no ego in that moment, no agenda, no exchange of energy, just the presence of pure love—the authentic connection between two Spirits who really *saw* each other. And just like that, I was given the opportunity of a lifetime. Today, my family runs a successful business out of that little store, and we do all that we can to inspire and be of service to our community. All of this happened —*I believe*—because I activated my pineal gland and made contact with the Divine source of creation. And you can do it too.

So, what are you waiting for? If you have that kind of power in your tiny pineal gland (and you do), let's activate that baby!

When it's not being used or stimulated, the pineal gland calcifies. That means that our most powerful gland basically turns to a stone in our heads. Heavy metals in our water, food supply, and atmosphere bind to the brain and cause our pineal glands to harden. If it's not really good for you, why *do* they put fluoride in our water? …Anyways.

To decalcify your own pineal gland, you might want to consider ridding your body of heavy metals, not drinking fluoridated water or brushing your teeth with fluoridated toothpaste, not heating your food in aluminum or non-stick cookware, and not eating conventionally farmed food. You'll also want to wash your produce with clean, filtered water. Aluminum is being sprayed into our atmosphere, so that means its in our food supply. It can also be helpful to take herbs and supplements like cilantro, spirulina, and chlorella to help decalcify your pineal gland.

There's also a natural way to stimulate the pineal gland without adding anything to your diet. You can use your own energy system. In his legendary work, Dr. Joe Dispenza teaches an incredible breath work technique that involves locking down your lower three energy systems. Basically, you squeeze the muscle between your genitals (like a Kegel exercise) and pull your energy up and in, lock down your lower and upper abdomen and breathe in slowly, deeply pulling your energy upward and focusing it on the top of your head.

Hold in that breath for as long as you can, putting pressure on the pineal gland in your third eye center, and then relax, letting it all out. Repeat this process a few times and it will begin to stimulate your pineal. There's a whole bunch of science as to why this works, but I'm not going to get into it here. If you're like me and you love the deep science of this stuff, just read Dr. Joe's book, *Becoming Supernatural*.

Psychic Intuitive Energetics

There are no character structures associated with the sixth chakra because we've essentially left the body behind. Here is where we integrate all the characters and awaken to realize we carry each of them within us. Once they have become conscious, we can call upon any of their qualities to serve as needed. I needed to call upon the *Creative Idealist* to tap into the higher consciousness this book came from, my *EIS* to ask for love and support along the way, my *Charismatic Leader* to inspire the mission behind the message, my *Team Players* desire to support humanity, and the motivational drive of my *Knowledgeable Achiever* to make organizing this book possible. These characters aren't personalities, they're archetypes of the soul; they're found inside everyone, and every one of them is found within us.

Now that we've covered just about everything you need to know relating to your sixth chakra and the consciousness that governs it—lets assess the health and function of your Psychic Intuitive System. I encourage you to look to the connection you have to your own body, and to use your life as a reflection for how well you manage the energy of your Psychic Intuitive System.

Remember from the chapter on the human energy system,

that energy behaves in a multitude of different ways—it can be *excessive*, running too much energy; *deficient*, not able to generate enough energy; or *blocked*, meaning no energy is able to transmit through the chakra at all. Chakras can have both *excessive and deficient* characteristics, so the energetic state of your chakra may also fall somewhere in between any of those three states, depending on the situation. In an ideal world, however, we want our energy to be balanced and able to flow freely throughout our system. If a chakra is out of balance, not holding enough, or holding too much energy, we will need to either charge, discharge, or otherwise reorganize the energy of that chakra in order to bring it into balance.

Excessive energy in the Psychic Intuitive System is going to manifest itself as an overactive mind. Those with an abundance of energy in the Psychic Intuitive System tend to analyze every little thought they have, and then they analyze the thoughts they're having about their thoughts. They get caught in a loop of their own cyclical thinking and will waste hours thinking about what they've been thinking about, never actually coming to an understanding, or taking action.

They will have a ton of awesome, fun, and creative ideas, and a vivid and wild imagination, but struggle to get the energy out of their head and into the world. They want more than anything to share their thoughts with the world, but often struggle in the lower chakras which makes grounding their ideas possible. They love the feeling of freedom and imagining things, but have a fear of containment or limitation. Ironically, their fear of limiting themselves is what keeps them from accomplishing their goals.

They are also super psychic! Somehow, they just know things others don't. They have easy access to their inner world and usually have vivid dreams. They will identify with many of the clairs, but mostly clairvoyance (the visual one.) Most of the time, their dreams will tell them all they need to know about what's going on around them.

To discharge some of their excessive energy, they'll need to learn to ground themselves, something they avoid doing. They'll also need to take some action on their ideas. Usually, their visions are huge, because they come from the limitless space of their imagination, so they fear taking any action at all because to ground something of that magnitude requires a lot of limitation and self-discipline, which they also fear. Those with *excessive* energy in the Psychic Intuitive System will benefit from taking small steps towards their large goals, like writing a poem or a chapter instead of trying to write the whole book or painting a picture instead of trying to present a collection in a gallery.

In contrast, those with a *deficient* Psychic Intuitive System won't be able to generate the energy required to change their mind at all. They're relatively closed to new ideas and might only be semi-open to seeing another way of living; they're able to honor it when other people do it but struggle to do it themselves. They usually just stick with what they know, and trust what they see with their eyes. They might be aware that they dreamt throughout the night but won't be able to remember once they've woken up. The majority of their psychic intuitive energy is still stuck in seeing the world the way their child-self was programmed to see it, and they have a hard time breaking out of that pattern. They want to connect with their imagination, they just struggle to do it.

In order to energize a *deficient* Psychic Intuitive System, one needs to allow new information into their mind that will expand their thinking. They need to become willing to evolve beyond their inherited mental programs. Taking up a meditation practice, reading new books, or signing up for some classes, particularly those that cover spiritual concepts, can help.

Energy that has become *blocked* in the Psychic Intuitive System will manifest as a mind that is completely closed off to new ideas. Nothing new comes in and the only thing that goes out is what's already in there. These people are not willing to take in another person's perspective and won't even allow themselves to listen to it. They know what they know, and that's all they want to know. They're sometimes religious, but aren't often spiritual, and have a difficult time embracing spiritual concepts. They won't be very imaginative and will question the sanity of those who are. The world is mechanical for those with blocked sixth chakras—life is lifeless, and void of deeper meaning.

If you believe that you have a block in your Psychic Intuitive System, start by analyzing your early childhood programming around the right to use your imagination. How were your ideas supported by those closest to you? Were you allowed to dream, and fantasize, or were you told that dreams aren't reality? In order to move a block that's manifested in the Psychic Intuitive System, one needs to reconnect to their inner vision and the world of their imagination. Meditation and dreamwork help, as does learning about symbolism and the language of archetypes.

Ideally, we want our Psychic Intuitive System to be *balanced*. Those with a balanced Psychic Intuitive System don't just see the world through their eyes, they're able to perceive the language of dreams and symbolism. They can see beyond the veil of illusion, but don't get trapped behind it either. They're very much in the world, they're just not caught-up in it because they're able to see through its drama. There's something magical about these people; they look like ordinary humans, but they feel like magicians. A lot of time they work as psychics and healers, and they help other people develop those gifts as well. Those with a balanced Psychic Intuitive System will be able to see things in their imagination and make them come to life in their reality. There's a fluidity about what they see inside, what they say, and what they create in the world. They serve to remind us that extraordinary magic exists in the ordinary world.

Questions for Reflection

I suggest setting aside some time to sit with each of these questions and journaling on the answers that arise for each.

- How free would you say your mind is?
- How was your right to imagination supported when you were younger?
- How often do you dream?
- Can you see the aliveness of the world you're in?
- How well do you manifest your ideas into reality?
- How spiritual would you say you are?
- Is meditation easy for you?
- Do you let new ideas into your mind, even ones that contradict what you already think you know?
- How vivid is your imagination?
- Do you think you have a clair? If so, which ones do you feel the most connected to?
- Can you see the symbolism in your life?
- Do you pay attention to synchronicity, or are they still coincidences?
- How analytical are you?
- Do you feel connected to your inner vision?
- What do you think when you hear the word psychic?

THE SEVENTH CHAKRA—
THE DIVINITY SYSTEM

"You are not a drop in the ocean,
you are the entire ocean in a drop."
—Rumi

Beyond the spectrum of light and sound, humanity is left with nothing but pure, limitless consciousness. Some might even call this infinite space God. Yea… I said it, *God*. I know, things can start feeling weird for people once they hear the *G* word, because some are really squeamish about religious dogma and the name God can be a huge trigger point for a lot of people. Luckily, the collective became free from a tight noose and all the jargon associated with organized religion when words like Universe, Creator, Great Spirit, and best of all, The Field came bursting onto the human divinity scene. All of a sudden, we have universal and dogma-free terminology for what our ancestors simply called *God*.

The force that we call God is unknowable to the human mind. We can get glimpses of it, but only the truly enlightened can sustain the connection. Asking a human to *know* God is like asking a fish to read the newspaper. They can't do it. Neither can we as humans truly know God, our physical form simply doesn't allow for it. If someone tells you they know what God is, they're mistaken. We can, however, perceive its presence all around us. That's why life and God remain the great mysteries. It's why the mystic, the poet, and the Saint dedicate their lives to these unseen magical forces, and then do the best they can with what they've been given to share what they experience.

Even then, they can't truly *know* God. What mystics, poets and saints have found is a way they can connect to the *feeling* of divine presence. Our ancestors were very much connected to this force that we call God and felt its presence strongly in nature. Somehow, we've lost sight of that. And because of our severance from God and all that's sacred, we're destroying the planet we live on. This force we call God is at work behind the scenes every moment of our lives, but we have to be willing to let ourselves awaken to its presence. Our single eye must be open, and we have to be willing to see our world symbolically. The Divine doesn't speak to us in words and phrases the way humans do. The Divine uses the language of synchronicity and symbols. In order to spot God's handiwork in our lives, we have to be paying attention.

How did humans get so screwed up about God anyway? Oh, yeah, that's right—*coorporate* religion. What was once created to encourage faith in the mystery became a rigid set of rules and guidelines to follow so you don't go to hell. Religion became a way to control human beings through the emotion of fear. We've been taught to *fear* God—to fear his wrath—to feel guilty for our sins against him. We were taught to be ashamed of our nakedness and not to enjoy the pleasures of the body. We were taught to believe that we're imperfect, flawed, and in need of forgiveness. Humanity came to believe that it had sinned against God and was now doomed to live in a state of perpetual fear. We are all children, terrified of being punished.

But where did all this information come from? Did it come from God, or did it come from someone else's interpretation of God? Sure, Christ was said to have reached Salvation, the ultimate union with the Creator, but that doesn't mean any of his followers achieved the same level of consciousness. A person can only allow information in that's equal to their emotional state, so if someone wasn't on the frequency of love, the frequency of enlightenment, or the frequency of Christ, then could they truly understand what Christ was trying to tell us?

Somehow, Christ's message of unconditional love and forgiveness has become so watered down that we started killing people in the name of religion. How does something like that happen? Surely, that can't be God.

The answer lies in the collective unconscious of humanity and the weight and fear of the human ego. The ego's limited self-perception doesn't always allow for the expansion into oneness that we experience in an awakened Divinity System. An un-awakened ego believes *itself* to be all-powerful, not necessarily God. If we view life solely from the lens of our ego, we haven't yet reached a level of conscious awareness that allows us to understand Christ's message or to connect to God—whose messages speak from compassion and divinity. These are systems that exist above the personal power of the ego.

My hope is that we may be a little closer to understanding now than we were 2,000 years ago. Perhaps, the stories are right though—maybe we did choose to separate ourselves from God. Maybe we did choose *against* the force of creation when we wanted to experience ourselves as separate from it. But what if God is something we can never truly be separate from? What if God is Love? And what if awakening our Divinity System, can lead us back to that place of oneness? I believe that it can.

Humans were *created* with a link between us and Divinity, between our humanness and a consciousness that is far greater than our own. Some call this link the holy spirit, others, the soul. However you choose to define it—it's a link that can never be severed. *A Course in Miracles*, the sacred text channeled through a woman named Helen Shucman, tells us that the humans of earth are the *separated sons*; although they cannot sever their link to divinity, they have lost sight of it in many ways. Many of us believe in our separation more then we believe in our connection to God; we believe in our egos power, more than the power of the divine. As a result of that painful disconnection, our lives are full of suffering. The Course also mentions the concept of *atonement*. The atonement is when the separated sons of earth return their spirits to the divine source that we call God. It sounds a lot like awakening, doesn't it? Awakening is an evolution of our consciousness and has great potential on our planet right now.

In order to understand our relationship to divinity, we may need to forget some of the things we've been taught about God, or the divine in general. When someone else tries to tell us what God is, we absolutely cannot believe them. In fact, you shouldn't believe anything I say about God either. Our connection to the Divine is unique and ours alone. It's a connection we must make and nurture for ourselves. But we can't do that if we're afraid of God, or if we can't trust or believe in anything greater than ourselves. The ego would have you believe that this is it—that you are all there is and when your life here is done, so are you—but I just don't believe that to be true. I believe that we are all immortal, spiritual beings, and we're here to be in service to something much greater than our ego would lead us to believe. But to discover what that greater purpose is for our lives, we need to reconnect to the divine source, the God within us—our own Divinity System.

The One Who Listens

"There is nothing more important to true growth than realizing, you are not the voice of the mind—you are the one who hears it."
—Michael A. Singer

Have you ever wondered who the perceiver is behind your eyes? Who sees when you look out into the world? And who thinks when you're thinking? Perhaps, it's more important to ask yourself, who does the perceiving when you're doing the looking—and who's the one who *listens* to your thoughts? If you're both the *thinker* and the *listener*, then there must be two of you. Is one of them *you* and the other one *not you?* Maybe they're *both you?* Who is it that's processing the words as you read them off the page, or listen to them as they're being read to you? Who's the one that observes us while we observe our lives? Some have called this perceiver the *witness*, others simply call it *consciousness*. The silent witness, the consciousness behind your thoughts, is your connection to divinity.

The divine witness has been present for us our entire lives, it's the constant when everything about us is changing. Our bodies change, our awareness remains. Our emotions fluctuate, but the one who experiences them doesn't. Our actions take many forms, but the witness takes only one. Our hearts break, and they break open, the divine watches it all. Our words will change as our minds expand, and still, the consciousness that watches us remains the same. Always silent, always listening. To place your awareness on the one who listens, and not necessarily the one who thinks, is what it means to expand your consciousness. What if connecting with the mind that observes all minds is what it means to merge with God?

We can't connect to the divine, however, if all we ever listen to is our own mental chatter. We have to learn to place our attention on something greater than our limited selves. We have to learn to listen to the one who listens and watch the one who watches; and then we will come to know God for ourselves and not simply listen to what our thoughts have been programmed to think *about* God.

Healing Our Relationship to the Divine

"I looked in temples, churches and mosques.
But I found the Divine within my heart.
—Rumi

In order to awaken the Divinity System, like we did with all of our other systems, we must look to how they've been programmed. We must look at how our relationship to God is formed in our early life. I believe that when we incarnate into a body, we do so under the agreement that we'll forget our connection to God, and we'll go through this life trying to manage our way back. We know there will be breadcrumbs for us to follow along the way, but we might get lost under the veil of forgetfulness. The earth is thick with dense psychic energy and the cloud of forgetfulness weighs heavy on our souls. This can make remembering our own divinity hard work.

Once our souls establish a link between our spirits and our bodies, our parents take on the positions of Gods, and their beliefs about divinity often become our own. To our child selves, the voices of our parents literally *are* the voice of God. Parents and other parental figures are our first experience of a power that's greater than our own. So, what our parents say about God must be the truth because they're the ultimate power in our lives. And because we forgot about our own connection to God, it's the voices of our parents that get stored in our Divinity System.

The way our parents related to God is often the relationship we'll project onto the divine, until we do our own spiritual seeking, that is. The stronger our parents felt about religion, the more likely it is that we will adopt the same attitudes and beliefs towards the divine as they do. Or we will simply reject religion all together, rather than explore the concept of spirituality for ourselves. It's often said that God is *our Father in heaven*, therefore, God is our parent and we are God's children. So, in order to reconnect with God, we often have to heal the relationship we have with our parents, more specifically, the way our parents viewed spirituality. We have to purify the parental figures living in our heads if we ever want to welcome in our own connection to the divine.

Our beliefs about God are getting programmed into our own Divinity System throughout childhood, they don't necessarily form at a specific age like some of the other lower systems. We pretty much just absorb the ideas about God that circulate around us, especially if our parents were churchgoers or followers of various other organized religion. We learn to connect to the divine in the way our families did and not always in a way that makes sense to us. A child that's made to sit still during long church services doesn't always feel God in the room in the way that his parents might. In fact, a child might even develop a distaste for God simply because sitting still for that long can be torture to a small child. A connection between the child and the divine doesn't always take place in a mosque or a synagogue either; perhaps for some it does, but not for all. And many children raised by strict religious parents will reject the notion of spirituality later in life because they were actually traumatized by it, especially if they were taught to fear God or made to believe that God was judging them or punishing them for being bad.

If we want the peace of God they talk about in the holy books, we'll have to establish our own connection to the divine and discover what divinity means to us. This usually means we need to learn to see our parents and caretakers as simply a way for us to get into this world so our souls could go on their own journeys, instead of the Gods our inner children made them out to be. Our parents had a job, and that job was to keep us alive until we could find our own way back to Source. Our parents were never meant to take God's position in our lives. We gave them that power when we stopped evolving our own consciousness. And our poor parents!

They take care of our bratty little selves our entire childhoods, and then when we grow up, we blame them for screwing us up. Our parents gave us the best they could with what they'd been given, even if what they gave us was wounding and dysfunction. It's our job to make the best of that. When we finally explore our own selves and merge our spirit with the true power of divine love, we'll all be thanking our parents for giving us life.

Spiritual Maturity

"With the disappearance of God, the ego
moves forward to become the sole divinity."
—Dorothee Solle

The Divinity System is where we evolve into our spiritual maturity, and because we're living in a time of very obvious change, a time of uncertainty and extremes, where everything about our world feels rocky and unstable, the grounded presence of spiritually mature adults are needed now more than ever. But what exactly does spiritual maturity mean and how does one go about achieving it?

First, a declarative differentiation needs to be made between spiritual wisdom and intellect. Simply because an individual progresses in age doesn't guarantee that they'll also grow in wisdom. To be intellectual is to be smart, but not necessarily wise, and being wise doesn't require one to be scholarly. *Spiritual maturity* can be found in understanding the difference. Spiritual maturity is a journey made in the conquest of truth—the symbol of its attainment: wisdom.

Spiritual maturity is gained by consistently learning the lessons that life offers. And the greatest lesson a human can learn is the lesson of surrender. Surrender is the highest form of spiritual maturity. Surrendering our ego's agenda for ourselves doesn't mean giving up power, in fact, it's quite the opposite. Surrendering the ego means we realize we are both the drop, and also the entire ocean. It's a relief when you think about it, for the drop to finally let go of control, and allow itself to merge with an even larger flow of life. To surrender the ego's limited agenda is to allowing ourselves to be used by something greater than us, to create something greater in the world. We don't *lose* ourselves in this process, we learn to *use* ourselves, and to let the divine use us.

Surrendering the ego to divine consciousness is also what it means to become selfless. There's a lot of talk in spiritual communities about selflessness, and I'm not sure we fully understand what being selfless really means. We think that selflessness means to give freely of ourselves, so we bend over backwards trying to make everyone around us happy, always think of ourselves last. Our unconscious assumption is that by putting ourselves last, we're expressing virtuous behavior, but this just ends up draining our batteries. In reality, to be selfless is to be free from the *unconsciousness* of our ego—to be free from the egos idea that it is separate from the divine. To surrender and to become selfless is to merge our personal will with the will of the Divine. Its surrendering to the divine plan for our life—the pinnacle experience of our Divinity System.

But this isn't always as easy as it sounds. Planet earth is a planet of free will. We basically get to do what we want down here; our world is full of temptation and this can be cause for a lot of distraction. People on earth are allowed to be complete assholes, kill each other, and trash the planet and no one can stop us, because we have the free will to do so. Not to mention, our planet is also heavy with fear, and those who've lived fearlessly in the pursuit of the divine have historically been killed for doing so. And so, a lot of spiritually minded people will choose to play small out of the unconscious fear of being annihilated. The freedom to choose our lives and how we show up for them is our divine birthright. But what if a higher plan was already chosen for us a long time ago and all we need to do is surrender to it?

Sadly, striving for selflessness just isn't on everyone's agenda. Most of the world is still trying to discover their happiness in realms outside of themselves, outside of their connection to the divine. Our world is full of people convinced that the key to happiness is found by following the status quo, brainwashed into believing that collecting possessions and acquiring wealth are the ways of success. If we're all lusting after luxuries, designer brands, perfected self-image, and personal recognition, how free from-self are we really?

And I'm not saying that worldly success is bad, it's definitely not. Life is a lot more comfortable with money than without it. What I'm saying is that it's really easy to get caught up in the pursuit of worldly achievement and completely lose sight of what we're really searching for. With the unconscious desire to fit in, follow suit, and not makes too many waves, most people just get caught up in the rat-race, marching along to an imperceptible rhythm without ever questioning who's beating the drum. In the quest to achieve the so-called American dream, many of our youth prematurely enroll themselves in college or start families and buy houses, amassing incredible amounts of debt and stress before they can even ask themselves the most important questions of all, "Who am I?" Perhaps the more important question is, "Why am I?" If we can't first *feel* our reason for being, then we can't ever be fully satisfied.

Too often, people unconsciously create entire lives before they're even aware of what it is they truly desire. But how can they know what they truly desire if they haven't maintained a connection to who they are throughout their early life? In order to awaken the Divinity System and anchor God onto our planet, our other systems need to be intact. We need to be awake.

If you're fortunate enough, you may be waking up halfway through life with a well-paying career, a house, a few cars, the kids, and all the other bells and whistles, but wondering why you're *still* not completely satisfied. What could be missing from your picture-perfect reality? Well, I'll tell you—it's YOU—it's the *you* that you were born to be. You knew this *you* when you were little, but you got swept away by the alluring nature of your own free will and lost connection to your true identity, to your divine nature.

When we're born, we already know who we are. We know what we were born to do, we know what we love, and we know how to do it. We felt who we were when we jumped rope in the driveway, sketched for hours, got lost in storybooks, made make believe, rode bikes, and played naturally. As children, we knew that who we are is an essence of *being*, and we knew it right up until we bought into the story that told us we weren't enough. We knew it until the moment we started looking for happiness in a world outside of ourselves. But life has a way of redirecting us back toward our divine self, be it through illness, trauma, hardships, or a quiet inkling in the back of our mind that says, "Is this really *it*? There's *got* to be more to life than this." The personal quest to answer the *more to life* question will ultimately lead you back to your divine will. In the words of the late, great, Joseph Campbell, *follow your bliss,* it will show you the way back to the you that you're looking for.

The realization of your divine will is the awakening of your higher self, the higher plan for your life—it's the discovery of what you were *created* to express. Free will is your birthright, but divine will is your gift from God. Free will gives you the freedom to choose what you think will bring you satisfaction and nothing will interfere with your free will without your consent. This is an essential rule to the epic game of life. But awakening to your divine will will lead you on a path to great adventure—your own hero's journey that lives in your heart and soul. The divine plan for your life can only be awakened when you request to know it. You have to ask and then be willing to follow the breadcrumbs. That's how the game works.

When I finally realized that my own will was actually trying to kill me, I prayed for a better way to live and my divine will took me by the hand and showed me the way. And here I am, ten years later, living a life I never imagined possible. Surrendering your ego and merging your will with the divine will for your life doesn't mean the end of pain, but it can be the end of suffering.

Divine Energetics

Now that we've covered just about everything you need to know relating to your seventh chakra and the consciousness that governs it—lets assess the health and function of your Divinity System. I encourage you to look to the connection you have to your own body and to use your life as a reflection for how well you manage the energy of the Divinity System.

Remember from the chapter on the human energy system that energy behaves in a multitude of different ways—it can be *excessive*, running too much energy; *deficient*, not able to generate enough energy; or *blocked*, meaning no energy is able to transmit through the chakra at all. Chakras can have both *excessive and deficient* characteristics, so the energetic state of your chakra may also fall somewhere in between any of those three states, depending on the situation. In an ideal world, however, we want our energy to be *balanced* and able to flow freely throughout our system. If a chakra is out of balance, not holding enough, or holding too much energy, we will need to either charge, discharge, or otherwise reorganize the energy of that chakra in order to bring it into balance.

Those with *excessive* energy in their Divinity System will tend to put God above all else. And although a connection to the divine is important, if a tiger is about to eat your child, it's not the time to put God first and simply trust that God would have your child be eaten. *Excessive* divinity types might deny the body's primal needs, along with their need for pleasure and even community. They may also give God all the credit for their lives and accept very little acknowledgement for what they themselves are capable of doing. They will devote themselves solely to God, and to God only. However, it's entirely possible to devote your life to God and still have a husband or wife and kids. You can definitely devote your life to divine service and not become a priest or nun. You can work an average job and do it in a Godly way. Just be a loving human and do onto others as you would have them do onto you. But those with *excessive* energy in the seventh chakra don't always see things that way, it's usually all God and nothing else.

Excessive intellectualism is also a characteristic of the excessive Divinity System. Those with expanded crown chakras are often deeply inspired by the world of wisdom and information, I tend to favor this realm, however, the energy of intellect must be able to connect with the other systems. One has to be able to ground the energy of intellect into the world and truly do something with it. Without the vehicle of the lower energy centers, excessive wisdom is just a show-pony for the ego.

In order to discharge *excessive* energy in the Divinity System to allow for more balance, it's not about connecting more to God, rather, connecting more to the ground. If those with excessive energy in the crown learn to ground it, it can bring stability and balance to the rest of their system. Usually they will benefit from finding an outlet to express their divine connection. They need to be able to move the energy out of their head and into their life.

In contrast, those with a *deficiency* in the crown already believe they know everything there is to know, especially on the concept of divinity. They're comfortable in their beliefs and won't feel the need to challenge them. People with too little energy in their Divinity System will very rarely open their minds to new ideas or spiritual concepts. They can also be rigid in their beliefs about God and will often identify as religious, but not usually spiritual. They're reluctant to allow any ideas into their mind that aren't already their own. They might even subconsciously fear new information that challenges their existing religious ideologies and fear anyone who presents them.

To bring more energy into a crown that is deficient, one might benefit from exploring various spiritual concepts. It doesn't necessarily mean they are going to convert from their current religion, rather, that they become open to exploring other ideas and measure those ideas against what they already believe. One who identifies as a Christian, might read a book on Buddhism, not to change themselves, but to simply understand others.

A *blocked* Divinity System will not be able to access anything higher than themselves. They might fear God or swear off religion all together. A person with a block in their crown chakra will usually tell you that life is full of pain and suffering and that's all there really is. There's an overall depression and cynicism about a person with a block to their Divinity System. They can feel really alone and isolated and as if they've been abandoned by life. A lot of times their cynicism is covering over a really deep sadness and lack of connection with their soul. If you feel as though your Divinity System is blocked, begin by addressing your early relationship to spirituality. How was spirituality addressed in your home? Were you raised religious? Did you ever feel called to explore your own spiritual path? In order to remove a block and open the crown one needs to reconnect with a power that is greater than themselves, a *higher power*, if you will.

Meditation is a wonderful tool for opening the crown; begin by simply observing your thoughts and watching yourself as you process the events of your life. This creates a new space within you, an added dimension to your mind, an expanding of your consciousness. Focusing your attention on the observer rather than the thinker will help you establish a connection with a greater consciousness. Finding that infinite awareness will allow you to explore what you think and what you believe.

Ideally, we want our energy to be *balanced*, especially in our connection to the divine. Those who have balance in their Divinity System strive to live their human lives in as Godly a way as possible. They have a natural connection to a source that's greater than themselves and will live their lives in service to that higher power. Although they know the immensity of the power they work with, they're also deeply humble, because they know that it comes through them, not necessarily from them. Those with a balanced crown are usually very spiritual, but not always religious, although they may identify with many religions. They are seekers of truth, not necessarily dogma.

Questions for Reflection

- How open are you to spiritual exploration?
- Do you believe that there is a divine plan for your life?
- Do you have a relationship with a power that is greater than yourself?
- How did your parents view spirituality?
- Are you open to the spiritual beliefs of others?
- How comfortable are you sitting in silence?
- How attached are you to the material world?
- Do you believe that there is more to you than your physical body?
- Do you follow any spiritual disciplines, practices, or rituals?
- Which practices allow you to feel the most limitless and free from yourself?
- Can you allow yourself to honor the sacredness in all things?

THE AWAKENING

Getting Your Shift Together

"The true revolution is the evolution of consciousness."
—Ram Dass

For those who are paying attention, it's become quite obvious, there's a massive paradigm shift taking place on our planet—one that's been prophesized for centuries—and we're all feeling it. Whether we have eyes to see it or not, *everything is shifting*. Technology is advancing at an incredibly rapid pace, while we simultaneously witness many old and outdated systems collapse—all in order to create space for new and better ways of living to emerge.

Thanks to the internet and unlimited access to vast platforms of knowledge and information, people on an individual level are finally waking up, taking their power back, and getting serious about making change happen. As more and more of us break free from our cultural and societal conditioning, we're collectively rediscovering the power of authenticity.

Many are liberating themselves from the stranglehold of big pharma, and instead, educating themselves about the power of nature, mindfulness, stress reduction, diet, and exercise to recover and heal from illness. Thanks to various social media platforms, we no longer need big corporations or advertising agencies to endorse or sponsor our work, which is allowing for creative entrepreneurs and out of the box thinkers to share their message and become financially independent. Today, we have independent access to infinite amounts of information on things that interest us, literally at our fingertips. As a collective we're becoming conscious of our ability to create the lives we truly desire. As more of us reclaim the power of creation, the possibility for a global awakening becomes more of a reality. It also becomes more of a threat to those who'd wish to stop it.

As we gently pull the wool from our own eyes, it becomes painfully obvious that the economic model for the world was created to benefit the few, while the majority struggle. The medical system reflects more of a sickness for profit industry than it does a healthcare system, and our environmental issues are reaching the brink of no return. We're clearly in the midst of a political shit storm with no end in sight, and with only *lesser of evils* to choose from. The educational system struggles to serve the highly sensitive youth that are emerging and demanding change. All the systems that keep culture as we know it in place are struggling to maintain their structure. More and more people are waking up to the truth, beginning to think for themselves, and demanding real solutions to pressing global issues. These systems of governance have been held in place by the limited consciousness that created them. But as consciousness evolves, so does the need for a cultural upgrade. What's motivating this change is a massive shift in our beliefs about power.

The *power of love* is slowly rising up against the *love of power*.

All the energies within and around us are changing, doing their best to come into a harmonious alignment. Once viewed as polarities, masculine and feminine energies are now seeking unity. Inner and outer worlds are coalescing, higher and lower selves are merging in the middle—the sacred space of the heart center. If we're going to be an influential part of this shift, we must get our own energies into alignment too. It means we first have to understand what's actually happening, and then we each need to show up to do our part. Every human who walks the earth has the potential to be a magnificent instrument for healing and change. If we can allow our music to flow through us unrestricted, we will contribute a unique and soulful sound to the epic cosmic orchestra. The problem today is that many have forgotten who they are. Instead of searching for their own music, many are busy trying to play the notes of someone else's song. Or if not, they're getting in their own way and blocking the flow of their song from being sung. Right now, instead of an elegant symphony, the earth sounds like an awful cacophony, a loud racket of disharmonious noise. But the power to change all of that is literally ours, it's in US! It's in the collective.

The planet herself is desperately seeking homeostasis as we have seemingly reached a critical point in our evolution. We now must either evolve differently or go extinct. The earth is a living, breathing entity. She is desperately trying to heal herself before it's too late, and we're all being called to assist in her healing. The vibration of the planet is rising in order to restore natural rhythm and harmony. Those of us doing the work to raise our own frequency and get into alignment with the energy of a new paradigm are anchoring in this new frequency and acting as catalysts for this shift to take place. You are being called to do the same, or you wouldn't be reading this book.

Awakening is a purification process. It means ridding yourself of anything that isn't authentically you. It's about moving from the head and into the heart—shifting from separation to unity—transforming fear into love and judgement into compassion. As you do this, you'll naturally start to uncover your deeper passions, your hidden gifts and talents. You will then be called to use them in a way that not only nourishes you as an individual, but also benefits the whole. I believe that human hearts across the globe are responding to the pleading cries of mother earth, begging us all to wake up and *remember who we are*. Many of us are being called to serve a spirit much greater than ourselves, a force that's far more powerful than the limited human ego could ever be. And we're being called to do it in a way that is uniquely our own. Although it may be buried under a lifetime of limiting thoughts, beliefs, and behaviors each and every one of us has an inborn passion, a soul calling, and a desire to create something real and authentic in the world. The challenge is that many obstacles can stand in the way of our pursuit of happiness, and it takes great dedication to seek our own joy and fulfilment. It's actually much easier to drift through life waiting for something to happen than it is to carve out your own path and *make* things happen.

But whether we like it or not, the shift is going to hit the fan! And in today's rapidly changing world, there seems to be two distinct types of people—there are the *shifters*, and there are the *resisters*. Even though it's obvious a large portion of creation is awakening, there are still a lot of people on the planet today living in a fear. They're disconnected from who they are and are committed to fear because fear is what they know. We've all been conditioned by fear, and as a collective we haven't fully embraced another way. People in resistance to the shift are desperate to keep the past alive because they can't yet see a new vision of the future.

Shifters are the people slowly coming to consciousness. They're waking up and becoming aware of themselves and choosing to break free of their limitations. They're questioning the deeper meaning of things and examining and challenging the origins of their outdated belief systems. They're creating a world of their choosing. Shifters are those willing to do the deep and sometimes painful inner work of awakening the soul.

Resisters, however, are simply resisting. Resisters aren't bad, they're just afraid. They were often wounded very deeply in childhood and they fear, more than anything, opening their hearts again. The best way to shift a resister is to allow them to be exactly where they are, while still living your life as a powerful example for the way out of fear.

There's an iconic scene in the movie *The Matrix* when Morpheus says to Neo, "*The Matrix is a system, Neo. That system is our enemy. But when you're inside, you look around, what do you see? Businessmen, teachers, lawyers, carpenters. The very minds of the people we are trying to save. But until we do, these people are a part of that system and that makes them our enemy. You have to understand most of these people aren't ready to be unplugged and many of them are so injured, so hopelessly dependent on the system, that they will fight to protect it.*" Morpheus is talking about the resisters.

Resisters are not our enemies, but I do believe that they're committed to living in fear and will fight to protect the system that enslaves them. If you're reading this, you're most likely a shifter, and as you're in the midst of shifting, resisters are not the people you should be concerning yourself with. There are plenty of fellow shifters out there—people unplugging from the system and tapping into their internal power source and then doing their part towards creating a better world. Go out in search of these people and surround yourself with them.

A shifting person has only one job, and its simple: to move through their own darkness so they can shine as brightly as possible. Shifters are like a lighthouse at midnight, a signpost for all other ships seeking refuge. The lighthouse doesn't go out in search of those in need of rescue, the boats in need of help will naturally be attracted to the light. As you begin to make this shift for yourself, you'll find that certain people distance themselves or may even disappear entirely from your life, while others will begin to gravitate towards you. You may discover that you've become more sensitive to negativity. The harmful habits you used to engage in like gossip and social drinking no longer interest you. You might even find that you now have a hard time being around it. Don't fret if your friend circles start shifting as you do. As your vibration changes, your point of attraction will be different, and therefore so will your experiences. If you are consistent, your new energy will attract a new circle, one that matches your new vibration. As you do the work of purifying your mind and body, your energy will be elevated and will no longer be a match to the lower frequencies of fear.

Fear and control are energies of the past.
The energy of the future is Love.

As the vibration gets higher, everything that isn't in harmony with this new frequency is going to experience a disruption. Whatever has been standing in the way of us becoming who we are meant to be in this lifetime is going to come to the surface to be cleared. Consider this a much needed deep cleansing. This shift into higher consciousness is happening whether we're in alignment or not, so the best thing we can do to make it a smooth transition is to get ourselves into alignment with it. Things on our planet can't continue on the way they have been. We're already experiencing multiple systems failure and things aren't going to improve unless *we* do. The shift taking place is a necessary recalibration.

But are we ready for a global awakening?

If you've made it this far, you're probably as dedicated to awakening as I am. You've come to know just about everything you possibly can on how to human, and now you have everything you need to awaken all of who you are, to reclaim all of your fragmented parts, to make your unconscious conscious, and to *heal.*

To be fully awake is to strive for balance in all our systems. Balance at all times, of course, is not always possible given the nature of our lives, however, we can certainly *intend* to live our lives in a state of balance and be an example for others who may be striving for the same. In this way, we can all pave the way for an awakened world.

When we can all honor our bodies as our vehicles for consciousness and treat them like the temples they are...

When we can nourish our sensual nature and honor our need for pleasure...

When we can understand the need for a healthy, well-developed ego and reclaim our personal power...

When we can open our hearts, and find true forgiveness for ourselves and everyone around us...

When we discover the power of our voice and allow it to express the creative essence of our soul...

When we activate our true sight and remember how to truly see each other, and our world...

When we use *all* of what we've learned throughout life, to heal ourselves and surrender our will to something greater than we are...

Then, and only then, will the lives outsides of us reflect the world we all desperately long for. Only then, will we, as a collective, finally heal.

For every human alive to be living their life from this awakened state of consciousness is the goal of Heal the People. From here on out, may life itself become your greatest teacher, your greatest practice, and the collective's greatest mirror. May our pain serve only to awaken us fully. My wish for you is total balance, in all of your energy systems, so you can go out and live your life as purposefully and powerfully as possible.

EPILOGUE

Choice Point

"Unless someone like you care a whole awful lot,
things aren't going to get better—they're not."
—Dr. Seuss

I started writing this book, or I *should* say that *Heal the People* started writing *me*, many years ago, long before the events of 2020 had taken place. These words are now more applicable than ever before. Change isn't just happening for *some* people anymore—change has been thrust upon *all* of us. The momentum for such radical change has been building for quite some time. The expansion of consciousness has been gradually increasing, so many could sense something coming, but I don't believe any single person could have predicted exactly how these changes would manifest.

In a few short months, our world was totally rocked by a viral pandemic, a global lockdown, and a massive movement of civil unrest. There's simply no more denying it, our world is *shifting*. Some will see this event as a great catastrophe, as with all great change comes discomfort and a bit of uncertainty. There is, however, another choice— to see this as a window of opportunity—a brief moment in time to pause, to surrender to *what is*, and to search for the silver lining.

Humanity is at a very critical crossroads, a choice point in our evolutionary journey, a cultural dark night of the soul, if you will. And although many of the events taking place have manifested themselves in our *material* world, a dark night of the soul is essentially a *spiritual* crisis. It's an *existential* dilemma. It's so often during times of loss, grief, change, and uncertainty that we find ourselves pondering life's deeper questions and searching for answers to life's greatest mysteries: *Who am I? Why am I here? What is the meaning of my life? Am I truly happy?* And if I'm not happy, *what can I do to change?* I think it goes without saying that the year 2020 snapped many of us to attention. It's awakened some to their inevitable mortality and encouraged many to stop waiting for tomorrow and to live their lives *today*, to make the changes they've been putting off, to take their health more seriously or tell that special person that they love them, to quit their job and move to another state or pursue their real passions. It's also opened the eyes of many to oppression, historical injustice, and other disturbing realities that have been lurking in humanity's collective shadow.

Could it be that all of this is happening so suddenly and intensely because we needed a major pattern interruption and this was the best way to get our attention? Perhaps this was the sharp wakeup call we needed. I think much of the world (and the earth herself) benefited from us stepping off the hamster wheel of modern living and gave many of us the space to perceive reality from a new perspective. When reading the stories of humanity's greatest heroes, you'll find a central theme; painful moments are often necessary for enlightenment to be achieved. It seems as though all of humanity is simultaneously experiencing deep and painful moments necessary for a mass awakening. What we choose to do now might be the most important choice we'll ever make. Will we cling to the familiarity and security of a dying world, or will we use this moment as the catalyst for the greatest awakening the world has ever known? Will we allow ourselves to evolve into something greater than ever before?

Are you willing to evolve right now?

I'd like to leave you with this:

This shift is a much needed one. We must allow positive change to continue through *us*.

It's no mistake that we're here at such a pivotal time in human history. *This* is the experience that many of us came for. We've each been tasked with the duty of witnessing the ways of an old world dissolve and to take responsibility for helping to usher in something greater. But this can only happen if we *stay awake*.

We're not here on this planet simply to survive, pay bills, and die—we're meant to *thrive*. That can only happen if we surrender our fears and choose to follow a different directive instead. We must be willing to get out of the way and let something greater than us do its work *through* us. Although it may not look like it on the surface, this moment in time is a *spiritual* one. If we're to find peace during these times of great change, we have to reunite ourselves with something deeper. We must learn to anchor ourselves to the shining jewel, the kingdom of heaven— *Anahata*—the unstruck place within ourselves. This unconditional seed of truth is buried deep within each and every one of us. It can never be erased, it can never be silenced, and we can never be severed from it. This space knows no fear, no lies, no anger, no greed, and no jealousy. It knows no famine or war.

When the people of the world make the conscious choice to live from *this* space, the great spiritual center, the *heart*—only then will the world know peace—and that's the only way to truly *Heal the People*. Love. *Always Love.*

ACKNOWLEDGEMENTS

This book wouldn't have been possible without the inspiration, guidance, wisdom and continued support of many others.

I'd like to acknowledge the spirit of iboga for planting the seed of this book in my mind long before it became a reality.

My first real life teachers, Rhys Thomas, Lisa Campion and the staff at the Rhys Thomas Institute of Energy Medicine for introducing me to a tribe of like-hearted healers, guiding me deeper into a spiritual life and helping me develop a sense of belonging in the world.

The various other teachers, many of whom appeared in the form of books, lectures, workshops and videos that inspired me to keep learning, growing and challenging myself.

My editors, Joan Schaublin, Lauren Sarat and Petra Wise. You've helped me refine and restructure my thoughts into a comprehensible book, for each of you I am eternally grateful.

I'd also like to acknowledge the strength and tenacity of the human spirit, and all of the incredible, powerful people on the planet today doing the great work of awakening and healing themselves so together we can create more peaceful and loving world.

REFERENCES

BOOKS:

Mate, Gabor, M.D. *In the Realm of Hungry Ghosts: Close Encounters with Addiction.* North Atlantic Books/The Ergos Institute, 2010.

Byrne, Rhonda. *The Secret.* Atria Books/Beyond Words, 2006.

Judith, Anodea, Ph. D. *Wheels of Life: A Users Guide to the Chakra System.* Llewellyn Publications, 2004

Judith, Anodea, Ph. D. Eastern Body Western Mind: Psychology and the Chakra System As a Path to the Self. Celestial Arts, 1999.

Kessler, Steven. *The 5 Personality Patterns: Your Guide to Understanding Yourself and Others and Developing Emotional Maturity.* Bodhi Tree Press, 2016.

Thomas, Rhys. *Discover Your Purpose: How to Use the 5 Life Purpose Profiles to Unlock Your Hidden Potential and Live the Life You Were Meant to Live.* TarcherPerigree, 2015.

Lowen, Alexander, M.D. *The Language of The Body: Physical Dynamics of Character Structure.* The Alexander Lowen Foundation, 2012. Originally published, 1958.

Reich, Wilhelm. *Character Analysis.* Farrar, Straus and Giroux; Third Edition 1980

References

Pierrakos, John, M.D. *Core Energetics: Developing the Capacity to Love and Heal.* Life Rhythm Publications, 2ⁿᵈ edition, 1990.

Brennan, Barbara Ann. *Hands of Light: A Guide to Healing Through the Human Energy Field.* Bantam, 1990

Myss, Caroline, Ph. D. *Anatomy of the Spirit: The Seven Stages of Power and Healing. Three Rivers Press, 1996*

Myss, Caroline, Ph. D. *Why People Don't Heal and How They Can: A Practical Programme for Healing Body, Mind and Spirit.* Harmony, 1998

Chek, Paul. *How to Eat, Move, and Be Healthy. Your Personalized 4-Stage Guide to Looking and Feeling Great from the Inside Out.* C.H.E.K Institute, 2004.

Ford, Debbie. *The Dark Side of Light Chasers: Reclaiming your Power, Creativity, Brilliance and Dreams.* G P Putnam's Sons 1998

Hawkins, David R. M.D., Ph. D. *Power vs. Force: The Hidden Determinants of Human Behavior.* Hay House 2002

Canfield, Jack with Switzer, Janet. *The Success Principles: How to Get from Where You Are to Where You Want to Be.* Collins, 2006.

Hendrix, Harville. *Getting the Love You Want: A Guide for Couples.* St, Martin's Griffin, 2007.

Powell, John Joseph. *Why Am I Afraid to Tell You Who I Am? Insights into Personal Growth.* Zondervan, 1999

Dispenza, Dr. Joe. *Becoming Supernatural: How Common People Are*

Doing the Uncommon. Hay House, 2017.

Dispenza, Dr. Joe. *Breaking the Habit of Being Yourself: How to Lose Your Mind and Create a New One.* Hay House, 2012

Lipton, Bruce, Ph. D. *The Biology of Belief: Unleashing the Power of Consciousness, Matter and Miracles.* Hay House, 2015

Pollan, Michael. *How to Change Your Mind: What the New Science of Psychedelics Teaches Us About Consciousness, Dying, Addiction, Depression, and Transcendence.* Penguin Press, 2018.

OTHER SOURCES:

Facing the Habit, documentary. 2008
www.dictionary.com
www.alvernia.edu
www.nutritionsimplified.com
www.cdc.gov

Made in the USA
Middletown, DE
06 October 2023

39833503R00201